D1607522

THE BERLIN
AIRLIFT

Dedication

In loving memory of our father and airlift veteran,
John Francis Sutherland (1926–2005).

The Berlin
Airlift

The Salvation of a City

Jon Sutherland and Diane Canwell

PELICAN PUBLISHING COMPANY
GRETNA 2008

Published by Pen & Sword Books Ltd, 2007
Published by arrangement in North America by
Pelican Publishing Company, Inc., 2008
First Pelican edition, 2008

ISBN-13: 978-1-58980-550-7

Printed in the United States of America

Published by Pelican Publishing Company, Inc.
1000 Burmaster Street, Gretna, Louisiana 70053

Contents

Introduction

It seems abundantly clear that the victorious Allies in 1945 had very different expectations of a post-war Germany than Europe. On the one hand, the Soviets wanted to exact punishment on the Germans for the carnage that they had inflicted on Russia since 1941. On the other hand, the Western Allies, led by the British and the Americans, wanted to rebuild Germany, stabilize Europe and stop the spread of Communism to the rest of Europe.

It had already been agreed at Potsdam that the Germans would have to pay a price for waging two world wars in three decades. For the Western Allies this did not mean that the German population would starve to death. The Soviets, it seems, had little interest in whether or not the Germans lived or died. The Soviets were more intent on taking anything that could be loaded onto a train or the back of the truck; the Western Allies were more concerned with getting Germany's economy back on its feet. As US Secretary of State, George C Marshal said in 1947:

'There is no question in my mind whatever that the German economy is the heart of Europe.'

The first violation of Potsdam as far as the Soviets were concerned was the joining economically of the American and the British zones of occupation in Germany. This was as a direct response to the Russians staging a coup in Czechoslovakia and was the first major rift between east and west.

The Allies also squabbled about imports and reparation payments. The Soviets simply took whatever money was available. The Western Allies, on the other hand, set some aside to provide vital imports to keep the German economy going. Ultimately it was an economic straw that broke the Soviet camel's back. The Western Allies wanted to create a West

1

German currency. This would help to stabilize the economy and give the Germans some buying power. The Soviets were offered the currency but they wanted to print their own money. It had already been proven that the Soviets were happy to print as many notes as they needed to pay for things during the initial occupation phases of Berlin, so the Western Allies were set against this path. When Berlin City Council adopted the western currency the Soviet blockade started to be put into place.

Once the Soviets started their harassment and blocking of Western Allies into and out of Berlin it became abundantly clear that the way in which Germany had been divided was impractical. It had simply not been thought through. Admittedly there had been no expectations of crisis arising between the West and the Soviets, but the Allied Control Council, or at least the *Kommandatura* should have solved the problem. But in the event they, too, had been poorly conceived and were dissolved as soon as an impasse reared its head.

As the blockade closed in only an airlift could sustain the garrisons and the inhabitants of the western parts of the city. The Soviets felt they had to shut down access to Berlin in order to force the issue in their favour.

The Berlin airlift began the first large-scale humanitarian effort to ensure the survival of a city's population. It was also the first international humanitarian coalition. Ultimately the success of the Berlin airlift would bring about the end of the Soviet blockade, but there would be no firm handshake or real end to the political tensions between the Soviet Union and the other, victorious allies. Whilst the Western Allies created a democratic and self-sufficient West Germany, the Soviet Union created a tightly controlled East Germany. Berlin would remain partitioned for another forty years. There would be increasing force to control the border and, in effect, for four decades, East Berlin and East Germany would be cut off from the western world.

The city was permanently partitioned in the early 1960s, when the Berlin Wall became the dominant symbol of east-west tension and the Cold War. The East German government fell in 1989 and immediately the hated Berlin Wall was stormed and, for the first time since the Berlin blockade, the city was free for its inhabitants to roam at their will.

The reunification of Berlin and Germany as a whole was really the end of the crisis that had begun forty years before with the Berlin blockade and airlift.

During the Berlin airlift life for the Berliners was hard. The winter of 1948 to 1949 left homes cold and industry idle, yet the Berliners in the allied sectors were determined not to capitulate. They had seen what it was like to live under the heel of Soviet soldiers. The Western Allies too were determined that Berlin would not be sacrificed just because they could not bring in supplies by conventional means. Brave and exhausted pilots flew fleets of aircraft around the clock into inadequate and dangerous airfields around the city. Mechanics worked day and night to ensure that the aircraft remained air worthy. At the height of the effort any aircraft that was not being stripped down for inspection or repair was aloft.

As Mikhail Semiryaga, a Russian who was of the Soviet Military Administration during the Berlin blockade and airlift said:

> We expected that the Allies could introduce the army, and some military units might accompany trains and cars. And we realised what might be the result. There might be some incidents with the soldiers, it might be used to start a fight between the armies. We felt it. And we had a directive from Moscow to have our families leave Berlin. That was the situation. And we also knew that some British and American people left their zones. Tension was high. Using that air corridor airlift, one plane arrived every minute. Where I was living they flew twenty, fifty metres over my house and touched down at Tempelhof, which was 2km away. We couldn't sleep, because the planes were huge B-29s. They brought everything to Berlin. Not only bread, meat, milk, but even coal and wood; and they saved the situation.

So in a Russian's own words, the airlift had averted what could easily have dragged the world into another cataclysmic conflict. This time former allies would face one another and with the spectre of atomic bombs in the background, who can know what may have happened?

The Berlin airlift, seen initially as a stopgap measure whilst political negotiations continued, proved for the first time that a city could be supplied by air. The Germans had failed to do it at Stalingrad during the war and the Soviets had lacked the aircraft to supply Leningrad, but now the full weight of the British and American air forces, supported by civilian aircraft flown by veteran pilots, would prove once and for all that humanitarian relief was an international peace policy in the post-war world.

CHAPTER ONE

Prelude to the Blockade

I n August 1944, the Eastern Front was relatively stable, but for
Germany total destruction was just eight months away. Even
before August the principal allies, Great Britain, the United
States and the Soviet Union, contemplated only unconditional
surrender and the partitioning of Germany.

A draft protocol, dated 4 August 1944, laid down the
partitioning arrangements. The outline agreement was based on
Germany's frontiers in 31 December 1937. The country would be
split into eastern, north-western and south-western zones. Each
would be occupied by one of the three major powers. Later a
fourth zone would be carved out of the two western zones for
France.

The protocol explicitly stated that Greater Berlin would be
jointly occupied by the three major powers. North-eastern Berlin
would be occupied by the Soviet Union, the remainder by the
British and the Americans, and later a zone would be allocated
to France. It should be borne in mind that by the end of the war
the Russians had overrun a considerable amount of Germany
and that Berlin, including the Western Allies' zones, would be
deep within Soviet-occupied Germany.

The Soviets had suffered greatly at the hands of the Germans
during the invasion and occupation from 1941. But steadily they
had begun to hold their ground and then launch massive
counter-attacks. They had taken Warsaw in January 1945. They

had launched a huge offensive, incorporating four army fronts, and within four days were steadily moving between 19 and 25 miles per day. They overran the Baltic states, East Prussia and Danzig and finally drew up on a massively fortified front just 60 km to the east of Berlin, along the Oder River.

On 24 February 1945, under the direct command of Heinrich Himmler, the hastily cobbled together Army Group Vistula launched an abortive series of counter-attacks. The Soviets responded by clearing the right bank of the Oder River and driving into Pomerania. To the south, Budapest had fallen on 13 February. The Germans again counter-attacked, in an attempt to recapture the Danube River. By 16 March the attacks had petered out and the Red Army counter-attacked. They crossed into Austria on 30 March and overran Vienna on 13 April.

With Hitler still in control of Germany, there could be no prospect of the Germans accepting unconditional surrender. Instead they fought on, buying valuable time for refugees to flee west to escape the Red Army. At this time the Western Allies were still considering dropping paratroops into Berlin. The general consensus of opinion was that the casualties would be extremely high and, in any case, according to the agreed protocols Berlin would be deep in Soviet territory.

The Soviets drove on and were now entering central Germany. They attacked on a broad front; their overriding objective was Berlin. Already Stalin was thinking about post-war Europe. There would be important German assets to seize in Berlin, and the more of Germany that could be overrun, the more of these assets could be removed and sent east.

Konigsberg fell on 9 April. This freed up an entire Soviet army, which could move west towards the Oder. During the first two weeks of April the Soviets reshuffled their troop concentrations. Collectively their armies boasted 2.5 million men and over 6,000 tanks, supported by masses of aircraft, artillery and other vehicles.

General Gotthard Heinrici had replaced Himmler on 20 March. He had an excellent reputation as a defensive commander. He correctly surmised that the Soviets would attempt to cross the Oder River and head for the east–west *autobahn*. He therefore set up his defensive screens some 10½ miles to the west of the River Oder, a perilous 56 miles from Berlin.

The Soviet offensive began on 16 April 1945. The initial attacks were a disaster. Swampy ground, deliberately flooded by the Germans, hindered the advance. Despite gaining about 4 miles in places, the German defensive line remained intact. Reserves were brought up from the rear and the pressure on the German defensive lines increased. They were still holding out by nightfall the following day. The Germans had retained mobile units to plug gaps in the line.

A series of massive new assaults began on 18 April. This time the Soviets broke through three German lines of defence, and on the following day they broke through the final screens and the road was open to Berlin. By nightfall on 19 April virtually nothing remained of the German Eastern Front. There were pockets of resistance, but nothing could now stop the Soviets.

By 21 April the 2nd Guards Army was just 50 km to the north of Berlin. It was now that they encountered the outer defensive rings around the city. Three days later the city was completely encircled. All attempts by German units near the city to break through failed.

The city was defended by what remained of several army and SS units, the bulk of whom were old men and boys.

The Soviets planned to attack the city centre from a number of different directions. The first would come from the south-east, heading towards Alexanderplatz, another from the south, heading towards Belle Alliance Platz. There would be a second from the south, heading for Potsdamerplatz and one from the north, aiming for the Reichstag. There would be vicious hand-to-hand fighting as the desperate German defenders denied the Soviets each and every building.

The situation had become so critical by 30 April that Hitler committed suicide. On 2 May General Weidling, the commander of Berlin, surrendered to the Soviets.

In the battle for the city alone the Soviets had lost upwards of 25,000 men. The entire operation had cost them over 80,000 dead, in addition to nearly 300,000 wounded. Some 2,000 armoured vehicles had been destroyed in the fight for the city. The total German losses are estimated to have been at least 450,000 including military personnel and civilians. The Germans continued to fight on for a few days, but on 8 May 1945 the German armed forces finally unconditionally surrendered. The liberation of Europe was over, but a new war between the Allies was only just about to begin.

In their various meetings throughout the war, the British, the Americans and the Soviets had remained steadfast in their demand for unconditional surrender. They were also certain that in order to exact reparations from Germany the country would have to be occupied. They finally agreed at Potsdam in July 1945 that the German army would be disbanded, the country would be de-Nazified and its capacity to build weapons would be destroyed. It was anticipated that the Allied military occupation of Germany would continue until all necessary government reforms had been instituted, a new constitution written and supervised elections held.

It was said at the time that 'the Russians received the agriculture, the British the heavy industry and the Americans the scenery.' What it meant was that the bulk of Germany occupied by the Western Allies was incapable of feeding itself, let alone their sectors of Berlin.

There were further complications: not only was Berlin 100 miles inside the Soviet zone, but Stalin had tinkered with the frontiers. He had moved the border between Russia and Poland to the west and had then moved the Polish border 50 miles into German territory. This meant that several million Germans were displaced and eventually found themselves as penniless and helpless refugees in the western zones. In this border move Poland had also acquired a great deal of Germany's most fertile agricultural land. As Churchill said: 'The Russians, pushing the Poles in front of them, wended on, driving the Germans before them and depopulating large areas of Germany, whose food supplies they seized, while chasing a multitude of mouths into the overcrowded British and American zones.'

It seems that the deal to partition Germany was distinctly one-sided. The Russians and the Poles acquired the coals of Silesia and the breadbasket of Germany, whilst all the Western Allies acquired were thousands of additional mouths to feed.

On 5 June 1945 the four military commanders in chief met in Berlin: General of the Army Dwight D. Eisenhower, Field Marshall Sir Bernard L Montgomery, Marshal Georgi Zhukov and the Frenchman, General Jean de Lattre de Tassigny. Together they signed The Declaration Regarding the Defeat of

Germany and the Assumption of Supreme Authority. This formalized the zones, their boundaries and the Allied Control Council.

Over the next month, until 4 July various Allied formations moved to their positions in their appropriate zones. The Allied Control Council met for the first time on 30 July. It was to be a four-power agency that would jointly govern occupied Germany.

As for Berlin itself, by May the population had dipped from a pre-war total of 4.6 million to 2.8 million. The working population had been decimated and barely 30 per cent remained. Pre-war Berlin had had 6,500 doctors; now there were just 2,400. The city had been pulverized by Allied aircraft raids throughout the war and had suffered huge damage in the battle for the city. Seventy per cent of the buildings had been damaged, but could still provide rudimentary shelter. Twenty per cent had virtually been demolished, whilst 10 per cent, with work, could be reoccupied. The capital's industrial base had been reduced to just over 40 per cent of its capacity. Hospitals had been severely damaged and there were barely 8,500 beds available.

The city had had eighty-seven functioning sewer systems; none of these now worked. This meant that dysentery and typhus were an ever-present threat. Fresh drinking water had been organized, but it was food, both now and later, that would be the major problem. The city could barely supply 2 per cent of its population's needs for food. It was extremely reliant on food being imported from the Soviet-occupied areas in order to survive.

For eight weeks after Berlin's surrender, no Western troops were allowed in the city. Whilst the frontline troops of the Soviet army had exacted revenge on the German nation, it was the reserve units that now occupied the city. They looted, raped and murdered civilians and it was only when the military police stepped in that this was stopped.

To their dismay now – and their horror later – the Allied planners realized that no formal agreement had been made with the Soviets for access to the Western zones of Berlin. On a number of occasions access had appeared on the agenda, but other, more pressing issues, had taken priority. It was assumed that because of the presence of Western troops access would be guaranteed.

There was no reason to believe that the Soviets would not honour even an implied agreement. It was to be this lack of a formal agreement and the Soviet insistence that the Allies were only in Berlin because they had been granted special permission to be there that would be the root cause of many of the problems.

In late 1945 the Aviation Committee of the Allied Control Council, primarily for safety reasons, established six 20-mile wide air corridors. These linked the capital with Copenhagen, Hamburg, Hanover, Frankfurt, Prague and Warsaw. The Soviets, during the negotiations, argued that only the Hanover, Hamburg and Frankfurt routes were strictly necessary. This agreement, in its revised form, was approved on 30 November 1945, and was to come back to haunt the Western Allies, as it only allowed limited freedom of aircraft movement into and out of the city. More importantly, Soviet aircraft routinely violated these corridors.

Because of the enormous cost in life to the Soviets, the occupation of Germany, and particularly Berlin, was imperative. To them Berlin represented Germany and its continued occupation represented a huge propaganda success. They had no great desire to share it with their Western allies. They had entrenched themselves in Berlin and had recruited thousands of German civilians to clear the rubble. They had repaired the airfields around Berlin. Initially the 515th Fighter Air Regiment had occupied Tempelhof, Berlin's civil airport, but later other units would also operate from the airfield.

Within days of the capital's surrender in 1945, the Soviets had begun to use it as a huge propaganda weapon. They were broadcasting from Radio Berlin for nineteen hours every day. The programmes were dominated by reports of Germans working happily under Soviet direction to rebuild the city.

The shape of things to come was illustrated by the proposal that an American survey be undertaken in June 1945. The Soviets had already requested that the British and the Americans should not move into Berlin until 1 July. However, in late June they agreed that an American convoy could enter the city. For political reasons it was called the Preliminary Reconnaissance Party, Berlin. Colonel Frank L. Howley, the head of the military government detachment, A1A1 (also known as the Berlin Detachment), commanded a party of around 100 vehicles and

500 personnel. Around 50 per cent of them were part of the US Military Government Administration.

The column set off on 23 June. It entered Soviet territory at Dessau, on the River Elbe, and was immediately stopped by Soviet troops. Hours of argument followed, but finally, the colonel was allowed to cross into Soviet territory with just fifty vehicles, thirty-seven officers and 175 men, only four of the officers, however belonged to the Military Government Administration. The convoy was given a Soviet escort as far as Babelsberg, where they were herded into a military compound. This was as far as the mission got after that they were told to return to the American occupation zone without having even entered Berlin itself.

This did not bode well for the future. More concrete and long-lasting arrangements had to be made. Consequently, General Lucius Clay, the commander of the Office of Military Government and the Military Governor of Germany, along with the British Deputy Military Governor, Lieutenant-General Sir Ronald Weeks, went to meet Marshal Zhukov in Berlin on 29 June.

Clay and Weeks explained to Zhukov that they needed his assurance that the Western Allies could use three railway lines and two highways, in addition to the air space. Zhukov did not think that these were essential and in any case he could not promise to police these routes, as he was preoccupied with the demobilization of Soviet troops. The two Western representatives asked merely for access. Both men knew that there were no agreements about access to Berlin and that something needed to be formalized. In the end they accepted a highway, a railway line and two air corridors. But they reserved the right to bring up the matter once again with the Allied Control Council. Both men were unaware of the fact that under the terms of the agreements to set up the Allied Control Council the Soviets had the right to veto any proposal that did not suit them. According to Clay himself:

> While no record was kept of this meeting, I dictated my notes that evening, and they included the following. It was agreed that all traffic – air, road and rail – would be free from border search or control by customs or military

authorities. I think now that I was mistaken in not at this time making free access to Berlin a condition to our withdrawal into our occupation zone, but I did not want an agreement in writing which established anything less than the right of unrestricted access.

Meanwhile, Howley had been patiently waiting at Halle. He now set out once again for Berlin, this time with eighty-five officers and 136 men. They approached Dessau and crossed the River Elbe. By the night of 1 July they camped to the south-west of Berlin. Howley would not accept any interference from the Soviets. His men were armed and prepared to defend themselves if necessary.

On 1 July the British detachment arrived at Magdeburg on the River Elbe. The Soviets maintained that they had no authority to let them through their lines. They would not let them cross, claiming that all the bridges in Magdeburg were being repaired. Undeterred, the British simply hunted for an intact bridge and after a short delay crossed the river.

Above all the Soviets were determined not to allow their erstwhile allies to make a triumphant entrance into the city. The US 2nd Armored Division had been assigned to stage an Independence Day parade in the capital on 4 July. Once again the Soviets tried to block them, claiming that the bridges were unsafe at Dessau and that the road to Berlin was closed. In the event the unit entered the city after making a detour via Helmstedt.

It was agreed that the Western Allies would take control of their zones of Berlin at midnight on 4 July. The Soviets promised to attend the formal ceremony of occupation and to witness the Independence Day parade planned by the Americans. But there was shattering news as the hastily organized parade was coming to an end. Zhukov told the Americans and the British that the Western sectors would not be turned over to them until the new Administrative Authority for Berlin had been established.

The Americans and the British were frustrated and angry; their men and equipment had been delayed and they were not about to play the Soviets' game any longer. The American garrison commander, Major-General Floyd L. Parks, ordered Howley to deploy his men in the American sector. When the

Soviets checked the following morning, American flags were flying and it was too late to do anything about it.

The city presented to the Western Allies was a scene of devastation. The stench of death hung in the air, the canals, polluted by ruptured sewers, were teaming with insects. The German civilians scratched a living amongst the ruins. Berlin citizens had been allocated 1,240 calories per day, but due to chaos and inefficiency they were receiving only 60 per cent of this amount. There was a thriving black market that would soon be fuelled by the Americans.

Allied military marks were the official occupation currency. Unfortunately the Soviets had been given copies of the printing plates. Whilst the British, Americans and later the French would strictly control the printing and distribution of these notes, the Soviets just printed as many as they needed and paid their soldiers with them.

The first meeting of the Administrative Authority of Berlin or the *Kommandatura*, took place on 11 July 1945. The immediate problems were obviously food and fuel. The Soviets initially refused to allow food to be transported from the Soviet sector into the Western zones of the city. Eventually they conceded, provided the western powers paid for it. Once this had been agreed the Soviets told their Western counterparts that there was in fact no spare food in their occupation zone and that any food would have to be brought in from western Germany.

This was to present an enormous problem. The Western occupation zones were barely capable of providing enough food for themselves, let alone the 1.5 million Berliners in the Western sectors. The Soviets insisted that the other Allies should maintain the rules and regulations they had imposed on the city. For the time being they agreed, with the proviso that they would make changes later. However, they were already trapped, as the Soviets had the power of veto and nothing in respect of Berlin could change without their agreement.

During 1946 the British, American and French garrisons rose to 20,000. During this time sixteen trains per day crossed the Soviet zone into western Berlin; later this would increase to thirty-one. In addition road and barge transport carried supplies.

The question of reparations had also reared its head. Stalin demanded the equivalent of $10bn in direct reparations. He also wanted access to the Ruhr coalfields, and to acquire German technical and scientific know-how. This led to an agreement at Potsdam for the Allies to seize reparations from their own zones of control. The British and Americans even went as far as to allow Stalin a sixth of any surplus production from their zones. Regardless of this, the Soviets systematically stripped all of Germany that was under their control. Three and a half thousand plants and factories were uprooted and shipped east. This included over 1.1 million pieces of equipment and with it 2 million jobs. By late 1946, thousands of German skilled workers were also being forcibly transported east.

It was clear right from the very beginning that Stalin wanted the German government to be pro-Soviet. Back in October 1944 he and Winston Churchill had sat, staring at a map of Europe, trying to determine its fate after the war. Stalin had demanded a protective belt of pro-Russian and anti-Nazi states, including Poland, Czechoslovakia and Hungary. He had initially demanded that Germany be entirely broken up. Neither Russia nor France wanted a unified Germany that was not under their control.

On 4 June 1945 Stalin had told German Communist leaders that he intended there to be two Germanies. He wanted a Soviet-dominated eastern occupation zone and would then work to undermine the British zone and then, after a year or two when the Americans tired of occupying Germany, he would pull all of Germany into the Soviet fold.

He had allowed the Red Army systematically to pillage and rape. Reparations had removed a full 30 per cent of eastern Germany's industrial output capability. There were millions of forced refugees fleeing west. Any German that opposed Soviet policies was arrested. Then abruptly, in mid-1946, from a policy of retribution Stalin moved to a policy of reconciliation. Nonetheless, eastern Germany was now in ruins and the Soviets showed little inclination to establish any coherent reconstruction policy.

What was developing was a truly unfair situation. Whilst the Soviets continued to bleed Germany dry, they refused to pool their surpluses and simply transported them east rather than redistributing them. Only the French and Russian zones were self-supporting in terms of food. Britain itself was suffering from

post-war economic problems. She had the most heavily popu-
lated area to contend with – the Ruhr – and, as a result, huge
amounts of supplies had to be imported, primarily from the
United States.

The Germans in the west called this period 'the great famine'.
Germans in the British zone received 1,040 calories per day. In
the American zone it was 1,275, whilst in the French zone those
carrying out light work received only 927 calories against those
doing manual labour, who received 1,144.

Not all of the devastation could be laid at the doors of the
occupying forces, certainly in terms of damage once Germany
had surrendered. The country's fanatical determination to
defend itself in the latter stages of the war led, for example,
to 28,000 farms being destroyed in the British zone alone.
Germans were starving, and what was worse was that because
they were starving they could produce even less. In Western
Germany, between 1 January 1946 and 20 June 1948, 143,000
people had their cause of death registered as exhaustion or
malnutrition. This was a full third of all deaths during that
period. Doctors figured that for every hospitalized individual
with hunger-related problems, forty-eight others were still
struggling elsewhere. In September 1946, 13,000 people from
Düsseldorf were hospitalized due to malnutrition; 25,000 others
in the area were turned away due to lack of beds.

The British and the Americans searched for a solution. It was
suggested towards the end of 1946 that rather than retain their
two separate zones, they should be merged. After all, they were
mutually dependent. Ernest Bevin, Britain's Foreign Secretary,
agreed with General Clay, Robert Murphy (US Political Advisor
in Germany) and James F. Byrnes (US Director of War Mobil-
ization and Reconversion) that the zones should indeed be
merged. Typically, the Soviets were critical of the plan and the
French refused to have any part in it.

The British and Americans, however, decided that regardless
of the Soviet reaction they would go ahead. General Clay, as the
spokesman, made a formal offer to the Allied Control Council
on 18 July 1946. He said:

Since the zones of Germany are not self-supporting of
themselves and since treating two zones or more as an

economic unit would better this situation in the zones concerned, the United States representatives in Germany will join with the representatives of any other occupying power or powers in measures to treat their respective zones as an economic unit, pending four-power agreement to carry out the Potsdam provision regarding the treatment of all Germany as an economic unit and the reaching of a balanced economy throughout Germany.

General George C. Marshall, the American Secretary of State, was clear about the US view on Germany:

The United States government does not want a piece of vengeance and it is convinced that the economic recovery of Germany, along peaceful lines, is necessary to the economic revival of Europe. It desires the de-Nazification of Germany, which will encourage democratic forces who otherwise may feel they cannot exert themselves with a fair chance. The sure way to encourage the growth of demo-cratic forces in Germany is to state in definite terms the conditions of settlement to fix German disarmament measures and the reparations which it must pay. The German people will then realize that the harder they work, the sooner they will be allowed to share in the benefits of European recovery. Germany's future boundaries should likewise be defined so that the German people may know that, as long as they adhere to the settlement, no interference will be given to their reconstruction efforts, which will help both themselves and all of Europe. While controls and secu-rity forces must remain for a long time in Germany, mass occupation and military government continued over a long period could defeat our own purposes. The German people must have the opportunity to minimize the certain difficul-ties and hardships of their situation by their own efforts so that they will learn not to blame their trials on Allied occu-pation but rather, and properly, on the devastating war of aggression which their leaders let loose.

In furtherance of these aims the British Military Governor, Sir Brian Robertson, and General Clay set up, in the autumn of 1946, a number of German committees. Under military guidance and supervision they would become responsible for food and agriculture, transport and communications, finance and economics and the civil service. At a later date, the German Economic Council, consisting of fifty-two members, was to be established in Frankfurt. These would be elected, the first democratic elections since the Weimar Republic.

Officially, the Anglo-American Bizone came into existence on 1 January 1947. It was clear that the Americans in particular were hoping for a rapid European recovery from the war and saw Germany as a key element in this goal. Marshall said: 'Economic unity was felt to be necessary to not only make Germany self-sustaining, but to help contribute to the recovery of Europe.'

George Kennan, a US foreign affairs specialist, stated: 'To talk about the recovery of Europe and to oppose the recovery of Germany is nonsense. People can have both or they can have neither.'

As far as the Americans were concerned their approach in Germany mirrored President Truman's address to US Congress on 12 March 1947. It was in this address that he announced the Truman Doctrine: simply it guaranteed US support for democracies that resisted enslavement by a minority.

There were other problems in Europe that were mirrored by their activities in Germany. The Soviets had effectively annexed the Baltic states. They had also helped themselves to liberal parts of Czechoslovakia, Finland, Poland and Romania. In 1945 they had begun to involve themselves in the civil war in Greece, where they supported Greek Communists. They were pressurizing Turkey over the control of the Black Sea and in Germany they insisted on Communist agents being an integral part of the Soviet zone, despite the fact that when the first elections were held in post-war Germany, the Communists were roundly defeated, even in the Soviets' own zone.

Elsewhere in Europe the Communist Party, sponsored by the Soviets, had seized power in Hungary. After forcing the resignation of the Bulgarian government, Communists gained power there as well. In Romania and then in Poland the trend continued, but it was not until February 1948 that the free and democratic Czechoslovakian government was finally undermined and Communists came to power.

As early as 1945 the Soviets had tried to merge a German Communist Party with the Social Democratic Party. In addition there were Christian Democrats and Liberal Democrats. The referendum in May 1946 showed that Berliners in the western zones were strongly disinclined to have anything to do with Communism. In the eastern sector, after intimidation against other parties, the Soviets closed the polling booths shortly before the election was due to take place. Despite this, they had agreed that a municipal parliament election would take place in the autumn of 1946, and would have 130 members. There was an enormous amount of bribery and corruption in the lead-up to the election. The result showed 47 per cent voting for the Social Democrats, 21 per cent for the Christian Democrats, 9 per cent for the Liberal Democrats and 19 per cent for the Communists.

Soviet attempts to engineer a Communist parliament had failed but they were to have the last laugh. Within two days of the election results mass deportations out of Berlin began. Some 25,000 skilled workers and their families were forcibly relocated into the Soviet zone of Germany, or even further a field.

The United States remained resolved to bring Europe back from the brink of destruction and to act against poverty, hunger and chaos. The US Secretary of State, General Marshall, proposed a raft of measures, which were to become known as the Marshall Plan, at Harvard on 5 June 1947. On 26 June the British and French foreign ministers met in Paris and began plans to create the Organization for European Economic Cooperation. The Soviets had already denounced the Marshall Plan, claiming it was simply America's attempt to pressurize countries by the weight of the dollar. Nonetheless, Vyacheslav Molotov, the Soviet Foreign Minister, attended the Paris meeting.

Theoretically the Marshall Plan was open to any country that wanted to participate and that included the Soviet Union and their Eastern European satellites. Predictably, Stalin poured scorn on it and through his influence prevented Eastern European countries from participating.

The Soviets had manoeuvred the United States and Western Europe into accepting effective political division, as well as economic and military separation, between Eastern and Western Europe. It was Winston Churchill who dubbed this division the 'Iron Curtain'. From that point onwards Germany would effectively be two separate nations, with different destinies. The Soviets had gained precisely what they had intended, and that was unrivalled control of the eastern portion of Germany. Their hopes that they could undermine the British and rely on the Americans to weary of occupation had failed, but what they managed to achieve was a creditable second best; for the foreseeable future there would not be a unified German democratic state under the influence of the Western Allies.

The Soviets still sought to undermine Western occupation of Germany and clearly saw the uncomfortable position of Berlin as a key card in this deck. They were determined to continue to exert pressure on the Allies, and it was clear that Berlin was particularly vulnerable.

Ernst Reuter, the newly elected Chief *Burgermeister* of Berlin's City Assembly, was unacceptable to the Soviets. He had once been a Communist, but disillusioned by Stalin and Moscow, had become a Socialist. Indeed he had been chosen by the Social Democrats. The Soviets repeatedly returned correspondence addressed to him at City Hall, as the building was in the Soviet zone of the city. Eventually he stepped down and was replaced by Louise Schroeder. She became Acting Mayor in May 1947 and was to hold the post for eighteen months.

Soviet actions in Berlin were designed to increase tension. Anti-Communists were kidnapped; there was even a clash that led to deaths between rioting Russian soldiers and American military police. British military police dealt with a similar incident, in an entirely different manner: they disarmed the soldiers, beat them unconscious and then dumped them back in the Soviet sector. Always there were rumours that the Western Allies were about to pull out of the city.

Normal life was impossible in the city. If a civilian carried a Western newspaper in the Soviet zone they would be arrested. Passenger trains were routinely delayed, and vehicles entering the Soviet part of Berlin required special permits, which the Soviets made almost impossible to obtain.

May saw the arrival of the new British Commandant, Major-General E. O. Herbert. His initial optimism of being able to work closely with the Soviets was quickly dashed. By this stage the Allies had occupied the city for two years, and there were few agreements about anything. One of the important issues Herbert checked was the status of the three air corridors. Under the Quadripartite Agreement of November 1945, three air corridors passed over the Soviet zone to the city. Each was 20 miles wide and they extended from ground level to 10,000 ft.

Herbert immediately saw problems. Two of the corridors, from Hamburg and Hanover, terminated in the British zone. They were relatively straightforward as they passed over flat countryside; the highest point on the route was barely 400 ft above ground level. The Frankfurt corridor, leading to the American zone, posed more problems. It passed over much higher ground, up to 3,000 ft. With the absence of radio and radar navigation aids in Soviet-occupied territory, the Hamburg corridor extended for 95 miles, the Hanover one for 117 miles and the Frankfurt one for 232 miles.

Western Allied aircraft had freedom of passage over the Berlin Control Zone, a circular area centred on the Allied Control Council's building and extending to 20 miles. The only exceptions to this were areas close to Soviet military airfields, of which there were three: Johannisthal, Staaken and Schonewalde.

The British airfield was Gatow. It had been used as a German fighter base during the war. When the RAF took it over in 1945 they discovered that it had no runways, so nearly 1,500 yards of pierced steel planking was laid to allow Avro Ansons and Dakotas to fly in and out. Tempest Mark V fighter bombers of No. 3 Squadron were initially stationed there, but they were redeployed in May 1946. The ground at Gatow was predominantly sandy; as a consequence, the pierced steel planking proved inadequate and a concrete runway was begun in 1947.

The Americans, on the other hand, had use of Tempelhof airport, the city's major civilian airport. During the war it had a hospital, a Messerschmitt factory and a huge administration block. Initially it had been occupied by the Soviets, but when the USAF took over they laid a 1,663 x 39 yards pierced steel planking runway. They added a concrete block apron and a taxiway.

The Soviets had initially been alarmed by the potential of the Marshall Plan. They had thought that the Americans were determined to undermine Soviet Eastern European gains, but it appears that by the autumn of 1947 they had finally come to the conclusion that the Western powers were content with their share of Germany. Molotov wrote in a memorandum on 3 October 1947:

> Analysis of the materials at our disposal and of steps which were taken by the United States and Great Britain in Germany gives grounds for the conclusion that we are speaking not about a propaganda manoeuvre or political blackmail but about a real threat of political and [economic] dismemberment of Germany and inclusion of West Germany with all its resources in the Western Bloc knocked together by the United States.

The Soviets were desperate for this not to happen. On the face of it they seem to have abruptly changed their stance, as the Soviet delegation to the Council of Foreign Ministers in London was told to drive home the concept of a united democratic Germany. Of course, they meant nothing of the sort. The meeting took place between 25 November and 15 December 1947. There were huge differences between the West and the Soviets. The latter were still demanding massive reparations and seemed immovable on all other issues. In order to face them down the United States announced that forthwith they would no longer be sending excess production from their zone as part of the reparations package to the Soviet Union. France had finally begun to see eye to eye with the British and the Americans, which slightly strengthened the Western powers' hands. The Soviets continued to refuse to put resources from their zone into a common pool. This was still vital, both for western Germany and for Western-held Berlin. Amidst accusations and counter-accusations, abuse and insults, the Council finally broke up and would not meet again until May 1949.

The winter of 1947/1948 was a harsh one in the western sectors of Berlin. A typical Berliner was reduced to a lump of sugar, 1½ oz of cheese, 10 oz of meat, 7 oz of fat, three slices of bread, 1 lb of potatoes, 1 pint of milk and 12 oz of vegetables each day. This was supposed to be a temporary measure, amounting to 1,000 calories, but it was still in place as a typical ration package six months later.

The beginning of 1948 saw continued Soviet agitation. On 24 January a British military train was stopped and a pair of coaches containing German passengers detached. Two weeks later this happened to an American military train and this time German citizens were subjected to searches. The Soviets were clear about their intention to continue to intercept transport in and out of the city. They claimed that as it passed through the Soviet zone they were entitled to stop and check the identity of all passengers. If they were resisted, then the trains were simply directed into sidings and left for hours. When the Americans put armed guards on one of their trains to stop the Soviets from searching it, the wily Soviets simply turned off the electricity and left the train dead on the tracks for several hours.

Travelling into the city by road was no easier. Sometimes documents would be accepted; at other times, with the same documents, drivers were turned away or detained. This continued harassment affected individuals going both into and out of Berlin.

The Soviets soon learned that the Western Allies were determined to create a democratic and independent western Germany. Indeed, on 20 February 1948, Marshall became convinced that the Soviets fully intended to create in eastern Germany a mirror image of the Soviet Union. In response to this he believed that western Germany should be brought into the Western European fold.

Western Germany too may be at some time in the future drawn into eastern orbit with all obvious consequences which such an eventuality would entail. It has long been decided, in collaboration with the British government, that desire for an undivided Germany cannot be made an excuse for inaction in western Germany, detrimental to recovery of Western Europe as a whole. It [the US] would regard such an eventuality [a united Germany dominated by the Soviet Union] as the greatest threat to security of all Western nations, including the US.

France had been brought into the fold and together with Belgium, Holland and Luxembourg, the Western powers held meetings to discuss the establishment of a western German Republic in London between 23 February and 6 March 1948.

The Soviets continued to threaten that they would ignore any changes to the status quo, but Stalin does not seem to have been prepared for this tough stance by the West. He had gradually tightened his control over Eastern Europe, and was funding French and Italian Communists in order to disrupt those countries' economies and try to bring about a Communist government. In February 1948 the Soviets engineered a coup in Czechoslovakia. Jan Masaryk, the Czechoslovakian patriot, was either murdered or committed suicide and the country's government was overthrown. There was a temporary war scare, but all this succeeded in doing was hardening the resolve of the West to unify the western zones of Germany and introduce a unified currency.

Meanwhile Stalin ordered a gradual tightening of the blockade around Berlin. He met Marshall Sokolovsky the Soviet Military Governor, and General V. Semionov, the political advisor to the Soviet Military Administration in Germany. To this day it is not clear precisely what was discussed, but it seems obvious that Stalin told the two men to step up their harassment of the Western powers and to blockade Berlin. Three days later an assistant to Molotov suggested an outline plan to regulate the West's access to the city. This, he believed, would bring about a favourable conclusion to the status of Germany in the Soviet Union's favour. Shortly after, at a meeting with German Communist leaders, Stalin hoped that 'we can kick them out'.

There was an Allied Control Council meeting in Berlin on 20 March 1948. Sokolovsky led the Soviet attack, complaining that the conference in London had dealt with important matters concerning Germany and that the Russians had not been invited to make their point of view known. Clay and Robertson countered that the Allied Control Council was always kept in the dark about activities in the Soviet zone. Sokolovsky had already made a prepared statement, in which he claimed that the British and the Americans were hell-bent on wrecking the Allied Control Council. He went on to say:

By their actions these delegations once again confirm that the Control Council virtually exists no longer as the supreme authority in Germany. This constitutes one of the most serious violations of the obligations devolving on the British, American and French authorities in

Germany by virtue of the four-power agreements on the administration of Germany during the occupation period. It is therefore clear that the actions which are being taken now, or will be taken in the future, following the unilateral decision of the London conference, cannot be recognized as lawful.

With that, he snatched up his papers and said, 'I see no sense in continuing this meeting and declare it adjourned.' The Soviet delegation swept out and the council was never to meet again.

Administrative meetings that were due to be held were postponed by the Soviets, although they attended a meeting of the *Kommandatura* on 24 March. Meanwhile, the propaganda war went into full swing and they attempted to disrupt the city assembly.

On 25 March Sokolovsky issued orders restricting Allied military and civilian traffic between the western zones of Germany through the Soviet zone to Berlin. The following day the Soviet Chief of Staff, Lieutenant-General G. Lukyanchenko, accused the West of encouraging illegal traffic into Berlin and on 30 March declared that the Soviets would take positive steps to protect the citizens of Berlin against 'subversive and terrorist elements'.

On 31 March the Soviet Deputy Military Governor in Berlin, General Mikhail Dratvin, informed his Western counterparts that from 1 April all Western nationals travelling into the city via the railway or road network would have to submit to a luggage inspection and show identity documents at control points. In addition to this, permits would be required for all military equipment entering or leaving Berlin.

The Western Allies suspended their military passenger trains and bussed personnel in or flew them into the airports. The French were forced to follow suit after the Soviets took sixty German passengers off one of their trains heading for Berlin.

Clay, meanwhile, angered by the Soviet response, proposed to the US government that his men be given permission to shoot if necessary if Soviet troops attempted to board any of his transports. James Forrestal, the US Secretary of Defense, Kenneth Royall, the Secretary of the Army, Stuart Symington, the Secretary of the Air Force and the Joint Chiefs of Staff turned down his proposal. They believed he was overreacting but they did authorize him to test the restrictions. Clay immediately sent a train, the commander having been given orders not to allow the Soviets to inspect it. The result was inevitable: the Soviets shunted the train into a siding, where it remained for several days.

The Soviets had also begun to restrict parcel mail leaving Berlin and were also interfering with waterway traffic. The captains of the barges were told that new papers were required. They were not told what the papers were or where they could be obtained. In this respect the Soviets lost out as much of the cargo was actually destined for Czechoslovakia, Soviet controlled Germany or Russia itself.

On 2 April Clay directed the US Air Forces in Europe and their commander, Lieutenant-General Curtis E. LeMay, to begin delivering military personnel into Berlin by aircraft. LeMay was a forceful individual. He had commanded a bomber in Europe and the Pacific during the war. He deployed the Douglas C-47 Skytrain, one of the pieces of equipment that General Eisenhower had described as the four key weapons that had brought about victory during the war (the others were the Jeep, the bazooka and the atomic bomb).

The C-47 was derived from a prototype DC3 airliner that had first flown in 1935. It was the most widely used plane in USAF history. It had a maximum speed of 230 mph, was powered by a pair of 1200 hp Pratt & Whitney R-1830-92 engines and could carry 3 tons. Some twenty-five C-47s, belonging to the 61st Troop Carrier Wing at Rhein-Main were immediately pressed into action. The British Air Forces of Occupation used their own version of the C-47, the Douglas Dakota for the same role. This became known as the 'little lift'. The USAF were bringing in some 80 tons of rations, including perishable items, such as vegetables, eggs and milk, each day.

Meanwhile, on 3 April, secondary rail routes from Hamburg and Frankfurt were now to be routed through Helmstedt at the insistence of the Soviets.

There was continuous correspondence between the Soviets, the French, the British and the Americans. The Western Allies claimed that the Soviets were illegally denying the right of un-restricted access to Berlin. The Soviet counter-claim was that there was no such agreement. As it transpired the Soviets were right. There was a verbal agreement, but nothing in writing. Brigadier-General C. K. Gailey attempted to set this straight in a letter to General Dratvin:

> The agreement under which we entered Berlin clearly provided for our free and unrestricted utilization of the established corridors. This right was a condition precedent to our entry into Berlin and our final evacuation of Saxony and Thuringia. I do not consider that the provisions you now propose are consistent with this agreement. I must also advise you that we do not propose to accept changes in this agreement.

Dratvin replied in similarly terse terms:

> There was not, nor can there be, any agreement concerning disorderly and uncontrolled traffic of freight and personnel through the territory of the Soviet zone. It is obvious that such disorderly and uncontrolled traffic could only lead to confusion, and would contribute to provoking unrest in the Soviet zone through which traffic between Berlin and the western zones is passing. You are without doubt aware of the many facts, which show that the lack of control has been used by shady individuals for all kinds of illegal operations, as well as by criminal and other restless elements, causing lawlessness and a condition of crime on the territory of the Soviet Zone of Occupation. This constitutes a threat to the general peace.

Ernest Bevin, the British Foreign Secretary told the British parliament on April 6:

> It should be explained that the regulations for travel to and from Berlin are not so clearly specified. When the arrangements were made a good deal was taken on trust between the Allies, and until this event travel has been reasonably satisfactory. On the roads British travellers have shown their documents. On military trains this has not been required, since the trains were supplied by, and were under

the exclusive control of, British military authorities. The new difficulty results from the Soviet demand that Soviet military personnel should board the trains and examine passengers' documents.

It quickly became obvious that should the Soviets choose to occupy the remainder of Berlin, the fight would be relatively brief. The United States, for example, only had 6,500 men in the Berlin area. This meant that they were immediately outnumbered three to one. Against this Clay was ordered not to use force unless absolutely necessary. This is why he opted for the LeMay solution, which brought about the little lift. LeMay had taken over from Brigadier-General John McBain in October 1947. He had access to some 275 aircraft, predominantly light bombers, Thunderbolts and Mustangs. At the same time he could rely on the support of the RAF, which had a handful of squadrons, including Tempests, Spitfires and Mosquitoes. Against this was a Soviet tactical air force amounting to some 4,000 aircraft.

Secret negotiations were underway with the French and Belgian air forces. They would make several airfields available to the Americans should the unthinkable happen and war break out against the Soviets.

The little lift itself illustrated to the Western Allies that a single agency was needed to co-ordinate and clear all cargo before it was shipped. The US army's Transportation Corps provided a shuttle service so that aircraft could be loaded immediately and so that companies of men were available at either end of the flight to facilitate fast unloading.

Meanwhile, fruitless conversations were continuing between the Western Allies and the Soviets. There was an optimistic report to Moscow on 17 April:

Our control and restrictive measures have dealt a strong blow at the prestige of the Americans and British in Germany. The German population believe that the Anglo-Americans have retreated before the Russians, and this testifies to the Russians' strength. Clay's attempts to create an airlift connecting Berlin with the Western zones have proved futile. The Americans have admitted that idea would be too expensive.

This was, however, a highly misleading report. Although the KGB was highly active, they were hamstrung by having to tell Stalin precisely what he wanted to hear. By believing Soviet intelligence, Stalin believed that Britain and the United States would cave in about Berlin and Germany, but he was mistaken. He had enormously underestimated the Western Allies' resolve. The British, in any event, were determined to retain a garrison in the city. Stalin, on the other hand, still believed that by pressurizing Berlin he could force the West to abandon any plans to create an independent West Germany. He felt certain that if he blockaded the city the rest of Berlin would eventually fall under the influence of the Soviet zone.

On 5 April, close to Gatow airport, a Soviet Yak 3 fighter buzzed a British Viking airliner, with ten passengers on board. When the Yak buzzed it for a second time the two aircraft had a head-on collision. The Soviets used the incident to demand further restrictions. The Western response was equally unequivocal: both Clay and Robertson ordered armed fighter escorts for all transport aircraft. In the end it was Sokolovsky who backed down and apologized for the incident.

A telegram, dated 17 April 1948, to Molotov from a military deputy, said:

> The plan drawn up, according to your instructions, for restrictive measures to be taken regarding communications between Berlin and the Soviet zone with the Western occupation zones is applied from 1 April, except for restrictions from communication by air, which we intend to introduce later.

Clay was equally sure that this would be the Soviets' next step. He was public in his statement: 'If the Russians wanted to prevent flights of American aircraft through the corridors, they would have to fire on the American machines.'

Many believed that the Soviets actually relaxed their restrictions on or about 10 April. This was the period of the 'little lift', but in actual fact it had begun on 2 April and continued until the main lift, called Operation Vittles, began on 26 June. The major difference between the two lifts was that the 'little lift' was aimed at supporting the military garrison, whilst

Operation Vittles supported the German population of the city.

Throughout April, May and June the Soviets continued to apply pressure. On 9 April Clay was informed that any US military personnel maintaining communications equipment in the Soviet zone would have to be removed and on 20 April that all barges would require individual clearances. On 24 April, two international coaches on a train due to leave Berlin were refused their exit. On 20 May new Soviet documentation was introduced, delaying all barge traffic. Trains were interrupted on 1 and 10 June. The *autobahn* bridge across the River Elbe was closed in June.

The most important provocation took place on 16 June when the Soviets walked out of the *Kommandatura*. They claimed that they could not achieve their goals by participating any longer.

Despite the build up in harassment and the Western Allies' admission of the vulnerability of Berlin, little had been done to prepare for what might come. Almost immediately after the war the United States had virtually disbanded its army. Its total military strength in February 1948 amounted to 552,000 army, 476,000 navy and 346,000 air force personnel. In April 1947 Clay had decided to turn law and order over to the German police so that his troops could concentrate on combat training. However, a handful of regiments were not going to stop a determined Soviet attack.

By July 1948 the US establishment of army personnel stood at 116,000, but they were under strength at 90,821. Most of these had a poor combat-efficiency rating. In Berlin itself the Allies could muster five battalions of infantry with limited combat effectiveness and no heavy weapons. Against them were four whole Soviet divisions within 25 miles.

As it transpired, it was not the harassment, aircraft interdiction, tight border controls or any openly aggressive act that triggered the Berlin blockade. The Soviets already knew that in order to establish a stable West Germany the Allies would have to introduce a German currency. A currency already existed, but it had been undermined by the Soviets printing as much of it as they wanted. On 18 May 1948 the Soviets decided to put currency reform into effect in their own zone. If another currency was introduced in the western zones, they would limit the circulation of money in the greater Berlin area only to

Soviet-occupation currency. Consequently, on 20 June, when a new currency was introduced to the Western zones, it did not apply to Berlin.

Both the day before and the day after, passenger trains and traffic had been halted. On 22 June armed guards were placed on a US military supply train, which was then returned to western Germany. On 22 June there was also a meeting between the Allies' financial representatives. The Soviet delegate said: 'We are warning both you and the population of Berlin that we shall apply economic and administrative sanctions which will lead to circulation in Berlin exclusively of the currency of the Soviet occupation zone.'

In response the West decided to extend the use of their own currency to their sectors of Berlin.

Soviet troops began manoeuvres around Berlin, which seemed to create an impasse. On 24 June the Soviets severed land and water communications to the city. The following day they stated that they would no longer supply food to the German civilian population in the Western sectors. Only motor traffic was permitted out of the Western zones of the city, but even this was subject to a 14 mile detour.

Stalin was hoping that he could humiliate the Western powers and at the same time force the Berliners to accept Soviet terms, but it is abundantly clear, that he did not want war with the West. He knew that they, too, were unwilling to enter another war, but firmly believed that pressure would lead to them conceding political points. What he did not know, and his advisors did not dare to tell him, was that the British and the Americans had the capability and resolve to find a way to ensure that the free population of Berlin remained that way, despite his machinations.

CHAPTER TWO

Meagre Beginnings

Stalin still hoped that the blockade, and the Allies' reliance on the air bridges, would ultimately lead to failure and their humiliation. He hoped that he could force the Western powers and Berliners to concede and eventually accept Soviet assistance on his terms. It should be reiterated that he did not want war, but he did not have accurate assessments of the Western Allies' air capabilities and their determination to remain in Berlin.

Although the airlift could sustain the inhabitants and the garrisons in Berlin, it could not provide a solution to the blockade. In some respects, therefore, it was nothing more than a stopgap measure, brought about by necessity during the political manoeuvring. Continued supply of Berlin meant that the Western Allies could negotiate with the Soviets on a more even basis and not from one of desperation.

Lucius Clay had successfully instituted an airlift on a limited scale during the April crisis. He began again in the June, without any permission from Washington. There were 2,008,943 Berliners, and there were 7,606 British, 8,973 Americans and 6,100 French in the city. The Western Allies were supremely confident that they could supply their own occupation troops for an indefinite period. However, they were also certain that it would be impossible to meet the needs of the Berlin population for anything more than a few days.

In comparison with the winter of 1946/1947, 1948 had been pleasant and there had been a bountiful harvest. Although there had been a drought in the summer of 1947, 1948 was good enough for rations to be increased. The German fishing fleet had been rebuilt and much of Western Europe was actually producing a food surplus. On the other hand, the Soviets were sure that the Western powers would have to evacuate Berlin and could not have anticipated the massive effort that was about to be put into the Berlin Airlift.

It is important to remember several key points, which frame the way in which the airlift was approached. On 18 September 1947, the USAF had become independent of the US Army, formerly it had been the United States Army Air Force. It had some fighter squadrons and various other aircraft scattered around Germany. Two squadrons had been equipped as troop-carrying units with C-47 aircraft, but these were the only aircraft based in Europe that the Americans could use to carry cargo.

The RAF had suffered swingeing cuts, and only three fighter squadrons were based in Germany. To their horror, many aircrews that had been returned to the UK for demobilization were now abruptly informed that their service period would be extended by at least another six months. There were, of course, thousands of aircraft available, scattered here, there and every-where, including RAF Dakotas. There were also huge numbers of experienced aircrew. As for the French, all they could muster were a few converted Flying Fortresses, a handful of Dakotas and some Junker JU52s.

It is generally accepted that the Berlin Airlift began on 26 June 1948. However, eight days earlier the US European Command Transportation Division set up an air-traffic control point at Rhein-Main. Consequently, on 19 June the 67th Truck Company brought 200 tons of supplies from the Quartermaster Supply Depot at Giessen. Fresh milk was delivered to Berlin on both 19 and 20 June. The following day the traffic control point at Tempelhof was expanded and links made to the control point at Rhein-Main.

General Huebner, who later became the last Acting Military Governor of the US zone in Germany (15 May – 1 September 1949), ordered Curtis LeMay, the commander of the

USAF in Europe, to use Tempelhof and bring in as many aircraft and supplies as possible. In response to this directive LeMay wrote:

> I am today providing all available aircraft to supply Berlin in the crisis created by Soviet action following the recent currency conversion. This commitment will undoubtedly continue until the Soviets again permit our rail and freight shipments to pass to Berlin without inspection.

An interesting sideline to these developments is the dispute over who originally came up with the concept of the airlift project. It has long been believed that it derived from someone in the offices of Clay himself. Increasingly it is now believed that Air Commodore R. N. Waite, who was the Director of the Air Branch with the British Control Commission in Berlin, came up with the idea. Some forty-eight hours before the blockade came into action he alerted RAF Transport Command HQ, warning that an airlift would almost certainly be necessary. He submitted a draft plan on 23 June, which outlined the probable Anglo-American airlift requirements, to Major-General Herbert, who was commander of the British sector in Berlin. Herbert told him that it was out of the question.

Waite would not be so easily brushed aside and he spent hours working out the availability, loading capacity and cargo priorities, and the following day he returned to see Herbert again. This time the plan was very detailed. General Sir Brian Robertson was unsure whether or not the plan would work, but as a precautionary measure he agreed to present it to Clay later that day. It was then, with Clay enthusiastic about the idea, that LeMay was instructed to prepare for an airlift.

What is still confusing, however, is that in Clay's memoirs, he states that the first C-47s with cargo arrived in Berlin on 25 June, whereas other sources state that supplies started to be flown into Tempelhof on Saturday, 26 June 1948.

Clay's people began working out the necessary figures. He reckoned that the maximum that could be flown in per day was 700 tons, but he knew that this was far too little to sustain the population and the garrisons. On 27 June he sent a cable to William Draper, the US Undersecretary of the Army. It read:

I have already arranged for our maximum airlift to start on
Monday [28 June]. For a sustained effort we can use seventy
Dakotas [C-47s]. The number which the British can make
available is not yet known, although Gen. Robertson is somewhat doubtful of their ability to make this number available.
Our two Berlin airports can handle in the neighbourhood of
fifty additional airplanes per day. These would have to be
C-47s, C-54s, or planes with similar landing characteristics,
as our airports cannot take larger planes. LeMay is urging
two C-54 groups. With this airlift, we should be able to bring
in 600 or 700 tons a day. While 2,000 tons a day is required in
normal foods, 600 tons a day (utilizing dried food to
maximum extent) will substantially increase the morale of
the German people and will unquestionably seriously
disturb the Soviet blockade. To accomplish this, it is urgent
that we be given approximately fifty additional transport
planes to arrive in Germany at the earliest practical date, and
each day's delay will of course decrease our ability to sustain
our position in Berlin. Crews would be needed to permit
maximum operation of these planes.

There had been much activity in a short period of time.
President Truman was in full support of Clay and ordered that
the airlift itself was to be given the greatest support. He, too,
however, thought that the airlift would be short-lived in order to
break the diplomatic deadlock. Ernest Bevin, the British Foreign
Secretary, quickly obtained parliament's support to allow the
Americans to base B-29 Superfortress bombers in the UK. He
argued strongly that every effort should be made to increase the
airlift capacity to 2,000 tons per day as soon as possible.

Meetings were being held both in Europe and in America.
Truman quickly approved the British request to create a joint
military planning team and the first meeting was held on 30
June. The person given the responsibility to run the airlift itself
was General William H. Tunner, considered to be the very best
air transport specialist. General LeMay, meanwhile, appointed
Brigadier-General Joseph Smith to take responsibility for the US
side of the airlift. Originally the Americans called their organization LeMay Coal and Food Company, but it became more
generally known as Operation Vittles.

The 60th and 61st Troop Carrier Groups were immediately available to LeMay. Effectively the Americans had reduced their transport capabilities post-war to one group of four squadrons. They were primarily used for airline flights within Europe and for various special missions. In the spring of 1948 LeMay had asked that a second group of transport aircraft remain in Germany, so therefore the 61st Troop Carrier Group consisted of three squadrons, the 14th, 15th and 53rd. They were based at Rhein-Main and Wiesbaden. At Kaufbeuren in Bavaria there was the 60th Troop Carrier Group. This consisted of the 10th, 11th and 12th Troop Carrier Squadrons. Nominally, these units were supposed to have ninety-six C-47s. The 61st still needed one squadron to act as an airline and another to support the needs of the military government, so only the third squadron would be available for the airlift. From April at least twenty of the 60th's aircraft were flying into Berlin each day.

Clearly something had to be done to support the over-stretched C-47s. In late June there was a call for as many Douglas C-54 Skymasters as could be supplied. This meant stripping existing squadrons of their aircraft. Amongst these was the 20th Troop Carrier Squadron, based in the Panama Canal Zone, the 54th Troop Carrier Squadron at Anchorage in Alaska, the 17th Air Transport Squadron based at Great Falls, Montana, and the 19th Troop Carrier Squadron in Hawaii. USAF bases in California and Alabama also provided C-54s. The response was comparatively quick and by 10 July, fifty-four C-54s could now be deployed in Europe.

The response by the British began with a telephone call in the early hours of the morning of 26 June 1948. The Air Ministry in Whitehall informed RAF Transport Command Headquarters, Bushy Park, of the need to prepare for the airlift. This was to trigger the largest peacetime RAF operation. On 30 June 1948, in response to Whitehall's requirements, Transport Command HQ Order No. 9 was issued:

1. Following the breakdown of surface communications between the British Zone of Germany and the British Sector in Berlin, the latter will be supplied completely by air
2. The airlift into Berlin to be built up as rapidly as possible

to 400 tons per day and maintained at that level until 3 July 1948. Therefrom it is to be increased to 750 tons per day by 7 July 1948.

3. In Phase I up to 3 July inclusive, Dakotas of No. 46 and No. 38 Group operating under the control and direction of Air Headquarters, British Air Forces of Occupation (Germany), will provide the 400 tons per day lift.

Avro Yorks of No. 47 Group would provide the additional required capacity for Phase II. The airlift became maximum priority; all training was terminated and scheduled services worldwide were cancelled. It was also anticipated that a new runway at RAF Gatow would coincide with the increase to the 750-ton daily lift. No. 34 Group were given Operational Order 7/48 dated 19 June 1948 to lift 130,000 lb per day. It was code-named Operation Knicker. This would cope with the demands of the British occupation forces and alone would need some twenty-four Dakota flights per day. Initially it was expected that this lift would last no more than a month.

Air Commodore J. W. F. Merer, the Air Officer Commanding No. 46 Group, called a conference to plan the effort. Later, No. 38 and No. 47 Groups would be incorporated into the airlift operation, which was initially code-named Carter Paterson. Later this code-name was changed to Operation Plainfare.

Aircraft were shifted to position. Dakotas belonging to Nos 46, 53, 77 and 238 Squadrons moved to Wunstorf, where they would join Dakotas belonging to No. 240 Operational Conversion Unit. These were the first aircraft to begin the lift.

On 12 July, under the command of Wing Commander J. F. A. Skelton, twelve Avro Yorks arrived at Wunstorf. The Transport Wing HQ at Wunstorf was replaced by the Transport Operations based at Buckeburg, which became the headquarters for the operation.

The British had not initially anticipated the vast scale of the lift and therefore on 28 June, the British Army of the Rhine at Wunstorf created HQ Army Air Transport Organization. A Rear Airfield Supply Organization joined them. To begin with the Royal Army Service Corps controlled some 1,500 movements of lorries each day. At Gatow a Forward Airfield Supply Organization was created.

Meanwhile, the Americans were primarily using C-47s, some of which, by technical and engineering standards, were very old and had had up to five years in service. Some had flown more than 2,000 hours, most of them in wartime conditions. Many were still showing their D-Day 1944 invasion stripes. Those that were initially available had limited cargo capacity, which simply frustrated the planners. Some had corrosion and cracks in their landing gear, which required some 850 hours of inspection and maintenance. There was a great shortage of spare parts. The only big advantage of the C-47 over the C-54 was that the doors were low and easier to load and unload. LeMay was desperate for more modern aircraft, but some of these would not be available until 1949.

On 21 June overnight deliveries to Berlin by the Americans amounted to a shade under 6 tons. By the 22nd this had risen to 156 tons. For the next week or so the C-47s managed to bring in 80 tons of supplies each day. This was just the beginning and the effort would be scaled up considerably.

On 24 June General Clay, after meetings with his staff, came up with a completely different idea to break the Soviet blockade. He proposed sending a unit of US combat engineers up the *autobahn* to fix the vital bridge the Soviets claimed was unsafe. He firmly believed that if he forced the issue in this way the Soviets would back down; he was of the opinion that they were bluffing. He appreciated that he would be taking a calculated risk, and that it would take time to receive Washington's approval – if they were prepared to give approval to the operation at all. When Clay presented the plan to his British counterpart, Robertson, the British officer was appalled and said, 'If you do that, it'll be war – it's as simple as that. In such an event I'm afraid my government could offer you no support – and I am sure Koenig [the French military commander] will feel the same.'

Clay shelved the plan and met with Ernst Reuter, the Lord Mayor elect of Berlin. He told the German: 'I may be the craziest man in the world, but I'm going to try the experiment of feeding this city by air.' Reuter was clearly sceptical, but he promised Clay that the Berliners would be prepared to make any sacrifice in order to help the effort. In truth Clay was doubtful too, and hoped that the effort would only have to last for a few days.

Food was the greatest essential. On 26 June he contacted Colonel Frank Howley, who commanded the American garrison in Berlin, and asked for suggestions as to what should be flown in first. Howley told him that flour was the best foodstuff and consequently, by the next day, Clay had ordered 200 tons to be flown into the city. Howley himself witnessed the first C-47s arriving at Tempelhof.

> They wobbled into Tempelhof, coming down clumsily through the bomb-shattered buildings around the field, a sight that would have made a spick-and-span air parade officer die of apoplexy, but they were the most beautiful things I had ever seen. As the planes touched down, and bags of flour began to spill out of their bellies, I realized that this was the beginning of something wonderful – a way to crack the blockade. I went back to my office almost breathless with elation, like a man who has made a great discovery and cannot hide his joy.

There were other, more sinister deployments. On 26 June Ernest Bevin recommended that the United States send heavy bombers to Great Britain in order to deter the Soviets. There had been thousands of American aircraft on British soil during the war, but they were virtually gone by 1946. There had been a gentleman's agreement between Air Chief Marshall Sir Arthur Tedder, Chief of the Air Staff, and the commanding general, US Army Air Forces, General Carl Spaatz, in 1946. The two men had recognized that the Soviet threat was a very real one and that preparations, even if not ultimately required, were necessary. Existing RAF airfields could adequately cope with the US B-17s and B-24s. They were not, however, wide enough or long enough to cope with the massive B-29s. Over the two-year period since 1946 several had been earmarked for lengthening and widening to accommodate these aircraft. Therefore, when the crisis began to loom in 1948, the stage was set for the reappearance of American bombers on British soil. Sir Brian Robertson heard of the discussions between Bevin and the US ambassador, Lewis W Douglas, and their joint feeling that US heavy bombers in Europe could act as a deterrent to the Soviets. Consequently, on 27 June Clay made a request for a group of B-29s.

General Hoyt Vandenberg, at the US Strategic Air Command, had wanted additional units for some time and therefore fully supported Clay. Truman did not stand in the way of the request and approved it on 28 June. There was a slight delay until 13 July, when the British cabinet formally approved the establishment of two groups of B-29s. Sixty aircraft, belonging to 28th Bombardment Group, began arriving from Rapid City Air Force Base, South Dakota, between 17 and 18 July. Additional aircraft arrived from MacDill Air Force Base, Florida, comprising the 307th Bombardment Group. The crews and support personnel were told that this was a month-long temporary deployment, but it was extended, first to sixty days and then to ninety. However, the intention, as far as both the British and the United States were concerned, was that this deployment would be long-term.

Just how much of a deterrent the B-29s were is arguable. They could deliver conventional bombs, but not atomic weapons. Around this time B-29s designated Silverplate and configured to carry atomic weapons, were just coming into service. None of them was sent to Europe until July 1949, at this stage, in 1948, only the 509th Bombardment Group, based at Roswell Air Force Base, New Mexico, was allocated Silverplate aircraft.

Whether the Soviets knew that the B-29s were capable of delivering nuclear weapons is unknown. They were certainly aware of the arrival of the 28th and the 307th. The mere fact that the United States had the capacity to deliver nuclear weapons prevented Stalin from forcing the Berlin issue by force of arms, but it did not prevent the Soviets from making aggressive demonstrations, particularly in September 1948, when two divisions moved perilously close to the border of western Germany. Soviet units were combat ready and on 30 June 1948 the Politburo met in Moscow to discuss the requirements for aircraft defence of the Soviet Union.

Clay's plan to force the blockade by ground units had not exactly disappeared. On 16 July the US National Security Council met and discussed the situation. They were of the opinion that after October, when the winter set in, the United States would consider using an armed column to force their way into the city by land. Three days earlier the Pentagon had completed an analysis of the situation. It looked at the *autobahn* route and the potential dangers along it. It was some 125 miles long and there were around three bridges per mile. They were uncertain as to whether the route could be seized and held; moreover it would require thousands of trucks. Looking at the rail and barge situation, the US Army would have to seize hundreds of locks, marshalling yards, switches and bridges. Not only would ground operations risk an outbreak of war, but the Pentagon was also unsure whether the US Army had either the combat ability or the transport backup to carry out such a mission in the first place.

If such an operation were to be contemplated it would have to happen soon, and Clay was ordered to prepare a contingency plan by the US Joint Chiefs of Staff on 22 July. He drew up a stategy for what he called 'Taskforce Truculent' and presented it on 8 September. He would deploy the 2nd Constabulary Regiment, the 1st Engineer Battalion and between five and six companies of British and French troops. Between them they would deliver 1,000 tons of supplies to Berlin each day. Above all, the convoy would be prepared to fight and to deal with any obstacles *en route*. This would be the test convoy and if it worked regular convoys would be set up along the same route to provide Berlin with 1,000 tons every day.

The plan was met with scepticism from the Joint Chiefs of Staff. They still thought it was not practicable; it could not be forced through by the US and British forces, particularly if they had to fight their way through to Berlin every day. In any case, neither the British nor the French were prepared to be involved until all diplomatic avenues had been exhausted. The United States was fairly confident that if a diplomatic solution failed the British would support the effort, but was also sure that the French would not.

As for the Soviets, they too had considered the possibility of the Western Allies trying to force armed columns through to the city. The Chief of Staff of Soviet forces in Germany at the time, General S. Ivanov, had received information from Soviet intelligence that the Americans were not making plans to mobilize columns for this type of effort. In his opinion, therefore, he did not need to put forward any plans to deal with such a threat. He was of the opinion that the Soviets would consider armed columns moving through Soviet-controlled territory as an invasion and they would have been fired on without question.

Meanwhile, Group Captain Noel Hyde was sent to Germany by HQ Transport Command to coordinate the initial British effort. In his report he said:

> I received instructions on the evening of 29 June from the AOC [Air Officer Commanding] 46 Group that I was to take over command of Transport forces operating in Germany as soon as possible. I reported to Group HQ the next morning to obtain my directive and then flew to Wunstorf, arriving there in the evening. After some confusion over the chain of command on 3 July AHQ [Advanced Headquarters] issued Operations Instruction No 14/48, which completely reversed the statements made by the C in C and SASO [Senior Air Staff Officer] on the two previous days. Para 9 of this Instruction states that BAFO [British Air Forces of Occupation] Advanced Headquarters has been formed at RAF station Wunstorf, and that the officer commanding this headquarters is to exercise operational control over the transport forces allotted to him by AHQ BAFO. This he will do through the Officer Commanding RAF Station Wunstorf, who will in turn exercise control through the Officer Commanding the RAF Transport Wing located at Wunstorf.

Confusion arose when Group Captain Wally Biggar arrived at Wunstorf having received exactly the same authority as Hyde from the British Air Forces of Occupation. Once this had been sorted out the task fell to No. 46 Group, who would assume control of the British airlift.

Wunstorf was not exactly ideal. It had been built in 1934 and a *Luftwaffe* bomber group had been created there in 1939. It was then used for operations throughout 1940. From 1941 onwards it was used as a training base and in the latter stages of the war some fighters operated from the airfield. No. 123 RAF Fighter Bomber Wing occupied it in May 1945. By July 1948 some forty-eight Dakotas of No. 30 Squadron were operating from there. This was in addition to Nos 46, 53, 77 and 238 Squadrons and

No. 240 Operational Conversion Unit. The airfield was primarily grass, apart from two concrete runways, perimeter tracks and aprons in front of the hangars.

No. 46 Group's requirements, based on their Operational Order 9/48 of 30 June, required 400 tons to be lifted using 161 Dakota sorties every day. Six additional ones would be flown each day into Berlin as scheduled flights. This would last until 3 July. From then on eighty-four Dakota sorties, carrying 210 tons each day, plus the six additional ones, would need to fly out of the base. Meanwhile No. 47 Group would fly 120 sorties with their forty Avro York aircraft.

As we have seen, Skelton's first twelve Yorks arrived at Wunstorf on the evening of 12 July. It was quickly decided that due to the state of the surface of the airfield only twenty could be deployed there. Several ditches needed to be filled in and other areas covered by pierced steel planking. There was also heavy rain, which caused even more problems, but the pierced steel planking was fitted quickly and the additional Yorks started to fly into the base on 4 and 5 July.

There were also issues relating to air-traffic control. Aircraft leaving Runway 09 at Wunstorf were required to climb for two minutes at 145 knots and stay below 1,000 feet. They would then turn towards Walsrode. Their height to Walsrode would be 3,500 feet, at an air speed of 160 knots. From there they would head to Egestorf, then to Restorf and then to the checkpoint from Frohnau Beacon. At this point they could contact Gatow. They would then descend to 1,500 feet, making sure that they did not drop below 2,000 feet before they reached Tegel. On the return they would fly via Prutzke and Volkenrode.

Air Commodore Merer visited Wunstorf on 5 July. He wanted to increase flying hours and suggested 112 sorties each day until 31 July. On 16 July the Dakotas were showing signs of strain and the daily rate was reduced to 102 sorties. The following day, however, HQ Transport Command gave orders that the Dakotas should fly 2,000 hours on the next seven days and from then on 1,700 hours per week. This meant that there would be 125 sorties every day.

The initial planned lift for Operation Knicker, up to 29 June, was 130,000lb, but this was routinely exceeded by 30,000lb each day.

Between 30 June and 3 July, effectively the first phase of Operation Plainfare, the RAF failed to reach their target of 160 sorties each day. Bad weather was the main cause, but some aircraft could not be serviced in time, there were problems affecting electrical equipment onboard aircraft due to the dampness, and other problems including starter trolleys, petrol bowsers and loading difficulties due to lack of manpower. Once No. 47 Group's Avro Yorks were deployed during the second phase of Operation Plainfare (4–19 July), however the totals on a daily basis rose from 474 tons (6 July) to an impressive 995 tons (18 July).

The RAF was still dogged by bad weather, however. Gatow Air Traffic Control often stopped all flying, and sometimes they refused to allow aircraft to land unless there was an interval of at least fifteen minutes between each. The airfield was boggy and several of the Avro Yorks experienced mechanical problems. During this period the daily average of sorties was some seventy-seven; the target was 120, but no more than 100 was ever achieved in a single day. There were considerable problems with the C-47s.

At any one time parts of nine squadrons were involved, including Nos 18, 27, 30, 46, 53, 62, 77, 113 and 238 (which in November was redesignated No. 10 Squadron). Aircraft and crews had been brought in from a number of different stations. Nos 18, 53 and 62 came from RAF Waterbeach, Nos 27, 30 and 46 from RAF Oakington, Broadwell provided No. 77 Squadron, Fairford No. 113 and Abingdon No. 238. Abingdon also provided most of No. 47 Group's Avro Yorks (from Nos 40, 59 and 242 Squadrons). Lyneham also provided Avro Yorks from Nos 206 and 511 Squadron. Finally, Bassingbourn provided Avro Yorks from No. 51 Squadron.

Servicing and loading personnel, prior to the arrival of the Avro Yorks, were able to deal with the C-47s at a rate of one every six minutes during daylight hours. They even managed a creditable fifteen-minute interval at night. Once the Avro Yorks arrived there were problems resulting from differences in speed. The different aircraft were separated in height, but there were always dangers when either ascended or descended. It was impossible to create a fixed flying programme. It was possible for the last C-47 in a group of aircraft to be overtaken by the first

Avro York of the following group. Eventually this was worked out and waves of aircraft were created so that it did not happen, but unfortunately this caused problems for ground crew. By the time the system was in place aircraft were arriving at Gatow every four minutes. During times of poor weather the C-47 flights were often cancelled, whilst the Avro York ones were maintained.

Due to the pressures on the aircraft and the crews there were often delays in either loading or servicing. Once delays occurred, they would often ruin the flying programme for the day, causing additional problems for Air-traffic Control, making collisions more likely and adding additional pressures to the loaders and the servicing crews. Finally, Air-traffic Control was given comprehensive lists of all proposed sorties for the day, indicating the take-off time and the type of aircraft involved. Henceforth the aircrew would have to obtain clearance from flying control in order to lift off. Air-traffic Control would then look at the list and find the next available slot for that particular type of aircraft. The aircraft would then be given permission to start up, approach the runway and then lift off at the appropriate time. If there were problems with timing and the aircraft did not make the runway in time the sortie would be cancelled. This system was implemented on 15 July 1948.

There were, of course, considerable differences between the C-47 and the Avro York. The C-47 had a provisional payload of 5,500 lb as its maximum landing weight was 27,000 lb. To increase its loading capacity, any extraneous equipment was stripped out of the aircraft, including safety equipment. It was also decided to reduce the amount of petrol carried. HQ Transport Command received authorisation on 16 July to increase the landing and take-off weights of the C-47s to 28,000 and 28,750 lb respectively. This now meant that they could carry 7,500 lb.

Theoretically, it was supposed to take some thirty minutes to receive and turn around a C-47. However, in practice this was usually forty-five minutes. The delay was mainly down to the positioning of the aircraft in relation to the loading area and hangars. It was slightly simpler at Gatow, where the aircraft did not need to be refuelled, so the turn-around rate averaged out at about twenty minutes.

The Avro Yorks were supposed to fly some 120 sorties each day, but it was quickly discovered that 100 was about the maximum possible. The aircraft was more prone to throw up servicing problems, as it was only undertaking short flights – it was, of course, primarily designed for long-range duties. This meant that parts, such as the brakes and the tyres, were not designed for constant take-offs and landings and therefore needed a more thorough servicing schedule. In theory there should have been around forty Avro Yorks available for work on any given day. Of these, thirty would be actively used. The Avro York itself had a maximum loaded weight of some 60,000 lb. HQ Transport Command increased the landing weight to 65,000 lb on 16 July. This now meant that the passenger-freighter version of the Avro York had a capacity to carry some 15,000 lb, while the freighter itself could carry 16,500.

Another snag with the passenger-freighter version was that its door was under the wing and relatively small. It was originally envisaged that an Avro York would need two hours' turn-around time, but in practice again it was longer, by half an hour. Without the need to refuel, it would be turned around at Gatow in less time – just under three-quarters of an hour.

There were grave difficulties with the maintenance of the telephones and landlines, despite the best efforts of the Royal Corps of Signals. The British were also still getting to grips with the requirements of the lift and the practicalities of flogging the aircraft and aircrews to death with so many sorties each day.

Ten Short Sunderland flying boats from RAF Calshot, belonging to Nos 201 and 230 Squadrons, joined in the operation on 5 July 1948. The RAF had set up a new base to the west of Hamburg, on the River Elbe, at Finkenwerder. Henceforth these aircraft would fly into Lake Havel, close to Gatow airport. Their role was to fly in food supplies and fly out refugees and manufactured goods. DUKWs [an amphibious truck]were used for unloading. This meant that the Sunderlands could be loaded or unloaded in just twenty minutes at Hamburg and twelve minutes on the lake. These flights continued until 15 December 1948. In all, they carried in 4,500 tons of supplies and carried out 1,113 malnourished children. In all they completed over 1,000 sorties, but were forced to terminate operations when the lake froze. The Sunderlands were important, as they were the only aircraft able to carry salt, because they had been treated with internal anti-corrosion chemicals.

The British occupation zone provided considerable flying advantages, as it was mainly over flat land. The British also had shorter distances to fly, which allowed them to make more trips to Berlin each day. The Americans, on the other hand, operating in the south, were required to fly over the Taunus Mountains. Here the weather was milder but prone to fog.

The April crisis had given both the United States and Britain considerable warning, which allowed them to build up stockpiles of supplies. On 30 June , for example, supplies in Berlin had been stockpiled to the following levels:

Commodity	Days' worth of supplies
Flour	25
Sugar	81
Meat	19
Fat	56
Potatoes	18
Cereal	54
Milk	19
Coffee	18

Decisions still needed to be made about exactly what to fly into Berlin. A typical trade-off occurred with bread. The Allies could either fly in a loaf of bread, which was 30 per cent water, or flour and coal to allow the bread to be made in the city. In the event flour and coal was chosen. Rather than manufacturing *ersatz* in Berlin, which required fuel, it was decided to fly in real coffee. Fresh potatoes were discarded in favour of dehydrated ones. Other efficiencies needed to be made, including the building of a bridge between Gatow and the city. This meant that less petrol would be used. Elsewhere, electrical plants were converted to use diesel fuel rather than coal. Every single little saving took a tiny amount of pressure off the airlift.

Despite all of this the basic daily food rations for Berlin were still staggering amounts:

Commodity	Daily requirement for Berlin in tons
Flour/wheat	646
Sugar	180
Meat and fish	109
Fat	64
Potatoes (dehydrated)	180
Cereal	125
Milk (powdered)	19*
Coffee	11
Yeast	3
Dehydrated vegetables	144
Salt	38
Cheese	10

* Plus 5 tons of whole milk for children

This was in addition to liquid fuel and coal. Other raw materials were also required for industry, not to mention newsprint and medical supplies. It was Howley's estimate that between August and October 1948 the city could just tick over with just less than 3,500 tons every day.

In the early stages the Soviet blockade, although rigorously imposed, was not complete. The railway system wound in and out of Allied and Soviet sectors. The canal-boat owners, routinely used the canal traffic that passed through the British sector of Berlin, to smuggle goods and supplies into the city. All they had to do was show the Soviets that the final destination was the Soviet zone when, in fact, it was not. As Howley himself commented:

Tight lines were drawn between the Soviet sector and the three Western sectors, but they did not prevent intermingling during the blockade. About 80,000 Germans, living in our sector and working in another, or doing business outside their own sector, went back and forth daily. Theoretically, the Germans were not permitted to bring anything into our sectors, but the Russians, so keen on searching people on the slightest pretext, shrank at the formidable task of searching 80,000 every day.

Many Germans became past masters at smuggling and truck-loads of food entered the western sectors of Berlin despite the blockade. Potsdammerplatz was the centre of the black market; almost anything was available if you had the money.

Marshal Sokolovsky met with members of the East German Industrial Committee on 28 June 1948. They explained to him that many of the industrial elements in the Soviet sector would cease to function very soon if they could not have guaranteed access to machine parts and raw materials from the western zones. At this point it seems that the Soviets had absolutely no idea that their zone needed the western zones' industry to continue to work. Sokolovsky learned the bitter lesson and that the blockade was a two-sided coin. When Howley discovered that Sokolovsky's home was supplied by a gas main housed in the western sector, he ordered it to be turned off. This forced Sokolovsky to move, and when his furniture was put on a van and the Soviets tried to sneak it across the Western sector, Howley ordered the van to be captured and the furniture impounded.

Gradually the Allies were able to apply a counter-blockade. The Soviets had cancelled the Berlin Food Agreement on 25 June. Henceforth any food supplied by the Soviet occupation zone would only be used in the eastern sector of Berlin. The day before, the Soviets had halted milk supplies into the western sectors of the city. In retaliation, the US authorities had cancelled meat deliveries to the east. Likewise, when the Soviets made their announcement on 25 June the United States shifted flour supplied by them to the city from warehouses from the eastern sector to the west. In addition they cut shipments of food and medicine into the eastern sector. It did not take very long before these counter-blockade measures began to cause severe problems to the Soviet military command and administration and the German people living in the Soviet zone of occupation.

LeMay flew a C-47 into Tempelhof on 29 June. He experienced many of the frustrations that Allied pilots would have to cope with over the coming weeks. He was initially cleared to depart from Rhein-Main at 1045, but due to problems obtaining runway clearance at Tempelhof he was delayed until 1200. His aircraft was unloaded in a creditable twenty minutes once it arrived in Berlin. During his discussions with Clay they decided that the only way to move sufficient coal into Berlin was to utilize B-29s, which Tempelhof was incapable of accepting. Therefore LeMay suggested dropping the coal at low altitude. This idea needed to be tested in practice, so the commanding officer at Tempelhof, Colonel Henry Dorr, was instructed to find a suitable drop location.

LeMay was also concerned with air-traffic-control issues and ordered standard instrument approaches to be eliminated in favour of straight-in approaches, particularly during bad weather. Every minute could count in maintaining flight schedules. Pilots would routinely have to go to the operations room at Tempelhof to fill in forms, but from now on LeMay ordered the operations officers to bring the forms to the aircraft, along with coffee and refreshments for the crew. As a parting shot, he also ordered that the C-47s would fly with a reduced fuel load and thereby increase their cargo carrying capacity by 1,500 lb.

As far as the Americans were concerned the man that shaped the Berlin Airlift was Brigadier General Joseph Smith. He was only in control of the operation between 29 June and 28 July 1948, but it was he who established the team that would define the way in which the Americans approached the whole operation.

On 1 July the first C-54's arrived at Rhein-Main, and the first one flew into Tempelhof ten hours later. By the following day seventeen had flown into Berlin. More were *en route* and follow-on waves were being flown out of the United States. The first twenty-five joined the C-54 squadrons at Rhein-Main base. Thirty were allocated to the 60th Troop Carrier Group at Wiesbaden. Gradually they were replacing the C-47s. Rhein-Main would continue to be the place where parts and spares were located for all aircraft, but by 12 July it was exclusively a base for C-54s. Ten C-54s were moved to Wiesbaden and the last C-47 squadron was transferred to Cyprus.

It was Smith who established what became known as the block system. He had to grapple with the problem of handling two very different types of aircraft, the C-47 and the C-54. The aircraft would fly in groups by type, the C-54s having priority simply because they could carry more. Initially a block of C-54s would leave Rhein-Main, followed by a block of C-47s. The C-47s at Wiesbaden would take off after the C-54s. Eastbound

C-47s were codenamed 'easy' and westbound ones 'willy'; east-bound ones were 'big easy' and westbound C-54s 'big willy'. These designations were followed by numbers assigned in order of take-off, starting with 1, followed by the last three digits of the aircraft's serial number.

There was other work for Smith to do in these early days. He decided that the aircraft spacing in each block should be three minutes. At least 65 per cent of all aircraft should be available on any given day and that any aircraft being flown should make three round trips. By 26 July all military-industrial supplies would be handled by Wiesbaden, Rhein-Main would be reserved primarily to supply the civilian population of the city. Finally, on 21 July Smith asked for improvements at Tempelhof with regard to the navigation beacon. From then on the American Forces Network would broadcast all night in order to help the crews gain a fix for radio compasses.

Despite all of these improvements, the Tempelhof airfield was beginning to show signs that it would not last much longer. The C-54s were exacting a heavy toll on the landing strip and Smith was warned that it was unlikely to last more than another couple of months. On 9 July he had authorized the construction of a second runway. Within ten days everything was in place to begin flying in the necessary construction materials. Smith had insisted that the planners incorporate the construction materials at a rate of 50 tons a day and by 31 July nearly 280 tons had arrived. On 23 July he had begun to make tentative investigations into whether the British would allow him to use RAF bases in the British occupation zone. He spoke to Group Captain K. B. B. Cross, who suggested Fassberg, Gutersloh or Wunstorf. Smith proposed to use one of these for C-54s.

The arrival of the C-54s was having a huge impact. At the end of June the Americans were managing around 500 tons each day. By 31 July this was up to 1,719.5 tons each day. Meanwhile the British were contributing 1,437 tons per day. This meant that the combined Allied total amounted to 3,156.5 tons per day, but this was still inadequate, as 4,500 tons were needed. The cumulative total by both the Americans and the British up to 31 July amounted to 69,005.7 tons. Of this, the Americans had contributed 39,971 tons and the British 29,034.7 tons.

Returning to British operations, Wunstorf was buckling under the strain of the number of C-47s and Avro Yorks it was handling, and the RAF transferred its C-47s to Fassberg. The Avro Yorks were beginning to suffer from maintenance problems. This would not be solved until the arrival of the Handley Hastings. The British soon realized that in order to maintain the airlift and reach the daily ton rate required they would need to press civilian aircraft into use. They placed these under contract. There were already several private companies that had specialized aircraft, foremost amongst which was Flight Refuelling Limited. They had extensive experience in delivering aviation fuel and owned several Avro Lancastrian tankers. These were transport versions of the commercial airliner and designed to carry liquid fuel. The first Lancastrian left Tarrant Rushton in Dorset on 7 July, flying into Berlin. Discussions were already underway between the Ministry of Civil Aviation and the Air Ministry to bring in more commercial aircraft. There was already ten C-47s at Fassberg, along with a pair of Short Hythe flying boats. At Wunstorf there was a Handley Page Halton and a Consolidated Liberator. A variety of other aircraft could be brought into use: the Avro Tudor was a liquid fuel tanker, the Bristol Freighter was capable of carrying 4 tons and the Halton itself was a version of the Halifax bomber and could carry 6–8 tons of liquid fuel. It could also carry a pannier under the fuselage for transporting salt.

One of the major problems in Berlin as far as aircraft was concerned was the extremely low stock of liquid fuel. It was proposed that by 1 January 1949 a fleet of thirty-one tankers would deliver some 220 tons of liquid fuel. As it transpired, the British only had access to eleven tankers with a maximum capacity of 148 tons at that stage. The civilian fleet, however, was to prove a decisive addition. In all they would fly 21,921 sorties into the city and would contribute 146,980 tons of supplies. This was for many of the small businesses, run by veteran pilots, a great opportunity. Unfortunately, by 1950 many of them were gone forever. The twenty-five civilian companies used 104 different aircraft during the lift. These included forty-one Haltons, nineteen C-47s, seventeen Lancastrians, nine Tudors, four Bristol Freighters, three Hythes, three Liberators, three Avro Yorks, two Vickers Vikings and a pair of Bristol Wayfarers.

On 16 July the US National Security Council heard a

pessimistic report from the Assistant Secretary of the Air Force for Material, Cornelius V. Whitney. They learned that if they used 180 C-54s and 105 C-47s, the maximum lift was 3,000 tons per day. It was now estimated that Berlin needed 5,300 tons per day; Whitney suggested that the British contribution could not be more than 1,000 tons, so they were 1,300 tons short of the target. There were other problems too. Tempelhof was breaking up, Berlin was sucking up the United States' entire transport reserve; in conclusion Whitney was certain that the air operation was doomed. In the end the National Security Council believed that it would be impossible to maintain the airlift after October 1948 and would not, at this stage, commit further aircraft.

Truman had an entirely different point of view. He was acutely aware of Soviet expansionism and meddling. They had been defeated in France, Greece and Italy, their activities in Finland had been reversed and Tito of Yugoslavia had caused them acute embarrassment. Truman now felt that they would not countenance failure in Berlin. Following on from the meeting he had with Secretaries Forrestal and Marshall on 19 July, Forrestal said: 'The airlift by that time had begun to demonstrate its power. Immediately the situation was a trifle easier; but the long-term possibilities were formidable.'

Clay met with Truman and the National Security Council on 22 July. He asked that the full support of the United States be put behind the effort in Berlin. He explained that he had the full support of the British and the French and that the German people in the city and their representatives were completely co-operative. He reported that fifty-two C-54s and eighty C-47s were managing to make 250 deliveries each day, but he needed more aircraft. If he was to have his complement of C-54s increased to seventy-five, he could deliver 3,500 tons every day and with the British providing a further 1,000 tons, 4,500 tons was within reach. He concluded by saying: 'The airlift has increased our prestige immeasurably. It has been impressive and efficient and has thrown the Russian timetable off. Two months ago the Russians were cocky and arrogant. Lately they have been polite and have gone out of their way to avoid incidents.'

The National Security Council approved Clay's recommendations and gave him a further seventy-five C-54s. They also agreed that new airfields should be constructed in Berlin. Decisively the National Security Council reaffirmed their desire that the United States remain active in Berlin.

On 26 July the US Joint Chiefs of Staff suggested that negotiations with the Soviets continue and that, if possible, an alternative to the airlift be sought.

> It is assumed that diplomatic effort together with all practicable counter-pressure will continue to be used to arrive at peaceful solution of the Berlin problems. In this connection, it may not be altogether out of the question to consider, during the time that is to be gained by concentration of major effort on air transport supply, the possibility that some justification might be found for withdrawal of our occupation forces from Berlin without undue loss of prestige.

There were, indeed, diplomatic moves afoot and there had been since 29 June. On that day Sokolovsky told General Robertson that the blockade could be lifted, provided the decisions of the London conference were scrapped. He reiterated this view on 3 July when he met with Clay, Robertson and Koenig. Clay later reported that for the first time Sokolovsky had given a reason for the blockade in the first place. It was simply that they required the abandonment of any plans to create a West German government.

There was a meeting on 2 August 1948, between the British, American and French ambassadors in Moscow, and Stalin. Stalin told them that he did not want the Western occupation zones to be unified. Provided he received a promise that the London conference decisions would be put back, he would lift the blockade.

On 15 August the Soviets proposed the publication of a joint communiqué, stating that the new currency would be withdrawn from Berlin, in the future meetings of the Council of Foreign Ministers would discuss any outstanding questions involving Berlin or Germany and the idea of a government for West Germany would be shelved. In effect, it was everything that the Soviet Union wanted. Clearly the West would not agree to such a communiqué.

Meanwhile, on 28 July Major-General William H. Tunner landed at Wiesbaden. He was the USAF's pre-eminent authority on air transport and firmly believed that the Berlin crisis was not a battle that the West could afford to lose. Later he described the Berlin Airlift in detail.

The actual operation of a successful airlift is about as glamorous as drops of water on stone. There's no frenzy, no flap, just the inexorable process of getting the job done. In a successful airlift you don't see planes parked all over the place; they're either in the air, on loading or unloading ramps, or being worked on. You don't see personnel milling around; flying crews are either flying, or resting up so that they can fly again tomorrow. Ground crews are either working on their assigned planes, or resting up so they can work on them again tomorrow. Everyone else is also on the job, going about his work quietly and efficiently. The real excitement from running a successful airlift comes from seeing a dozen lines climbing steadily on a dozen charts – tonnage delivered, utilization of aircraft and so on – and the lines representing accidents and injuries go sharply down. That's where the glamour lies in air transport.

The first thing Tunner insisted on was the efficient use of the day. He figured that, as there were 1,440 minutes in each day, the ideal would be to organize 480 landings each day, in other words one every three minutes. He viewed the air corridors between western Germany and Berlin rather as conveyor belts.

No one could escape Tunner: he worked for eighteen hours a day, seemed to be everywhere, talking to everyone and jollying people along. He had an eye for the small things, the things that made a real difference. When he visited coal barges he saw that the workers filling the bags were not checking each weight. He ordered fifty bags to be checked straight away and found that on average they weighed not 100 lb but 115 lb. This meant that the aircraft were taking off with around 15 per cent more weight than was expected; henceforth every bag would be weighed.

Tunner did not come alone: there were more C-54s on the way, as promised by the National Security Council on 22 July.

On 23 July a task force, comprising nine squadrons of C-54s, was created. Three crews were allotted to each aircraft. This soaked up some two-thirds of all C-54 aircrew available to the United States worldwide. At this stage they could lay their hands on 866 C-54s, and civilian airlines had a further 267. Calculations were made of the availability of aircraft and the planners discovered that there was a ready pool of 393 C-54s. This meant that the first squadrons could be sent to Germany. By mid-August they had access to 126 C-54s for the airlift.

Tunner established his headquarters on 29 July. Two days later Airlift Task Force (Provisional) was activated. As we have seen, General Smith had approached the British in July about using one of the RAF bases in their zone. Eventually they focused on Fassberg. It had huge advantages: it was just fifty-five minutes by air to Berlin, half the distance from Frankfurt, it was close to the port at Bremen, and the weather conditions were better. The United States believed that they could operate twenty-seven C-54s from there. In an eight-hour day they could deliver 988 tons. This compared favourably with the twenty-seven based at Wiesbaden, which could only deliver 518 tons.

Negotiations began at the beginning of August and by the 6th it was agreed that Fassberg would be used for the C-54s. The RAF would load all the aircraft and maintain the runway, hangars and other facilities, whilst the United States would provide personnel to man the fuel pumps, maintenance staff and rations. In effect it was to become a joint operation between the RAF and the USAFE. US personnel from 7496th Air Wing began to arrive at Fassberg on 13 August, supplies began arriving three days later and the refuelling units were ready on 18 August. The first flight of twenty-seven C-54s flew into Fassberg on the 21st.

CHAPTER THREE

Black Friday

On 2 August the Berlin Airlift task force began looking at procedures to direct RAF or US aircraft to either Tempelhof or Gatow, whichever had the least amount of traffic at the time. A US liaison detachment was set up at Gatow and by the end of August US aircraft were routinely using the RAF base.

There had been several meetings during August to try and resolve command and control problems. The control centre in Berlin was providing adequate coordination for the city. It was finally decided that Air Commodore John W. F. Merer would co-ordinate all Allied efforts operating from the British zone and that the US Transport Command task force would cover the US zone.

From the beginning the US operations out of Fassberg were co-ordinated with the RAF effort. The C-54s lifted off at 0100, 0500, 0900, 1700 and 2100. The aircraft in each block would take off at three-minute intervals, up to five minutes if there was poor weather. They were ordered to fly at three different altitudes: 2,500 ft, 3,000 ft and 3,500 ft. Once a block was airborne, the RAF would be informed that the corridor was available for C-47s and Avro Yorks.

Additional C-54s, crews and ground personnel meant that there was going to be congestion. The Rhein-Main base and Wiesbaden were overcrowded and this caused efficiency problems. There would have to be a long-term plan to modernize the facilities and construct new runways and buildings. As a result, two main decisions were made in August. Fassberg was opened as a priority and the United States began to dispense with C-47s.

Tunner was already developing plans to base some forty C-54s in the British occupation zone at Celle by the beginning of December 1948. Berlin was also a problem. Neither Tempelhof nor Gatow was sufficiently developed to cope with the amount of aircraft landing every few minutes (see Chapter 6). Under Tunner's direction the first airlift task force began to monitor the flow of traffic. They kept a close eye on the corridors and made sure that diversions were made when necessary. There were three centres that controlled the rate of flow along the corridors: one in each occupation zone and a third in Berlin. What Tunner wanted was for that system to be fully integrated. At the moment he felt it was simply too complicated.

There were two methods for regulating take-off. The first entailed each base receiving blocks of time within which to take off, this took account of different aircraft with different air speeds and distances to travel. The second, operated when the bases were close together. There needed to be a way to ensure that each aircraft entered Berlin at the proper interval, so standard air speeds for climb and cruise were brought into effect. However it was not until 30 September 1948 that the last C-47 left US airlift operations. After that date the block system was abandoned and Tunner's conveyor-belt approach was adopted. The British, meanwhile, had widely spaced bases and many different types of aircraft and needed to rely on the block system.

Ideally, aircraft flying at the same speed and heading for the same airfield would approach at least 500 ft apart and with an interval of six minutes between them. This should have provided sufficient safety and was enough for long-haul flights, but for short-haul trips a three-minute interval was introduced. A problem arose when aircraft with different speeds were involved. They had to approach at radically different altitudes for safety reasons and to ensure that there was still a smooth flow of aircraft into the base.

Bad weather threw all of this into chaos, with Air-traffic Control grounding aircraft or diverting them to other airfields as far as 600 miles away. If aircraft missed their landing time at either of the Berlin airports they would be stacked. This meant that they had to circle in order to land again, whilst those behind held their pattern over the base. If there were further delays then more and more aircraft would be circling, stacked higher and higher into the pattern. This would inevitably cause delays. In effect, if nine aircraft were stacked at up to 9,000 ft, they would take upwards of ninety minutes to land. It was a dangerous procedure, particularly as they were heavily laden.

On Friday, 13 August 1948 the airlift had been in operation for seven weeks and Tunner had been in command for two. He was to fly into Berlin to present an award to a pilot who had made the highest number of flights into Berlin at that stage, a Lieutenant Paul O. Lykins. He took off from Wiesbaden amongst black clouds and in rainy conditions. He could see ahead of him, at three-minute intervals, a line of heavily laden C-54s. Behind him the line stretched back into the distance. As Tunner's aircraft approached Berlin the weather closed in. Very little could be seen as the clouds dropped to rooftop level and sheets of rain confused the radar operators.

A C-54 came into land; it missed the runway, crashed and burst into flames. A second made the approach and as it landed its main tyres blew as it was attempting to swerve out of the way of the first wrecked aircraft. A third arrived and began its approach. It missed the runway completely and just about managed to land on an auxiliary runway. It was at about this time that the stacking was brought into effect. Berlin Air-traffic Control put Tunner into a slot at 8,000 ft. Other aircraft following his were stacked up to 12,000 ft. In a relatively short period of time there were dozens of aircraft going round and round from 3,000 to 12,000 ft.

Tunner grabbed the radio and called Air-traffic Control: 'This is 5549, Tunner talking and you better listen. Send every plane in the stack back to its home base.'

There was a moment's silence and then a voice asked him to repeat. Tunner complied. 'Send everybody in the stack below and above me home. Tell me when it's OK to come down.'

Air-traffic Control complied. Tunner had realized that stacking was both dangerous and counterproductive. He concluded that aircraft that missed their approach should be sent back through the centre corridor and then re-routed to Berlin. This needed new procedures and Lieutenant-Colonel Robert D. Forman, who was Tunner's chief of operations, worked out the details. Lieutenant-Colonel Stirling P. Bettinger, Tunner's chief pilot assisted him.

From this point, aircraft attempting to land at Tempelhof would be given just one chance. If they could not land they would head back towards their home airbase along the centre corridor. Still loaded, they would fly at a different altitude from the aircraft returning to base unloaded. They could then be re-routed back to Berlin. This now meant that the aircraft would fly towards Berlin at three-minute intervals and would be expected to land at three-minute intervals. If the aircraft missed its approach, it would head back to the home base, land and then be given a new slot. It made a considerable difference. Nine stacked aircraft would take ninety minutes to land, but by using this straight-in approach the aircraft could land at three-minute intervals and, therefore, rather than nine C-54s landing in the ninety-minute period, thirty could land.

The crews had to be trained and made aware of these standard techniques and operating procedures. Towards the end of the airlift each month around 17 per cent of the crews were replacements. This meant that around eight pilots each month had to be upgraded to cope with the new operating procedures.

The first British civilian charter flight came in from Bückeburg into Gatow on 27 July. Elsewhere there had been tremendous progress and transport aircraft were actually far outstripping the facilities at Wunstorf. Consequently, all of the RAF and civilian C-47s were moved out to Fassberg on 29 July. Four-engined civilian aircraft remained at Wunstorf, along with the RAF's own Avro Yorks.

Fassberg was a former *Luftwaffe* bombing school training base and had been completed in 1936. It was later used for technical training and operational *Luftwaffe* aircraft used it before the Allies overran it in 1945. The RAF had used it as a fighter base but it now needed to be considerably enlarged. The twelve-barrack blocks were renovated, along with the former technical school. A pair of office buildings became accommodation and two hangar annexes were converted. Expansion also required considerable clearance. Some 5 acres of forest were levelled and 180,000 square yards of pierced steel planking was laid, along with around five miles of railway sidings. Hard standing was added and, incredibly, under the watchful eye of Group Captain Biggar, the work was completed in just seven days. In the event, however, the British C-47s only stayed there until 22 August, when the base was handed over to the USAF and the first detachment of forty C-54s.

The British aircraft now moved to Lübeck, which the Germans had built in 1935. Initially Heinkel He 111 bombers had used it, and later night fighters were based there. When the British took control of the area after the war it was used as an armament practice camp. Again the work needed on this air base was extensive, but was rapidly completed. Around 88,000 square yards of parking apron was laid, along with pierced steel planking. The railhead was expanded, a concrete road laid to bulk petrol storage installations and comprehensive lighting installed for the runway and the loading areas. It is important to note, however, that Lübeck was just 2 miles from the Soviet zone of occupation. This meant that pilots had to pay particular attention to their approach to the base and take-off from it.

The routine for take-off from Runway 26 was to climb to 400 ft at around 110 knots. They would then turn to starboard, holding their course for a minute. The pilot would then have to make a climbing turn to starboard and set a course at 2,000 ft. Equally explicit instructions were required for other runways. Aircraft inbound from Gatow would come in at 5,500 ft at a speed of around 135 knots. They would head first for Ruhen, then Lüneburg and Tremsbuttel and then complete the final 16-mile leg to base.

There were no less than seven RAF squadrons operating from Lübeck. Nos 18, 27, 30, 46, 62 and 77. They were primarily concerned with bringing in coal, newsprint and materials and equipment in order to keep Berlin's industries going. In addition to the RAF squadrons, Air Contractors, Air Transport, British Nederland Air Services, BOAC, Ciros Aviation, Hornton Airways, Kearsley Airways, Scottish Airways, Sivewright Airways, Trent Valley Aviation and Westminster Airways all operated from Lübeck. In all they contributed around eighteen C-47s.

Within a very short period of time, however, even Lübeck became congested, and the civilian operators were transferred to Fuhlsbuttel on 5 October. Fuhlsbuttel was controlled by the Civil Aviation Control Commission of Germany and was the civil airport of Hamburg.

Australians, South Africans and New Zealanders arrived in mid-September 1948. The first to arrive were twelve C-47 crews of the Royal Australian Air Force of No. 1 (Dominion) Squadron. Ten South African crews arrived in October, belonging to No. 2 (Dominion) Squadron of the South African Air Force. Three New Zealand crews arrived in the November, belonging to the Royal New Zealand Air Force. They were assigned to fly RAF C-47s and throughout the airlift would make a considerable contribution to the effort.

Just as Tunner had witnessed potential disaster over Tempelhof on 3 August, the British were not immune to problems themselves. There had been a handful of accidents spread across the first few months of the airlift. A C-47, heading for Great Britain for servicing, was forced to make a landing at Schiphol when it suffered engine failure on 21 July. On 22 July there was another engine failure on a C-47, which had to make a forced landing at Gatow. On 26 July a C-47 caught fire in the air and crashed near Fassberg. The crew, fortunately, were able to walk away from the crash.

An Avro York was damaged during a loading accident at Gatow on 28 July. Another Avro York was involved in an incident at Wunstorf when a fuel bowser hit the aircraft's wing on 3 August. There were two other accidents that day: a C-47 was damaged when it swung off the runway at Bückeburg and another C-47 caught fire shortly before landing at Gatow.

A pair of C-47s was damaged on the ground on 17 and 18 September at Lübeck, and an Avro York's engine failed during a night take-off on the 19th and crashed at Wunstorf, killing all five of the crew.

RAF Transport Command wrestled with a difficult problem in August. They were not sure that they could replace the pilots that were being lost; the training organization that brought new pilots through had been reduced to a bare minimum as the trainers were working on the airlift operation themselves. The decision was made to try to draw back some of the instructor aircrews and run the Transport Command at around three-quarters efficiency. This led to ten Avro Yorks and twenty C-47s, along with thirty-six aircrews being withdrawn from the airlift operation in the September. The effect was immediate and the tons being delivered by the RAF dropped significantly. As it was, the RAF could do little about this until the first Handley Page Hastings arrived in November.

As we have seen, there were problems with co-ordination. Servicing was an issue, as were loading and despatching, and operational control had no overarching authority. The men working on the airlift lived in cramped accommodation and worked long hours. Discussions were underway about trying to create a combined operation between the British and the Americans, which led to the arrival of Tunner and the establishment of the Combined Airlift Task Force at Wiesbaden.

On 1 November the first Handley Page Hastings arrived at Schleswigland. They had a cruising speed of just over 300 mph, and these aircraft, with a greater load capacity, could improve the airlift operation for the British. The first aircraft duly flew in from RAF Dishforth in Yorkshire, belonging to No. 47 Squadron. The squadron began operations on 11 November with eight aircraft. No. 297 Squadron arrived a month later. There was to be a third squadron of Hastings, No. 53, but they were not re-equipped properly until August 1949.

A further boost to the airlift took place on 15 December when Tegel, the third airport in Berlin, was opened. Squadron Leader Johnstone had made an initial flight there on 19 November (see Chapter 6).

AOC No. 46 Group assumed responsibility for the five RAF bases in the British zone on 1 December 1948. They became responsible for Celle, Fassberg, Lübeck, Schleswigland and Wunstorf. In addition to this they were of course responsible for Gatow. Celle was only made operational on 15 December. It was opened in 1935, and the Germans used it as a training base during the war. In the latter stages of the war Junkers 88s operated from there. In 1945 the RAF's No. 36 Wing and No. 84 Group Communication Flight occupied it, and its conversion into a base had begun in mid-September 1948. They had brought in 2,000 Germans to construct the facilities and necessary housing. The base needed 5,400 x 150 ft of runway, a pierced steel planking loading apron covering a massive 190,000 sq ft and, in addition to this, another pierced steel planking taxiway of some 9,500 x 50 ft. In addition to all of this a fuel storage complex was needed, rail facilities and other sundry buildings.

It was decided to develop this base for the USAF's C-54s, mainly because the Americans lacked suitable sites close to the Frankfurt corridor. It also meant that the C-54s would only have to fly short distances. The move was not complete, owing to different weather conditions in the zones, and it was therefore decided that only half of the US force would move into the British zone.

Initially Celle and Fassberg were under RAF command, certainly in terms of administrative duties, but Fassberg was handed over formally to US control in March 1949.

A significant milestone for the British occurred on 17 December 1948. An Avro York, flown by Flight Lieutenant Beeston, brought into Gatow what would normally be a fairly standard cargo of canned meat. However this consignment was the 100,000th ton of supplies brought into Berlin by the British since the beginning of their Operation Plainfare. The Deputy Mayor of Berlin, Louise Schroeder, met Beeston and the Avro York.

Another milestone was achieved on 23 December. Incredibly the British achieved their 50,000th landing at Gatow during the Operation Plainfare airlift. In the Christmas week alone the British made 2,031 landings; the total for the month of December reached 6,737. Although this was a lower figure than the previous two months, this was mainly due to fog that had shelved C-47 operations between 22 and 24 December.

The British had even been able to institute Operation Union. Several British servicemen's families had intended to join their husbands and fathers in Berlin shortly before the Soviet blockade. They had now been waiting for six months, but twelve families were reunited just in time for Christmas.

There was a formidable raising of the stakes in the period July to August 1948. It will be recalled that B-29s arrived in Britain on 17 July. They were not alone, however; General Curtis LeMay had secured the deployment of Lockheed F-80 Shooting Stars. Towards the end of July sixteen of the aircraft, commanded by Lieutenant-Colonel David Schilling of the 56th Fighter Group, left Selfridge, Michigan. It was to be a gruelling journey. They flew to Bangor, Maine, then to Goose Bay, in Labrador. From there it took them just under two hours to get to Greenland. A further hour and three-quarters saw them in Reykjavik and they arrived in Stornoway just an hour and forty minutes later. They had crossed the Atlantic in five hours fifteen minutes. From Stornoway they flew to Odiham, Hampshire, refuelled and headed for Germany.

They had, however, been pipped to the post in terms of being the first jet aircraft to cross the Atlantic. On 12 July, six de Havilland Vampire F3s had left Odiham on a goodwill tour of the United States and Canada. These aircraft, belonging to No. 54 Squadron, had actually taken the reverse route of the Shooting Stars.

Some seventy-five more Shooting Stars arrived on 14 August, and this time they were carried across the Atlantic on board USS *Sicily*.

The Americans were certainly increasing both their personnel and their defensive capabilities in Europe. The USAF announced on 25 August that Burtonwood would become their main base in Britain. Three B-29 groups would operate from there. In all, there would be something like 2,500 USAF personnel, under the command of Lieutenant-Colonel Walter Ott. In fact by the end of August the total number of US aircraft in Europe had risen to 466; around 6,000 men were based in Britain of the 18,000 USAF personnel in Europe as a whole.

Burtonwood proved to be an extremely important base for the Americans in Europe. Maintenance technicians were brought over from the US Air Material Command Centre, based at Tinker Air Force base, Oklahoma City. They arrived in September 1948 effectively to replace the rather primitive maintenance depot facilities used for the Berlin Airlift at Oberpfaffenhofen. Up until this point 200-hour inspections had been carried out on the aircraft; they were washed down and checked, but they had to be kept in the open air. Ultimately, at Burtonwood, eight aircraft a day could be handled by being cleaned with industrial vacuum cleaners and then hosed down using detergents. This all took place on what eventually developed as a ¾ mile long assembly line.

This development coincided with the withdrawal of the

American C-47s. The primary aircraft now being used by the Americans was, of course, the C-54 Skymaster. In theory, twenty man-hours of maintenance were needed on these aircraft for every hour flown. They would be given a thorough check after every fifty, 100 and 150 flying hours. These initial checks, including the 100-hour check when the oil and sparkplugs were changed, would take place at the aircraft's own base. A more complex and time-consuming 200-hour inspection required the aircraft to be flown back to Burtonwood. Here the engines would be run and any maintenance work done on pipes, while ignition, instrumentation, cables, electrics, hydraulics, rigging, tyres, brakes and wheels were all thoroughly inspected.

The 301st Bomb Group replaced the original B-29 group that had arrived in Britain, the 28th Bomb Group. These groups, based at Scampton, finally left on 15 January 1949. Scampton then became RAF No. 230 Operational Conversion Unit, equipped with Lincolns and Lancasters. The Americans were also operating two other British airfields, Marham and Lakenheath.

As we have seen, in August 1948 some of the Americans' C-54 aircraft were relocated from Rhein-Main to Fassberg. The entire 60th Troop Carrier Wing (Heavy) was moved, including the 313th Troop Carrier Group (incorporating the 11th, 29th, 47th and 48th Troop Carrier Squadrons), the 513th Airbase Group and the 513th Maintenance and Support Group. This involved around 6,000 men.

Group Captain Biggar had, of course, organized the extension of Fassberg to cope with the C-54s. The operations between the British and the Americans there always worked comparatively well. Once the airlift was over an Air Ministry report said:

The USAF wing was responsible to 1st ALTF [Air Lift Task Force] for operations and technical matters. This meant there were two senior officers of the same rank, neither responsible to the other and neither having a very clear idea as to where his responsibilities began or ended. The situation was bound, sooner or later, to cause minor difficulties. To counter this, an experiment was carried out at Fassberg, where the command of the station, including the RAF administrative element, was vested in the USAF wing commander. This experiment worked very well, but it must be recorded that this was largely due to the personality and efforts of the US commander [Lieutenant-Colonel Paul A. Jones]. A great handicap in the operation of an integrated RAF/USAF force is the lack of any legal machinery for the maintenance of discipline. It would be an excellent thing if some form of agreement, such as exists between the British Dominions and the UK, could be entered into between the US and ourselves. It is of interest to note that, under existing conditions, the only action that can be taken in the event of insubordination or assault between members of the two services is the preferment of a civil charge.

In fact the situation as Fassberg was rather more complicated. The British were considerably outnumbered, with only thirty RAF and army officers and around 450 other ranks. The Americans were not very popular with the British, and they in turn felt that the base was primitive and that some of the rules and regulations were unnecessary. In addition, around 2 miles away, under the command of a British army officer, was a labour camp that housed 5,000 German civilians, who were responsible for loading coal into the C-54s.

The Americans continued to look for other suitable aircraft that could be used in the airlift. Their eyes fell on the Fairchild C-82 transport aircraft. It had a large, hangar-like compartment and rear loading doors. Unfortunately there were very few of them available, but they would have been ideal to carry in construction equipment. As it was, just five joined the airlift, on 16 September.

A month earlier, on 17 August the first Douglas C-74 Globemaster began operations from Rhein-Main. It carried 20 tons of flour to Gatow. The Americans only had one squadron of these aircraft in service, and just one was directly involved in the airlift, although several were used to bring spares and supplies across the Atlantic and land them at Burtonwood.

The typical American pilot involved in the airlift was expected to fly between six and eight hours each day. In addition to this he would have to be on standby for a similar number of hours. Effectively this meant that each pilot would usually make two or three trips to Berlin each day. There was, however, an awful lot of sitting around and waiting. Typically, a pilot would have to wait around for up to four hours before his first take-off slot. He would wait to take-off, wait to unload, wait to reload, wait to take-off again and then probably wait with his aircraft in a maintenance queue. They were also not given a great deal of leave. They had a seven-day schedule and would be assigned to the lift for something between four and five months. In effect their working day was anything up to sixteen hours, after which they could have anything up to twenty hours free. This was the theory, but in practice pilots were often on duty for as long as thirty-six hours.

Very few had their families with them. Enlisted men, in any case, lived in quite cramped accommodation. The general pressures on the pilots was great, particularly if they had to shift from day flights to night flights and back again. Over 60 per cent of all accidents took place at night, when the men were tired and had probably been on duty for eight or twelve hours, or more.

By October, the US Airlift Task Force found itself 180 aircraft short of requirements. The US Military Air Transport Service had decided not to commit any more of their dwindling reserves of C-54s to the airlift, so aircraft had to be found from elsewhere. A solution was found in a pair of US Navy R5D squadrons, VR-6 and VR-8. These were given very short notice to move from their airbases in the Pacific at Guam and Honolulu, first to Moffett Field, California, where their passenger versions of the R5D were swapped for R5D freighters. They then flew to Jacksonville, Florida, where additional radar and radio equipment was fitted to the aircraft. They then flew on, the first reaching Rhein-Main on 9 November.

The navy squadrons were assigned to different troop carrier groups based at Rhein-Main. VR-6 joined the 513th Group and VR-8 the 61st. US Navy technicians carried out all maintenance, up to and including the R5D's 1,000-hour checks. This would cause problems because the C-54s were required to return to Burtonwood for their 200-hour checks. In order to allay problems the navy aircraft were ordered to go to Burtonwood when their 200-hour check became due. This was an unmitigated disaster, because when the aircraft returned from Burtonwood the captain refused to accept it as being a serviceable machine. From that point onwards the captain returned to Burtonwood with his own aircraft and kept an eye on servicing, which meant the standard improved and the turnaround time quickened.

The US effort in terms of tonnage was beginning to rise in a satisfyingly steady way. In the period 26 June – 31 July the USAF mounted 8,117 sorties and managed to carry 41,188 tons into the city. The next period, the month of August, was even more impressive: 9,769 sorties, carrying 73,632 tons. By September this had risen to 12,905 sorties and the 100,000-ton barrier had been broken with an impressive tally of 101,871 tons. This was, of course, the point when the C-47 was withdrawn. From now on it was to be an almost exclusively C-54 affair. The only notable exception to this was a single Boeing C-97A Stratofreighter, a C-74 and five C-82s. The Stratofreighter was only used for a short period, but was withdrawn after an accident in May 1949.

September 1948 saw the number of US personnel directly assigned to the airlift at 1,320 officers and 3,605 airmen. These figures were to more than double by the end of 1948, when the Americans would have assigned 2,374 officers and 7,563 air men. Men were being drafted in from all corners of the world. Many were given to believe that their tour of duty would only last forty-five days, but in practice the vast majority were assigned to Europe for at least ninety days and, in more cases than not, 180.

There were sinister moves afoot, far beyond the humanitarian effort being directed at Berlin and its inhabitants. President Truman had authorized a crash programme to stockpile nuclear weapons. At this stage, of course, the Soviet Union did not have a viable nuclear device. It is certain that the Soviets were perfectly aware of Truman's new directive, and perhaps this forced them not to increase the tension in Germany. They refrained from making overtly aggressive moves, but still maintained their grip around the throat of Berlin. But it came as an enormous shock to the United States and the other Western powers when, many years ahead of the predicted date, the Soviets detonated their own first test atomic weapon in 1949.

CHAPTER FOUR

Berliners and Volunteers

T he search for food was a consuming passion for the inhabitants of Berlin. As far as the Western Allies were concerned it was always a question of balancing the quality and quantity of food they could deliver against the weight on each aircraft.

One of the best ways to provide sufficient carbohydrates, a good source of calories, was bread. Berliners favoured rye bread, but wheat was easier to source. As already mentioned, it was decided at an early date to fly in flour and coal rather than bread. Not only did this mean savings in weight as no water was being carried, but to some extent the Berliners could have the limited luxury of freshly baked bread. This meant that yeast had to be flown in too. It was now a question of fresh or dried; fresh yeast was three times heavier than dried and ultimately dried yeast was substituted.

The assumption that the bread was providing fresh and nutritious food was actually wrong. They were being supplied with Canadian wheat, which had lower vitamin C content, thus necessitating the airlift of vitamin C tablets.

There were also problems with other basic essential items, such as macaroni and noodles. They were heavy and bulky and packed in paper bags. Some 40 per cent split during the loading and unloading process. There were other problem foodstuffs. In August 1948 60 tons of oatmeal was flown into Berlin, only for it to be discovered that it had gone musty. There had to be a solution and what seemed to be an adequate one was biscuits instead of bread. In the event, these were reduced to pulp by the time they had been shipped into the city, and were even bulkier than bread.

The Berliners would have loved fresh potatoes, but they were far too heavy and bulky to transport in. It was therefore decided early on to send dehydrated potato flour. Again in August 1948, the Berliners received 600 tons of ready-cooked potato flour. It did not go down very well and little of it was distributed to the inhabitants. 3,835 tons of potato powder was also found to be virtually inedible, and some 600 tons of stripped, dried potato proved equally unpopular. The most popular form of dried potato was the British pom, essentially dried mash. The British emptied their UK stocks in August, some 4,000 tons in total, and then ran out. They managed to scrape together another 340 tons, found in British stores in Egypt, but meanwhile the Berliners had to wait while the manufacturers made more.

By early September supplies of dehydrated potatoes were perilously low. The Hungarians provided some, having to route deliveries around Berlin to land them in the western zone, from where they could then be flown into the city. As a desperate stopgap measure the US Army offered to loan a million pounds of dehydrated potato from its own stores, requiring payment of fresh potatoes in return.

Dried pea soup was delivered in huge quantities, but this needed two hours to cook and put a strain on fuel. Forty-three tons of very poor quality dried tomato soup was delivered, which was not only expensive but also revolting. A multitude of other soups were tried, but all tasted very poor and smelled stale.

Within the new bizone the Germans were producing their own dried potatoes. These turned out to be twice as expensive as imported dried potatoes and in any case the maximum output was no more than 50 tons a day, about 25 per cent of the needs of the zone and Berlin. In addition to this the dried potatoes from Germany were never packed in standardized sacks, which made it almost impossible to work out the correct loading for aircraft without weighing each bag individually as it was brought up to the aircraft.

There was a need to supply Berliners with a multitude of vitamin supplements, primarily to offset the fact that they were eating dried vegetables and were unable to get fresh food. In November 1948 there was a considerable push to persuade Berliners to take vitamin tablets and to eat cod liver oil.

There was also considerable debate about whether Berliners should be growing their own vegetables. As far as the Americans and the French were concerned, dried vegetables only took up 75 per cent of the space that fertilizer would take up. In any case there was a shortage of fertilizer. In the Berlin area there was the staggeringly low figure of 3,250 cows. In order to produce 5 litres of milk per day each, some 200 tons of food had to be flown in each day. They produced manure and it was probably this factor alone that prevented them from being slaughtered for fresh meat.

Horses in the city were fed on the oats that were not fit for human consumption. When they died the Berlin inhabitants did not often eat them, but instead the meat was turned over to the police for their dogs and distributed to blind owners for their guide dogs.

The animals in Berlin Zoo were a special case. Prior to the blockade it had used up some 8,000 lb of hay every month and its carnivores needed 6,000 lb of meat each month. By August the carnivores were only getting a meal every other day. In November the zoo was finally promised meat, vegetables and several tons of sunflower seeds. It was felt by its officials that its extensive gardens should be turned over to food production. Luckily, it was not under threat from those seeking a rather more exotic cut of meat, as had happened when Paris was besieged in 1871.

The Berliners had to cope with tinned food. It was easy to load and did not require any particular sort of storage to keep it fresh but some of it was as unpalatable as the cereals and dried vegetables. There was a huge consignment of tinned blood sausage in September but officials found it incredibly difficult to persuade anyone to take it. There was a similar reaction to liver sausage and to fake meat products, primarily made of dried egg.

For the planners it was always a question of how to balance food and fuel. On average, Berlin needed some 1,500 tons of food every day, and the city's public services alone needed a minimum of 2,534 tons of coal. As soon as the cold weather set in homes would need an additional 550 tons of fuel each day. Basically, as far as the planners were concerned, they could either fill Berliners' stomachs and let them sit in the dark, and cold, or keep them warm but hungry.

During the very poor winter of 1946 Berliners had made do with very little brown coal and wood and, as a result, several hundred of people had frozen to death in their homes. The planners promised at least four times the amount per household that they had achieved during that cold winter. But even the most optimistic planners realized that they could not provide this amount. On 7 October 1948 the occupation authorities suggested that some 260,000 cubic yards of forest in the sector should be cut down. They also suggested that trees in parks, along streets and in people's gardens would net another 195,000 cubic yards of wood. This was a drastic suggestion, as the wooded area in Berlin would be cut by two-thirds. In the end they agreed to reduce the tree-felling to 160,000 cubic yards. This may have produced heat, but nothing could replace gas or electricity; for those they needed coal.

In the immediate aftermath of the war it was not just the Berliners who had been hungry. As far as the United Nations was concerned, adults should receive an average ration of 2,650 calories each day. In reality, however, Germans in the western zones were lucky to get 1,500. Both then and during the blockade most energy went into finding food. There was a constant hunt for a handful of potatoes or even some kindling to start a fire.

Between 1945 and 1950 Germans in the Soviet zones were also subject to rationing. Politicians, officials, intellectuals and those doing manual labour were allocated 2,485 calories each day. Those unfortunate enough to be old, unemployed, seriously injured or otherwise not of any value to the occupying forces, were given just 1,248 calories each day. The Russians had begun the redistribution of land and anyone found to own more than 250 acres had it confiscated. Much of this land was used to set up collective farms and the theory was that in time the Germans would be able to feed themselves once again.

The Western Allies found that by the beginning of 1946 the Germans were slowly starving to death. There was a distinct shortage of food, and they could not buy any from abroad. Their industries were crippled and many of the experienced members of the workforce had simply disappeared. In January 1946, for example, General Clay began importing food from the United States, just to provide 1,550 calories per person per day. Even with this additional food supply he had to cut rationing down to 1,275 in March.

The British found themselves in an even worse situation. They had to cut the ration to just 1,000 calories per person per day. Even then 300 calories had to be imported from Great Britain. Rickets, anaemia, retarded growth in children, tuberculosis and a host of other diseases were commonplace.

It should be remembered that even in late 1946 Berlin was essentially a city of piles of rubble. During the winter the city's temperature had dropped to 30 degrees of frost. Electricity supplies were cut and the only way to keep warm was to pack into one of the public buildings. Berlin was not alone. Over 60 per cent of Hamburg's population had no gas or electricity throughout the whole winter. The British were forced to bring in 25 per cent of the required food and the Americans cut their average daily ration to just 900 calories. It was a deplorable situation and there did not seem to be any immediate way out of it.

By the autumn of 1947 some two-thirds of the average 1,000 calories per person per day in the bizone had to be imported. It was placing an intolerable strain on Britain in particular, as the country was indebted to other countries at that stage to the tune of £3,355m. Lend-lease had stopped abruptly in August 1945, imports were expensive and certainly by July 1947 it looked as if it was about to collapse economically. In order to save their own country the British really needed to stop aiding the rest of the world.

By the early weeks of 1948 the average calorie intake in the bizone ranged between 900 and 1,200 calories per person per day. The Germans really had to begin to produce more of their own food or earn hard foreign currency in order to buy it. By the spring industrial production was showing signs of recovery. In the western zones it was creeping towards 50 per cent of the 1936 figure. Coal production had reached 74 per cent. Exports were increasing, so finally imports could increase and rations improved.

One of the major reasons the Soviets had cited for establishing the blockade, the introduction of the new Deutschmark, was about to begin. In a secretive operation, code-named Bird Dog, the new notes were printed in the United States and sent to Frankfurt. What remained was to agree how to distribute the new currency. There was no confidence in the old Reichsmark and, as a result, the population tended to barter and manufacturers stockpiled finished goods and raw materials.

The major bone of contention was what would be used in Berlin. As it was, in June 1947 Berliners were already waiting for someone to make a decision. It seemed that the Soviets were planning to introduce their own currency in their own zone and it was this clash that would eventually lead to the blockade being firmly established. On 18 June Sokolovsky laid down the new exchange rate for the Soviet Deutschmarks. Sixty old Reichsmarks would buy forty new Deutschmarks. On that very night the blockade began.

By late June the airlift was barely meeting Berlin's basic needs. It was difficult to bring in certain items. Rolls of newsprint weighed 4 tons each and the decision was quickly made not to place newspapers ahead of food. Berlin newspapers eventually went out of production. On 3 July there was an urgent signal that many medical supplies were fast running out. The city needed 2,800 lb of ether each month, 20 tons of plaster of Paris, 24,000 square yards of x-ray film and around 1,300 gallons of alcohol.

In July 1948 the US Military Government commissioned an opinion poll of Berliners. Eighty-four per cent believed that the Allies could bring in adequate food for them. Interestingly, the remaining people, largely the more educated, believed that the airlift would not be able to cope with the needs of the city. Nearly 90 per cent believed that the city could not last out through the winter and that surrender to the Soviets was inevitable.

There was an interesting development on 21 July when the Soviet military administration offered to begin feeding the entire city from August. They said that Berliners in the western sectors could register in a district in the Soviet sector and thereby receive rations. Bearing in mind that many of those in the western sectors had been living on dehydrated vegetables, it was a tempting offer. The Soviets failed to realize, however, that the Berliners in the west were perfectly aware of the plight of their fellow citizens in the east. It was clear to them that if the Soviets were incapable of feeding their own people they could not possibly feed those in the west. There had indeed been shortages in the eastern sector. Some districts were out of meat, potatoes were hard to come by and the Soviets were resorting to importing food from Russia or from other Eastern European countries. In the event, by the cut-off date of 31 July 1948 just 2,050 people had signed up to receive Soviet rations.

Most of the Berliners were prepared to sit the blockade out, despite the cold, the anxiety, the hunger and the dark. They knew that their fellow citizens in the western zones were fully behind them, but in truth those outside Berlin had worries of their own. Currency reform had had a massive impact on people's savings, and price controls had been abolished. However, goods that they had not seen for years were appearing in the shops. Wages were increasing, employment was booming and importantly rations were increasing.

A dangerous series of events occurred in August 1948. Soviet troops began mounting raids in the western sectors of Berlin. Anybody that tried to intervene was dragged into the Soviet sector. Two men tried to kidnap a former city prosecutor, but they were arrested. The most dangerous place was Potsdamerplatz, which was where the Soviet, American and British sectors met. The Soviets claimed that they were making these incursions to catch black marketeers. On one occasion they rounded up 2,000 people and on another police from the east came under a barrage of stones from a crowd on Potsdamerplatz. They opened fire, killing one and wounding several others. The British and the Americans were forced to draw a thick white line and cover the boundary with barbed wire.

By September 1948 the airlift was still only bringing in about 40 per cent of what the city had been consuming prior to the blockade. It was generally accepted that the airlift was not even holding its own, despite good flying conditions. The experts assessed that the drop in delivered supplies during the winter months could be anything from 30 to 40 per cent. On average Berliners were already 8.5 lb underweight and many were on the verge of malnutrition, as they were now eating around 1,600 calories each day. They were still living in bomb-damaged buildings and had little coal or wood to burn on their fires.

During the winter of 1948/9 someone came up with the bright idea that if Berliners were kept occupied they would not think about being hungry or cold. The idea was to keep the women occupied during the winter in making clothes. A monthly order was put in for reels of cotton thread, 30,000 sewing and darning needles, 880 lb of steel pins, 150,000 gross of safety pins and 40,000 packets of machine needles.

The Berlin population had complex food needs. A prime example is what remained of the city's Jewish population. They needed kosher meat brought in instead of simply tinned meat. Diabetics were not forgotten: they were provided, after three months of pleading, with saccharine. In the run-up to Christmas the authorities spent a good deal of time and effort making sure that every Berlin child would at least get some chocolate to eat over the festive period. Planners even managed to work out a formula for the number of sanitary towels needed by the women.

Getting around the city was a major problem. There were virtually no private cars, and due to electricity and petrol shortages public transport was rare. Businesses and factories only operated during the four hours in which they were allocated electricity. There was nothing to light the streets so people walked home in the dark after work. The Soviets did, however, continue to run the S-Bahn, the local electric railway. This was not out of kindness, but to ensure that their own people could travel from the suburbs to their offices in the centre of the city.

Like any people under siege, the Berliners were resourceful. Many dug up their gardens to grow vegetables. Some resorted to walking around the streets with any valuable item, including cigarettes, to swap for food. Some even crept into the Soviet zone to find eggs or buy vegetables. It was not always possible to afford the prices on the black market; kerosene was 4 Marks a litre. The universal currency, however, was not the Mark in whatever form, but the cigarette.

In their homes Berliners eagerly awaited their four-hour allocation of electricity. This either came as a single four-hour block or as two two-hour segments. This meant that food had to be prepared when electricity was available. It was common to eat at midnight or to cook food in batches so that it could be served cold over the next few days. One of the most valuable items in a Berlin household was the Thermos flask. Hot drinks could then be enjoyed for several hours, even after the electricity had been turned back off again.

Those homes that had gas stoves, some 90 per cent of all households, fared no better. There were cuts and unpredictable pressure, but by December 1948 gas supplies had increased to around 75 per cent of what it had been before the blockade.

At this stage it was impossible to separate the two parts of the city. Upwards of 110,000 residents of the western zones worked in the eastern sector. At the same time, 106,000 living in the eastern sector worked in one of the western sectors. There were surface and underground railways to connect the two parts of the city, as well as eighty or so roads that went into and out of each side. The Soviets did try to clamp down on illegal movement; eastern lorries were forbidden to cross a zone line. Routinely, the authorities would search passengers on public transport to see if they had stolen, or acquired, food from the east. Little by little the restrictions were tightened and Soviet authorities set up seventy-one roadblocks. This was the beginning of the division of the city that would last until the late 1980s.

Miraculously, Berlin survived the winter and the new year brought increased production and higher levels of delivery by the airlift each day. In the third week of January 400 tons of airlift capacity was allocated for seeds. Despite the unpalatable nature of some of the food being sent into Berlin, the tuberculosis rate had been cut by half and for the first time there was an increase in the average weight of Berliners, males over sixty now weighed 6.2 lb more. Black market prices dropped considerably at the beginning of February, and food was becoming more plentiful.

We have already mentioned Flight Refuelling Limited, with its Lancastrian tankers. This company had been founded in 1936. At the helm was the aviation pioneer, Sir Alan Cobham. He had begun practising flight refuelling back in 1933. He and Wing Commander H. Johnson became collectively known as Cobham's Flying Circus. Johnson was at the controls of a Handley Page W10, which was refuelled mid-air by Cobham flying an Airspeed Courier. Later, on 20 January 1938, Cobham demonstrated to the Air Ministry that in-flight refuelling was perfectly possible. He transferred fuel from an Armstrong Whitworth AW23 bomber transport into an Imperial Airways C Class Empire Flying Boat.

By the time the Berlin crisis was beginning, the company had just completed some trials for the Ministry of Civil Aviation with its Lancastrians, with a view to using them to refuel BOAC Liberator Transports. Cobham however, immediately offered his services and those of his company to the Foreign Office.

Captain D. Hanbury, DSO, flew the first flight by one of their Lancastrians on 27 July 1948. He carried a load of petrol from Tarrant Rushton, the new headquarters of the company in Dorset, to Berlin.

The Air Ministry, the Ministry of Civil Aviation and the Foreign Office began discussing the use of other civil aircraft. Colonel G. Warton, OBE, the Charter Superintendent of British European Airways, was brought in as a technical advisor. The net result of this was a small fleet of C-47s, which would be based at Fassberg. A pair of Short Hythe Flying Boats would operate on the River Elbe at Finkenwerder. Also chartered were a Liberator and a Handley Page Halton. For a trial period they would work alongside the RAF's Avro Yorks at Wunstorf.

Initially the C-47s would be provided by a number of volunteers, including Air Contractors (three aircraft), Air Transport (one aircraft), Kearsley Airways (two aircraft), Scottish Airways (two aircraft), Trent Valley Aviation (one aircraft) and Westminster Airways (one aircraft, but they would later provide a second C-47).

Later more civilian C-47s would be chartered, including British Nederland Air Services (one aircraft), British Overseas Airways Corporation (BOAC) (three aircraft), Ciros Aviation (two aircraft), Hornton Airways (one aircraft) and Sivewright Airways (one aircraft). BOAC had decided that there was no future for flying boats and therefore Aquila Airways provided the Short Hythes. Bond Air Services provided the single Halton and Scottish Airlines provided the Liberator. Pilots from the Second World War had created the vast majority of these companies by acquiring surplus transport aircraft in order to continue flying.

The civilian aircraft were due to arrive *en masse* in Germany on 4 August 1948. The first proper sortie into Gatow landed at 0310 on 2 August. During its first twenty-four hours of operation the Halton, flown by Captain Treen of Bond Air Services, made five return flights between Wunstorf and Berlin. Almost immediately, however, many of the operators chartered for the airlift ran into difficulties. There was no time to send anybody out to Germany to check out the situation and find out about basics such as wireless frequencies, operational procedures or loading arrangements. Consequently it was a great surprise that when the bulk of them arrived on 4 August they expected to begin operations the following day.

Despatch riders were sent to various RAF stations in Germany in order to obtain radio crystals for the civilian aircrafts' radio sets, so that they could tune in to the correct frequencies. There was a slight problem about the load to be carried by these aircraft. Under the terms of civil aircraft's Certificate of Air Worthiness, they could not carry more than 6,000 lb, but the army wanted them to carry the same as the RAF C-47s, which was 7,480 lb. Applications were hastily sent off to the Air Registration Board and clearance finally arrived on 15 April.

The civilian C-47s arrived in Germany with an enormous amount of dead weight, including passenger seats and other equipment. These had to be stripped as soon as possible. None of the companies providing aircraft had brought administrative personnel and a captain, who was also engaged in flying duties, controlled each company. This meant that any operational problems that the RAF had with the aircraft had to be dealt with through the company's head office in London.

Taking part in the airlift was a hazardous financial risk. After all, the companies' only assets were their aircraft and experienced crews, both of which could easily have been lost. Many of the aircraft were very ill-equipped so the RAF quite willingly took the strain initially to make sure they were fulfilling their roles. There was also a problem with spare parts. The aircraft companies using C-47s needed American spares. Unfortunately the private companies were somewhat slapdash in their preparation for purchasing spare parts. Most of the time they were obtained on an as-needed basis.

It was not immediately clear at the beginning just how long

the private companies would be needed, particularly if they were proving to be creating operational problems. The Liberator was indeed withdrawn, mainly due to servicing problems. On 8 August the Lancastrians joined the Halton at Wunstorf. The civilian C-47s were moved to Lübeck on 28 August. This finally put paid to any suggestions that the civilian C-47s were about to be phased out of operations. For the first fortnight at Lübeck the civilian C-47s were only allowed to fly during the day due to the overstrained facilities at the base. Each lost flight meant a loss of income for the company, but it gave the aircrews a chance to rest and the companies an opportunity to set up adequate servicing facilities.

The Hythe flying boat operation out of Finkenwerder was working extremely well. They operated during daylight hours and the crews were drawn from demobbed Coastal Command crews. Experience was obviously a big advantage, but they also knew many people still in service at the base. The aircraft proved to be hugely reliable and the company itself, Aquila Airways, made continued efforts to increase the amount of supplies they were bringing in. To begin with they managed 9,982 lb per flight, by the end of August it had risen to 10,900 and by the end of October it was 12,400 lb.

It was abundantly clear by the autumn that the airlift would have to continue. British European Airways surveyed all available charter aircraft in Great Britain, looking for aircraft capable of carrying liquid fuel to Berlin. They were hoping to find adequate numbers of four-engined aircraft but in the event what they found was that the Halton, which was being used by a number of charter companies, was the only choice.

Another possibility would have been the Avro Tudor, but there were reservations about its airworthiness. A pair of the aircraft belonging to British South American Airways had disappeared. It was a considerably newer aircraft than the Halton and in time would prove to be very useful during the airlift. Air Vice-Marshall D. C. T. Bennett flew in a Tudor belonging to the Airflight Company on 3 September 1948. Towards the end of the month a pair of Tudors began operations out of Wunstorf. These were reinforced during September by a pair of Wayfarers belonging to Silver City, two of Skyflight's Halton Freighters and a pair of Vikings belonging to Trans-World Charter.

The next major problem for the civilian aircraft was the increase in military aircraft belonging to both the British and the Americans. This was beginning to have a serious impact on operations between October and November 1948. It was felt that the civilian fleet would have to be moved once again. The shifting around caused a loss in tonnage delivered, but it was an essential redeployment. On 6 October the civilian Dakotas were moved to Fuhlsbuttel, where the airfield facilities were in the process of being improved, including a 5,850 ft concrete runway and other building work to add to the 5,250 yard pierced steel planking airstrip. In the event, the new runway was operational by 21 December. Other improvements were made, including a new approach path and lighting.

By late October it was Gatow that was proving to be the choke point. Three more C-47s belonging to BOAC had arrived on 20 October, but their contract was withdrawn between 10 and 23 November because of the congestion. Skyflight's Haltons had also had their contract cancelled, as they had not been able to meet targets. The first civilian aircraft to be written off, a Halton belonging to World Air Freight, broke its back on take-off at Gatow on 6 October.

More civilian aircraft were still arriving. Eagle Aviation provided a pair of Halifax Transporters, Airwork a Bristol Freighter and Bond Air Services were now providing four aircraft. On 16 October, three Halton Freighters belonging to Lancashire Aircraft Corporation joined the effort. The company added a Halton Tanker at the end of the month. Airflight also took possession of a second Tudor, which would be used as a tanker.

Lancashire Aircraft Corporation's effort began on 16 October. They were to contribute a large number of airlifts into Berlin. Captain Dennis Richards clocked up 229 flights, Captain Nash 222 and Captain Franks 216.

A notable landmark was achieved by the civilian aircraft operators on 11 November 1948. They had been directly involved in the airlift for 100 days. Collectively they had flown 3,944 sorties and delivered 18,585 tons to the people of Berlin.

A new series of redeployments was in the wind. The Haltons were moved out of Wunstorf as Avro Yorks, belonging to Skyways, had arrived on 16 November. Also arriving around that time were British South American Airways' Tudor Tankers. The freighters belonging to Eagle Aviation and Bond Air Services shifted to Fuhlsbuttel between 14 and 20 November. The Vikings and Wayfarers were withdrawn. Only Avro aircraft, the Lancastrians, Tudors and Yorks, henceforth used Wunstorf. On 24 November the Lancashire Aircraft Corporation shifted their Halton aircraft to Schleswigland.

Schleswigland had two runways, but some fairly serious problems. It was situated very close to the Baltic and suffered from low cloud and sea mist. It was also a considerable distance from Berlin compared to other bases. From Wunstorf, it took two and a half hours to get into Berlin, and from Hamburg two, but a flight from Schleswigland would take nearly three and a half hours. It was a question of efficiency and contribution. Aircraft flying out of Schleswigland would have to fly fifty more hours than Hamburg aircraft and thirty more than those from Wunstorf to complete forty sorties. Nonetheless, it opened for operations on 25 November, and was initially home to the civilian airlines' Haltons and Hastings belonging to the RAF.

One of the other problems with Schleswigland was that it only had one small hangar available for the civilian aircraft. During the cold months it was incredibly difficult to service and maintain the aircraft outside.

Another problem reared its head on 17 December 1948. It was realized that not all civilian aircraft were fitted with the Rebecca navigational aid, a requirement that had been foreseen in August.

> For obvious reasons, it is essential that the civilian aircraft should be equipped with the same navigational aid, Rebecca, as other aircraft flying at the same altitude in the traffic flow. Arrangements will have to be made to fit this equipment in the UK, as lack of technical personnel will make it impossible for the RAF to equip the whole fleet out here. In anticipation, I recommend that the opportunity should be taken to carry out this work as aircraft return to the UK for major checks.

It seems that this advice was ignored and, in any case, at that stage it was not anticipated that the civilian aircraft would be needed for very long. However, towards the end of October the Air Ministry had been asked by the Foreign Office to see if the RAF could supply the Rebecca Mark II sets. The question was who was going to be paying for them. In any case only twenty-six were ordered. An unserviceable batch was found at No. 14 Maintenance Unit, Carlisle in December. It was not until 13 January 1949 that the Haltons were finally equipped with these sets. Luckily the civilian aircraft based at Wunstorf (the Avros) already had Rebecca sets.

Aircraft had to be withdrawn from service to have the sets fitted, which of course meant not only a drop in tonnage but also additional pressure on workshops and maintenance units. This, in turn, slowed up the number of civilian aircraft being brought into the effort.

All this came at an extremely bad time; by the end of December Berlin's liquid fuel stocks had dwindled to almost nothing at all. From 1 January the city would be reliant on air deliveries by the civilian fleet. It needed some 220 tons per day, but initially only 148 tons could be achieved. This target would have easily been reached if the thirty-one allocated tankers had all been available, but by 1 January 1949 there were only 11. Even by the 14th there were still only twenty and by the end of that month twenty-seven.

Compounding the delays were problems arising out of the conversion of passenger Tudors to tankers. It was assumed that five of these aircraft could begin their operations on 1 January 1949. However, by the 7th only three had arrived. It took until 2 February for the fourth to arrive and the fifth did not enter service until 14 February. From the end of November 1948, one of British South American Airways' Tudors had to be withdrawn for training purposes. The remainder of the tanker fleet was a mixed bag of several different private charter companies. Skyways was already using three Yorks, and reinforced them with two Lancastrian tankers. Flight Refuelling was now running seven Lancastrians, and British American Air Services, which had just joined the airlift operation, had a pair of Halton tankers based at Schleswigland. The Lancashire Aircraft Corporation was now, by the end of January 1949, running ten tankers and Westminster Airways had a single Halton. This meant that there were twenty-seven tankers in operation by the end of January and seventeen freighters, which meant that the total civilian fleet amounted to forty-four aircraft.

The fuel-loading facilities at Wunstorf and Schleswigland were somewhat primitive. They used bowsers from a cistern wagon and pumped the fuel into the aircraft through flexible hoses, using a portable pump powered by an engine. It was a slow process and assuming there were no complications it would take forty minutes to fill up a Tudor Tanker with 2,100 gallons of diesel oil. Unfortunately there were a number of breakdowns. On fifty occasions between 21 January and 21 April the aircraft were not filled within the forty-minute window. This meant that the sortie was lost. It is worth pointing out, however, that fifty lost sorties was a drop in the ocean as it only represented less than 2 per cent of all of the tanker sorties flown out of Wunstorf during that period.

Schleswigland had an underground system which had been used during the war by German night fighters. Six pumps were fed from ten tanks to the eighteen refuelling bays. Unfortunately none of the pumps worked at the same rate. After some tinkering around by the commander of the RASC [Royal Army Service Corps] Detachment, Major Craig, instead of taking twenty to twenty-five minutes to fuel up a Halton, it was now taking twelve to fourteen minutes. He achieved this by the simple expedient of coupling a pair of the bays together so that two pumps could be applied to each bay.

Construction work had begun in September 1948 and was completed in March 1949 to make five large underground tanks at Gatow. Throughout the whole summer of 1948 Gatow had been restricted to a pair of petrol tanks with a capacity of just 22,000 gallons between them. What the Berlin end needed was a rapid de-fuelling terminal. What they got were these five large underground tanks connected to eighteen de-fuelling points. It was arranged in such a way that fourteen tanker aircraft could be de-fuelled at any one time. The fuel was then pumped into storage tanks and distributed by tanker lorries.

The RAF was responsible for all liaison with the civilian aircrews. The problem was that many of the civilian operators had their own preferred procedures. Most of them had a distinct preference for flying during the day and they tended only to operate at night to make up for sorties lost during bad weather in daylight hours, or when they had spare aircrews. This brought with it a number of problems. Whilst the civilian aircrews were very keen it was difficult at times to rein them in. As they were primarily flying during daylight hours this put an additional strain on the maintenance schedules.

Towards the end of 1948 there were moves afoot to try and remedy some of these problems. The Foreign Office received a paper on 12 October, which recommended that the civilian charter companies be pulled together. This would mean that they could use the same type of equipment and that any additional resources could be redeployed to make up for deficiencies in other areas. There was also a suggestion that some aircraft provided by the civilian operators actually be phased out if they did not meet minimum tonnage requirements. The suggestions met with opposition from the Treasury and from the operators themselves. There would be extra costs involved in redeploying and pooling resources that would have to be met by the British government. In any case, the companies wished to remain independent units, providing for themselves and maintaining their identity.

As a possible solution to the coordination issues British European Airways, for example, placed the control of their airlift operations in the hands of a manager based in Germany. He sent someone to No. 46 Group HQ at Buckeburg, to liaise with Air Commodore Merer.

By mid-November 1948 the Berlin airports were buckling under the strain of the number of flights coming in. It now became a priority to convince the civilian operators to begin flying both day and night sorties. It was finally agreed that blocks of time would be set aside for civilian flights.

The first civilian casualty of the airlift occurred on 8 December 1948, a senior pilot of Airflight, Captain Utting. He was not killed in the air, but was knocked down by a lorry on the tarmac at Gatow while walking towards his aircraft. The person driving the truck was never identified.

Ice finally closed the Havel Lake operation on 15 December 1948. The three Short Hythes flying out of Finkenwerder had managed to complete some 265 sorties, carrying in around 1,400 tons of supplies.

There was a notable landmark on 16 December when a

Skyways Avro York made the 5,000th landing in Berlin. The worsening weather conditions had made December something of a nightmare for the civilian operators. Many of them lacked de-icing equipment. There had also been delays, as a large number of the aircraft had had to return to Great Britain in order to be converted into tankers. There was also the problem of the lack of Rebecca sets.

The strains on the crews were immense. On average each civilian aircraft only had 1.3 crews allocated to it. This meant that they would have to fly a far higher percentage of the time than their military counterparts. For example, Air Vice-Marshall Bennett was the only Airflight pilot that was qualified to fly a Tudor at night. There had been two qualified pilots but of course Captain Utting had died on 8 December. On average Bennett was flying two or three sorties each night over a period of two months.

The new year saw marked improvements as the civilian operators stepped up the number of sorties per aircraft per day. But on 15 January 1949 they suffered more casualties. Six ground engineers employed by the Lancashire Aircraft Corporation were being driven to the dispersal area at Schleswigland. The German driver drove in front of an RAF Hastings that was moving on the perimeter track. The pilot could not react quickly enough and there was a collision. The aircraft's propeller killed three of the engineers and the German driver. There had been other accidents that month too, when a Halifax and a Tudor were also damaged by vehicle collisions.

It was decided during January 1949 that the civilian operators working out of Schleswigland and Fuhlesbuttel would now fly into Tegel. They would use the northern corridor for both journeys and operate at 1,000 ft on their outward journey and 1,500 ft on their return. This would have another major advantage, as ice would no longer be a major problem. By February 1949 the civilian operators had increased their number of sorties per day to around fifty-four, and nearly as many aircraft were being flown during the night as during the day. In the last week of February the civilian operators had reached a target of nearly 400 tons of liquid fuel per day.

Throughout February civilian operators working out of Wunstorf flew 816 sorties into Berlin. This amounted to over 50 per cent of the total number flown by civilian aircraft, despite the fact that only around 40 per cent of the civilian fleet was based at Wunstorf. Other operators, such as Skyways, continued to battle on with their five aircraft, with only eight or nine crews available.

The Airwork and Silver City Bristol Freighters were withdrawn from the airlift between 5 and 12 February. Effectively they had been replaced by the arrival of RAF Hastings in November 1948 and the Americans' deployment of the Fairchild C-82 Packet.

January had also seen the decision to deploy a pair of Liberator Tankers. They were to arrive at Schleswigland on 19 February. This reinforced the civilian liquid fuel tanker fleet. By 20 February the civilian operators had been directly involved in the airlift for 200 days. Over the period they had flown 7,800 sorties and brought 44,387 tons of supplies into the city. Their second 100 days of operations compared extremely favourably to their first 100; over the first period they had averaged a daily tonnage of 186, by the second 100 days this had been increased to 258.

By March 1949 the teething problems with incorporating the civil aircraft into the overall operation had all but passed. The civilians were using their serviceable aircraft at least as well as their military counterparts. Most of the aircraft were flying at least three sorties each day and the average number of sorties flown by the civilian operators had leapt from fifty-four to seventy each day. A prime example of this was Airflight's pair of Tudors. In February they had flown ninety-two sorties; during March they had increased this to 144.

The civilian operators had been given a new target for liquid fuel deliveries for March: they were to bring in 350 tons each day. This target was met and over the course of the month 10,000 tons of liquid fuel was delivered to the beleaguered city.

However tragedy struck in March. On the 15th Captain Golding's Skyways Avro York stalled as he was making his final approach into Gatow. The aircraft spun into the ground and killed him. On the 21st Captain Freight, employed by the Lancashire Aircraft Corporation, was making a return flight from Tegel to Schleswigland in a Halton Tanker when he struck high ground. The only survivor of the crew was Radio Officer

Hamilton, who miraculously was thrown 40 ft over a hedge. Despite his injuries he walked 2 miles to Schleswigland airfield and reported the accident. After a stay in hospital he returned to duties on the airlift.

On 12 April 1949 it was decided , after a meeting in Berlin, that it was possible for the existing civilian tanker fleet to bring in 450 tons each day. With the addition of eight Lancastrians, a new target of 550 tons by 1 July could also be achieved. A few days before the Foreign Office had also decided to fit fuel-carrying tanks to four Tudor Mark Is and two Tudor Mark IIs in addition to another eight Tudor Mark IVs, which were already under conversion.

With several months' successful operations under their belts, the civilian aircraft were now using regular maintenance and other measures to ensure that their aircraft always remained in service. Skyways was now using four Lancastrian Tankers and improvements to the underground fuelling installation at Wunstorf meant that the new pressure-fed hoses could fill the Tudor at 100 gallons per minute, filling its tanks in around twenty minutes.

Compared to March 1949, the average number of sorties flown each day in April rose from seventy to nearly seventy-four. Unfortunately, on 30 April a World Air Freight Halton Freighter crashed in the Soviet zone some 9 miles to the west of Oranienburg. The pilot, Captain Lewis, and his three crew members were all lost. The civilian operators had now lost a total of twenty-one people. Back in November 1948, whilst *en route* to a routine overhaul at its home base at Tarrant Rushton, a Lancastrian Tanker belonging to Flight Refuelling crashed into a hill near Thruxton. This had considerably added to the death toll as eight had been killed, including three aircraft captains.

May brought several more accidents, but fortunately no casualties. On the 10th Captain Tucker force landed his Lancastrian into the Soviet zone some 7 miles to the west of Ludwigslust. The aircraft was a write-off. The Russians hospitalized the men, but allowed them to return to the British zone and an RAF salvage party was sent to recover the aircraft.

Despite accidents and losses, May saw some outstanding results. British South American Airways, which had prior to

May set their own record at 304 sorties in a month, managed to rack up 420. Lancashire Aircraft Corporation did equally well. Their previous best had been 323 and in May they managed to exceed this significantly, with 464. Skyways likewise did extremely well in May with 500 sorties compared to their previous month's best of 346. In all, the civilian operators managed to lift in 22,800 tons during the month, the vast majority of it liquid fuel, at 17,988 tons. This meant that the civilian operators were bringing in a staggering average of 578 tons of liquid fuel each day. In all, throughout the month, they had averaged 100 sorties every day, 900 more in the month than the previous record. In total they had achieved 3,104 sorties. They had no only managed to exceed all expectations, but had also shattered the tonnage rate set for July, which was 550 tons.

The Tudors belonging to Airflight were withdrawn from the airlift at the end of the month, because the Foreign Office was not offering enough money. In exchange, Airflight brought in a single Lincoln, which did not arrive until 24 June. It flew its first sortie on 30 June out of Wunstorf, after it had been converted into a tanker. It managed to take in 2,500 gallons on its first flight.

During May the Soviets had complained that civilian aircraft were overflying their airfield at Perleberg and coming in as low as 100 ft. These complaints were investigated but proved to be incorrect.

By the time the Soviets lifted their blockade on 11 May 1949, the civilian operators, over a ten-month period, had brought in 86,252 tons of supplies. They did not end their operations, however, but continued to work at full capacity for another two months. In the twenty-four hours to midday on 22 May, civilian operators had carried in 1,010 tons in 133 sorties. On 31 May the 100,000th ton of civilian operator lifted cargo came into Gatow. The aircraft was a Lancastrian Tanker, which touched down at 1610, flown by Captain D Hanbury, DSO. Air Marshall T. M. Williams, the Air Officer Commander in Chief flew in with him to mark the occasion.

Between 1 June and 15 August the final phase of the civilian airlift took place. The fleet had been reduced, but June's tonnage was 380 tons more than the May figure. The aircraft had also flown more sorties, with 3,205 clocked up for the month. On average, the civilian operators were bringing in 586 tons of liquid fuel each day. This was no mean achievement considering there had been a number of accidents that had put aircraft out of commission for several days.

Amongst these accidents was a Halton Tanker of the Lancashire Aircraft Corporation that was written off on 1 June at Tegel, during a landing accident. On 10 June a Halton Freighter belonging to World Air Freight was put out of action for the rest of the month during a landing accident at Fuhlsbuttel. On the 12th another Lancashire Aircraft Corporation Halton Tanker was written off at Tegel and on the 19th an Avro York belonging to Skyways crash-landed in a field shortly after take-off at Wunstorf. On the 26th a Skyways Lancastrian Tanker was gutted by fire after a landing accident at Gatow.

A number of contracts came to an end on 13 July, or were cancelled. This effectively brought civilian operations at Schleswigland to an end, putting British American Air Services, Lancashire Aircraft Corporation, Scottish Airways and Westminster Airways out of work in Germany. Airflight's single Lincoln Tanker also came out of service on 13 July, and Skyway's four Lancastrian Tankers were withdrawn on the 17th. The main reason for these cancellations was that the liquid fuel requirement for Berlin had now been reduced to 140 tons each day. Officially, the liquid fuel, or wet lift operation, terminated on 15 August 1949. Up until this period Flight Refuelling Limited had brought in 40 tons per day and British South American Airways 100 tons to make up the total.

In the meantime, the civilian-operated freighters bringing in supplies other than liquid fuel had continued throughout July. Throughout the month they had brought in 5,945 tons.

Captain Villa of Eagle Aviation flew the last official civilian sortie on 15 August in Halton, carrying 14,400 lb of flour. He landed at Tegel airport at 0145 local time on 16 August.

In total, some twenty-three private charter companies had been involved in the civilian lift. Around 103 aircraft had been used, but at any one time anything from thirty-one to forty-seven were in operation. It is remarkable that between 1924 and 1947 all British civilian aircraft carrying mail and freight only managed to carry half the tonnage that this handful of aircraft managed to cope with in just over one year. In all, the civilian

General Lucius D. Clay, Commander of the Office of Military Government (US) and the Military Governor of Germany (left) with Brigadier General Frank L. Howley, the US Commandant in Berlin.

Lieutenant General Curtis E. LeMay, Commander in Chief United States Air Forces in Europe. In command during the April Crisis to the early part of the airlift.

Douglas C-47 Skytrains unloading at Tempelhof in June 1948.

B29 Superfortresses of the 28th Bombardment Group (Rapid City, South Dakota) over Dover.

Tempelhof before the expansion programme. It was to become the main USAF airfield in Berlin.

Brigadier General Joseph Smith, who assumed the role of temporary commander of the airlift.

Air Marshal T. M. Williams, Air Officer commanding British Air Forces of occupation (from November 1948).

Avro Yorks, the transport version of the Lancaster bomber, outside unloading hangars at RAF Gatow (September 1948).

Avro Lancastrian of Flight Refuelling Ltd, discharging liquid fuel at RAF Gatow.

Major General William H. Tunner, USAF's air transport specialist.

Lieutenant General John K. Cannon, Commander in Chief USAF Europe (from mid-October 1948).

RAF and USAF radar personnel at RAF Gatow.

Runway construction at Tempelhof.

Parking ramp being constructed at Tegel in the French sector of Berlin. C-54s continued to use the runway.

Douglas C-47 Globemaster at Rhein-Main Air Base, September 22 1948.

Discussions about navigational problems in the air corridors take place amongst USAF staff.

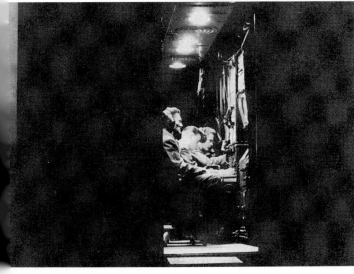

Ground control operators are the eyes of the airlift pilots attempting to land at Tempelhof.

Some of the thousands of tyres required for the C-54s, maintained, inspected and supplied by Rhein-Main.

A C-47 receiving maintenance and servicing at Tempelhof.

C-54s in the specially constructed wooden docks at Oberpfaffenhofen air depot, Germany.

A Douglas C-54 Skymaster flying low at the Replacement Training Unit at Great Falls Air Force Base, Montana.

American trucks, provided by the 66th Heavy Transportation Truck Company, with German crews at Wiesbaden on July 20 1948.

Coal for Berlin being loaded from a British lorry to a US C-54 by a German crew at Fassberg.

The Easter Parade on April 16 1949.

Coal being unloaded from a C-54 at Tempelhof.

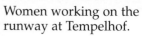

Women working on the runway at Tempelhof.

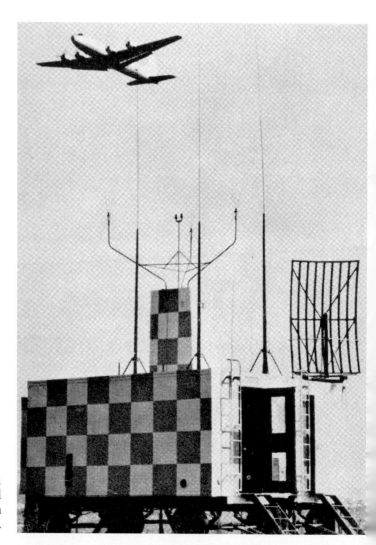

A C-54 flying over a mobile ground control approach station at Tempelhof.

C-54s being serviced at Burtonwood, Lancashire. Services were carried out every 200 hours.

Onboard a US Navy R-5D.

RAF pilots take a break.

A British York landing at
Wunstorf.

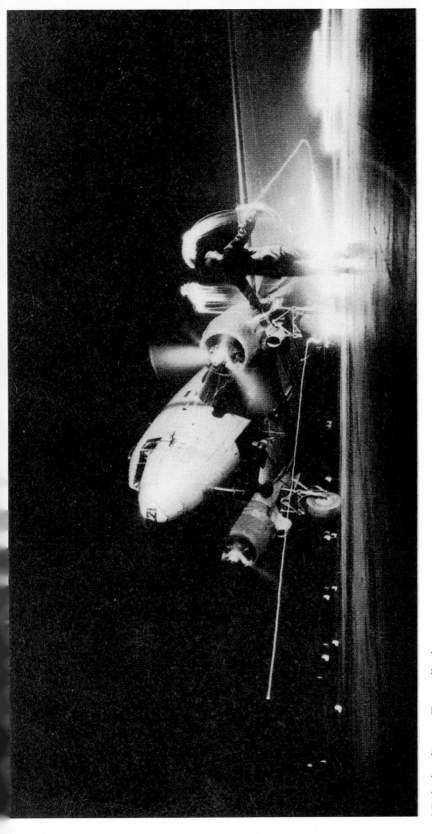

Night landing at Tempelhof.

Sunderland flying boat.

US C-47s at Tempelhof.

Coal being loaded for Berlin.

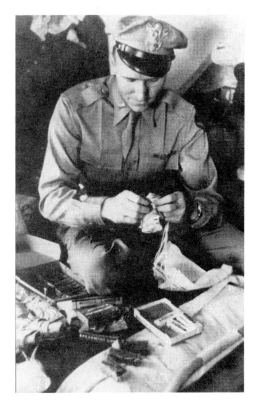

Lieutenant Gale D. Halverson preparing
chocolate parachutes.

Berlin children watch US aircraft landing.

Watching the expansion of Tegel airport.

German children re-enacting the airlift.

Supplies being unloaded from a York.

US General Lucius D. Clay, who initiated the airlift.

Some goods were made in Berlin during the blockade, as the crate proudly announces.

US C-54s at Tempelhof airport.

The Sunderland flying boat would be unloaded using DUKW amphibious vehicles or barges.

A Globemaster I at Gatow in 1948, showing the large fuselage.

US C-54 Skymasters at Tempelhof at night.

Corporal Margaret Fisher, BEM, from Poole, Dorset, and another engineer working on an RAF Dakota, which was operating during the airlift.

C-54 Skymaster being refuelled at the Rhein-Main airbase, near Frankfurt.

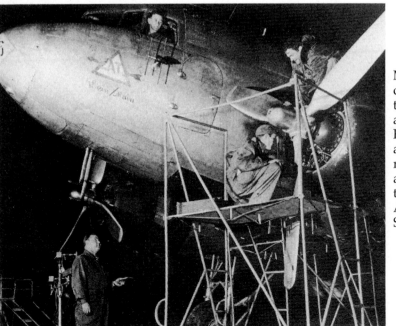
Maintenance crews at work at the Rhein-Main airbase near Frankfurt. They are carrying out a routine check on a C-47 belonging to the European Air Transport Service.

A Douglas C-54 Skymaster undergoing an engine change at Rhein-Main airbase. The aircraft was not in operation prior to the airlift and, as a result, spares, including engines, had to be shipped in from the US.

The USAF's workhorse during Operation Vittles. This Douglas C-54 Skymaster, with its double cargo doors, is being unloaded at Tempelhof and belongs to the 20th Troop Carrier Squadron.

SSgt Claude Richeson, San Antonio, Texas (left); 1st Lt James R. Davis, Los Angeles, California (centre) and Capt. Alfred Rumberg, Phoenix, Arizona (right), celebrate at Rhein-Main the news of the lifting of the Berlin blockade.

An RAF Air Sea Rescue and Marine Craft Section seaplane tender at Waltershofenhafen, Hamburg, in 1948.

The HMAFV Bridport, part of the airlift operation ferrying supplies into Hamburg.

Brig. Gen. Edward H. Alexander, commander, 61st Troop Carrier Wing, shakes hands with the crew of the last flight of Operation Vittles on September 30 1949.
Left to right: Capt. Harry D. Immel, Pittsburgh, Pennsylvania; 1st Lt. Charles N. Reece, Athens, Texas; 1st Lt. James C. Powell, Fort Worth, Texas; SSgt. Jerry G. Cooksy, Chicago, Illinois and TSgt. Matthew M. Terenzi, Lynn, Massachusetts.

Sunderland being unloaded on the River Havel.

A ceremony to commemorate the end of the blockade (shot taken May 12 1949).

Firewood was in short supply during the winter of 1948.

The end of the US occupation zone of Berlin.

The last airflight into Tempelhof.

Celebrating the one millionth tonne of supplies flown into Berlin in February 1949. Shot taken at Gatow airport.

Much-needed food being distributed after the blockade.

General Lucius Clay with the Berlin Mayor Ernst Reuter (May 1949).

Truck moving freely into Berlin after the lifting of the blockade.

The C-54 Skymaster and C-47 Skytrain on display outside the terminal building of Tempelhof.

The unveiling of the Berlin Airlift Memorial on July 11 1951, outside Tempelhof airport. The memorial was designed by German architect, Professor Eduard Ludwig.

The Berlin Airlift Memorial in Airbridge Square, next to Tempelhof Airport. The three prongs represent the three Allied powers involved in the airlift operations.

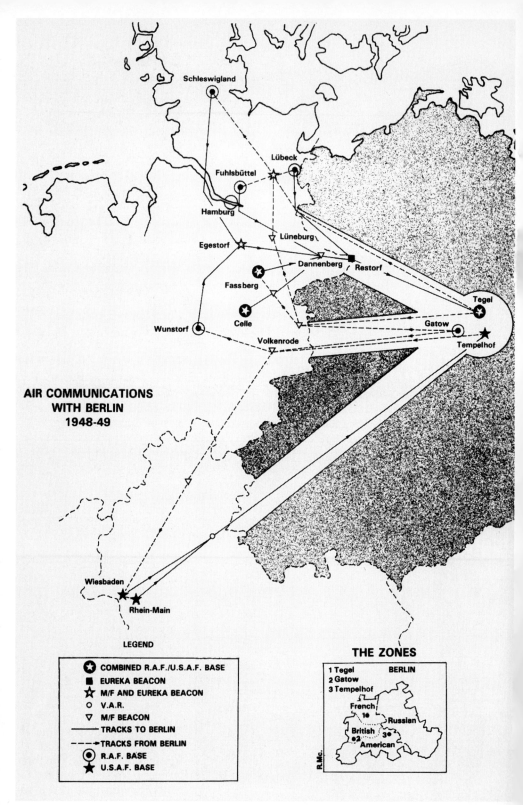

AIR COMMUNICATIONS
WITH BERLIN
1948-49

LEGEND

⊛	COMBINED R.A.F./U.S.A.F. BASE
■	EUREKA BEACON
☆	M/F AND EUREKA BEACON
○	V.A.R.
▽	M/F BEACON
——	TRACKS TO BERLIN
---▶	TRACKS FROM BERLIN
◉	R.A.F. BASE
★	U.S.A.F. BASE

THE ZONES

BERLIN

1 Tegel
2 Gatow
3 Tempelhof

French
British
American
Russian

R.Mc.

Air communications and routes into Berlin during airlift.

aircraft had carried into the city some 146,980 tons and had flown a staggering 21,921 sorties in all winds, weathers and conditions.

When the airlift began in 1948 there were a number of highly experienced Commonwealth aircrew, from Australia, New Zealand and South Africa based in Britain. They belonged to No. 24 (Commonwealth) Squadron and were primarily equipped with Avro Yorks and Douglas Dakotas.

From 29 June 1948, sixty-four Dakotas of RAF Transport Command were sent to Wunstorf. On 1 July, sixty-five Avro York Transports joined them. Australians flew either as entire crews or as part crews on missions out of Wunstorf. Flight Lieutenant Cornish and a Royal Australian Air Force crew made the 3,000th sortie into Berlin on 19 July. Flight Lieutenant Mal Quinn, who was later to be promoted to fly his own Dakota with an RAF crew out of Lübeck, accompanied him. Quinn unfortunately died along with his crew on 22 March 1949, when his Dakota crashed in the Soviet zone whilst attempting to land at Lübeck. His was the only Royal Australian Air Force death during the entire airlift. The Soviets returned his body and those of his crew and the men were buried at the British War Cemetery in Hamburg.

On 29 August 1948, five Dakota Transport crews arrived in Great Britain for attachment to the RAF. A total of forty-one men, they had been drawn from Nos 36 and 38 Squadrons. They were assigned initially to RAF Bassingbourne in Cambridgeshire for training. They were ready by 10 September and were flown to Lübeck to join RAF crews, along with aircrew from New Zealand and from South Africa. They began flying sorties into Berlin five days later.

To begin with the Royal Australian Air Force crews had been told that their attachment to the RAF would last just six weeks, but in the end they served for fourteen months. Generally, they flew in bags of coal, newsprint and fresh and dehydrated vegetables. The RAAF Dakotas flew in blocks of eight aircraft from Lübeck to Gatow. When they arrived at Gatow, German workers could unload them in as little as three minutes. They also flew out export goods from Berlin during this time. Between November and December 1948, they flew into Tegel, rather than Gatow.

On average, each RAAF crewman flew between 220 and 240 sorties to and from Berlin. They made their last flight into Berlin on 19 September 1949. After this they flew to RAF Manston in Kent and left for home on 20 October, in an RAF York. During the entire airlift period in which they had been involved, they flew 2,066 sorties, carried 6,964 passengers, and 15,623,364 lb of freight and racked up 6,041.5 flying hours. When they arrived back in Darwin they were read a copy of Air Force HQ Signal A763:

> I wish to express my congratulations and my appreciation to the very fine performances by all members of the 86 Wing Berlin Airlift Detachment in Europe. Your hard work, efficiency and devotion to your duty have set a fine example to the Royal Australian Air Force and have contributed greatly to the prestige of your Service and your country.
>   Air Marshall Sir George Jones, Chief of the Air Staff

There were New Zealanders serving with No. 24 Commonwealth Squadron and they flew Avro Yorks and Dakotas into Berlin. The senior officer was Group Captain R. J. Cohen, who was on a two-year exchange with RAF Transport Command. To begin with there were three Royal New Zealand Air Force crews directly under the command of Flight Lieutenant C. J. Fraser, Flying Dakotas out of Lübeck, working a twelve-hour day in order to fly three sorties into Berlin. They often carried coal, newsprint and cigarettes. On the way back they packed in many malnourished children.

The New Zealand aircrews were drawn from No. 41 Transport Squadron. In all they flew in around 1,500 tons of coal between the period October 1948 and July 1949. The Royal New Zealand Air Force flew their last sortie to Berlin on 11 August 1949 and by that stage they had carried in 1,577 tons of coal on 473 flights.

The South Africans left in two batches, on 22 and 23 September. Initially they were told that they would be needed for a short period and that relief crews would replace them in four to six months. They arrived at Oakington in Cambridge-shire on 26 September and were sent to Bissingbourne for training. On 18 October they left to join the airlift, operating out of Lübeck. They operated Dakotas into either Gatow in the British sector or Tegel in the French sector. Experienced RAF crews accompanied them on their first flight in but from then on they flew in blocks of five or six Dakotas.

On 5 April 1949 the first batch of South Africans completed their tour of duty. Over the period of time they had carried in 4,133 tons of supplies in 1,240 sorties. As promised, a second contingent arrived, under the command of Major J. P. D. Blaauw. The South Africans flew their last sortie into Berlin on 24 August 1949. By this date they had carried 8,333 tons of supplies into the city in 2,500 sorties.

The contribution of the South Africans was greatly appreciated. A message from the AOC No. 46 Group read:

We in 46 Group will miss you. You have fulfilled your task with high skill and invincible determination, which is the hallmark of the veteran squadrons of the airlift. But what has impressed us most has been your cheerful enthusiasm and your readiness to volunteer for additional missions on your rest days.

This vote of thanks was reinforced by a personal message from the AOC the Berlin airlift: 'We have all been tremendously impressed by the South African squadron. Not only have they taken their full share in the task of supplying Berlin, but the self-less devotion of all ranks has been an inspiring example.'

CHAPTER FIVE

Flying the Corridor

M any of the pilots were, of course, highly experienced, yet flying supplies into a beleaguered city was new to nearly every one of them. In the spring of 1945 the RAF had dropped 1,560 tons of food to a starving population in Holland. It had also supplied its own ground troops during the Pacific war against the Japanese, primarily during the campaign to recapture Rangoon in Burma.

The Americans had also had experience of mass supply drops. They had flown over 600 aircraft per day over the Himalayas from India to China, where US forces were supporting Chiang Kai-shek against the Japanese in April 1942.

Flying into and out of Berlin offered slightly more demanding conditions, however. Admittedly the pilots were not under fire from an enemy, as the British Lancasters had been from the Germans in 1945, or the Americans from the Japanese in 1942. The Americans had had corridors at least 50 miles wide and in many cases as much as 200 miles. Considerably more precision was now required.

Moreover, once the aircraft were over the city, they had to share air space with as many as seven Soviet airfields, three of which had circuits that intersected those of Tempelhof or Gatow.

Group Captain Noel Hyde, who was appointed Officer Commanding Transport Wing Wunstorf, kept a diary, clearly identifying some of the early problems with the airlift operations.

1 July: Well behind schedule chiefly owing to loading diffi-culties. Petrol and fuel section completely overworked and in a muddle. Yorks going to be difficult to handle with present congestion on airfield. Insufficient oil and petrol bowsers.

3 July: Gatow asked if we could speed up rate of flow at night to one every ten minutes. Petrol and fuel could not cope. Plumbers behind with serviceable aircraft, chiefly rectifications. It appears that night flying under present conditions costs us more than we gain because of diffi-culties of loading, servicing etc. at night. Big gap of over an hour in flow due to unserviceability and petrol and fuel loading unserviceable aircraft.

4 July: Combined Ops room not working well as Flying Control cannot cope with traffic and let operations know when aircraft are taking off and landing. Telephone went unserviceable at 1720 hrs. Tried to get it repaired but Army apparently have no one available.

5 July: Part of Dakota parking area badly cut up – arranged to have it covered with psp.

7 July: Army lent us two jeeps and trying to get us a walkie-talkie set. Wing Commander Technical says we cannot with present manpower cope with ten-minute inter-vals between take-offs. Marshalling and refuelling are difficulties.

Despite the difficulties, men who had been bombing Berlin three years ago were now feeding the city.

American aircraft carried two pilots and an engineer. They did not need a navigator as they used something confusingly called a radio compass. It was not a compass in the generally accepted meaning of the word, but a low-frequency radio link with the ground. The aircraft had to pass over a radio beacon to activate it, and as it did so the pointers on the instrument panel turned from 'full ahead' to 'dead astern'.

The American pilot would be fully briefed on weather conditions, wind direction and strength, as well as the recom-mended flying speed, before he took off. Once airborne, the aircraft then climbed to the beacon at Darmstadt. Here the pilot adjusted course and made for the beacon at Aschaffenburg. It was at this point that he climbed to his assigned altitude. The next destination was the beacon at Fulda, which allowed the pilot to line up with the southern corridor. He would now have to listen for the position and time of the aircraft just ahead of him. He would check his own position and report it back to base. Once everything was checked he would then be left to his own devices along the corridor. He would use dead reckoning to guide him along the prescribed route.

The crew would have to make constant adjustments to take turbulence and wind into account. Theoretically, if the aircraft remained at a steady 170 mph, it would be able to contact Tempelhof in around forty minutes. Once Tempelhof was in contact the pilot could confirm his height and obtain a time check. Once he reached the Wedding Beacon, he slowed to around 140 mph and waited for landing instructions from Tempelhof.

On the way back, the aircraft would fly along the central corridor, passing over Braunschweig Beacon and turning south over Fritzlar. Just before it reached Staden it would lose height and make contact with base. The last beacon to pass over before touching down was at Offenbach.

The system relied on the pilot's ability to use the radio compass and then make calculations and time the course accurately. American crews did fly with a high degree of accuracy – they had been very well trained. It was vital that they kept a close grip on the course and times, and the landing intervals between aircraft, as this would ultimately determine the success or failure for the airlift.

The RAF used a mixture of navigational aids. Some, like Transport Command aircraft, used radio compasses to check their turning points. Some navigators used a map, compass, watch and pencil in the time-honoured tradition of working out the exact position of the aircraft, taking speed and direction into account.

The most sophisticated system was the Rebecca-Eureka. Effectively this was a radar direction and distance finder. Pathfinder paratroopers had used Eureka beacons during the war. They would establish a beacon so that successive waves of aircraft dropping in paratroops could home in on the correct spot. The beacon emitted a signal that could be picked up and interrogated by the Rebecca set in the aircraft.

Each aircraft had a pair of antennae that would receive signals from the Eureka beacon and turn them into a blip on the navigator's screen. These blips showed the distance to the beacon. If the screen showed the blip longer on one side of a vertical line then the pilot adjusted course until both sides were equal. The British had placed beacons at Gatow and the other airbases, as well as at strategic points at the beginning of the northern corridor. There were also beacons at turning points close to the run-ins to the airbases.

Once the aircraft was close to one of the bases and the pilot was making his approach, he could then use the Beam Approach Beacon System (BABS). Two beams were transmitted from the ground and picked up by a single antenna. This showed a string of short and a string of long pulses. The pilot turned the aircraft until the pulses were the same size, which gave him perfect positioning for landing. Initially, BABS was installed at Gatow and Wunstorf, and in November 1948 a mobile system was flown into Tegel.

Many other RAF Transport aircraft had Gee equipment. A pair of simultaneous signals were sent from the ground and the pilot could position himself so that they arrived at the aircraft at the same time. The system worked perfectly well in the occupied zone, but was less useful over Berlin, as it was outside effective range.

An RAF aircraft would undertake the journey to Gatow in what could be described as a series of short hops. First they would check their position using the beacons at Celle, followed by another check at Danenberg and finally at Frohnau. The aircraft would either slow down or speed up if it was ahead of or behind its required timings. When it was about twenty minutes out from Frohnau the pilot would call Gatow. He would tell them what his cargo was so that the unloaders could be prepared for his arrival, and would then make a final turn and see the runway just ahead. The aircraft just ahead of him would be taxiing up to its position on the unloading apron. The pilot would touch down, taxi to the unloading apron and then grab some tea and a bun whilst his aircraft was being unloaded.

Once Allied aircraft reached Berlin they came within range of the Ground Controlled Approach (GCA) system. This was a means of seeing the arrival of aircraft and the direction in which they were approaching, and was a vital piece of equipment for times when there was poor visibility.

The GCA system was operated from trucks parked near the runway at Gatow or Tempelhof. The radar screen showed the height, bearing and distance of all aircraft within a 40-mile range. Aircraft could be contacted by radio and told to adjust their height and speed to make sure that they arrived at a regular, separated rate. An amplified picture of the immediate approach was picked up 20 miles out with an azimuth tube.

In poor weather, with bad visibility, the GCA controller contacted the aircraft and gave instructions as to the distance before touchdown. The pilot was also told whether he was left or right of the approach centre line. He could then be told how many degrees to turn to regain the centre line and the height needed to make a perfect approach.

Once the aircraft was some 6 miles out the GCA controller made sure that the pilot had his wheels down and that the flaps were locked for descent. Over the next few crucial minutes, he would continue to talk to the pilot, informing him about height changes, position and speed. In this way it was almost possible for the pilot to land with zero visibility. To begin with the GCA controller had to handle an aircraft every fifteen minutes. As the system was expanded and the controllers became more experienced, this increased to a rate of one nearly every five minutes.

Over the course of the airlift more and more aircraft became involved. The Americans began flying from the British zone and a number of new airbases were opened. For a while the crews would operate on adrenalin alone, but after weeks the strains were beginning to show. In effect, they worked until they were physically and mentally incapable of doing another thing. Certainly in the early weeks of the airlift there were no shifts as such, which caused all sorts of problems for the pilots.

In many cases the aircraft would land, taxi to the unloading apron and by the time the unloaders got there the pilot would be sound asleep. Pilots often fell asleep in the air, only to be woken when the aircraft suddenly lost height. One American pilot flew for some 156 hours in the first month of operations and said: 'Pretty soon I said to myself "Boy you aren't grouchy, you're just about on the verge of being done in."' This was not unusual. The USAF discovered that some of their men were on duty for seven days a week. If they were lucky they got seven hours' sleep in a thirty-two hour period. They kept awake by drinking coffee; their food was of poor quality, consisting of hastily gobbled snacks on the airfield. Even the vitamin pills they were issued with only helped to a certain extent.

During July and August 1948 the RAF issued a medical questionnaire. It became clear that the crews were eating more but still losing weight, a sure sign of exhaustion. It was also noted that the aircraft were landing much faster than before and that many of the landings were bumpy. Pilots were careless in the way they taxied their aircraft. These problems were particularly obvious during the last sortie of a crew's day.

Exhaustion was certainly taking its toll. Pilots routinely forgot to take their engines off boost, put down their flaps or feather their engines, and they were more irritable, as one pilot admitted: 'I also notice that when I am tired, people I normally dislike mildly I begin to dislike very much indeed.' It was clear that the crews could not be expected to keep this up for very much longer. They needed leave periods, sleep, proper food and rotas.

Pilots and planners were also trying to come up with ideas to improve performance. One pilot suggested radioing positions at fixed points and then making adjustments so that accurate timing and spacing could be achieved. Indeed accurate timing and spacing were the key to ensuring that Berlin was fully supplied around the clock.

In the early days of the blockade getting more aircraft and crews involved would not have improved performance in tonnage delivered or enabled some kind of rota periods for pilots. The organization of the airlift could not cope with what was needed and with what they had, let alone throwing more aircraft into the equation.

Despite the tiredness, by October 1948 the crews were far more adept at flying and navigation. Moreover, the air traffic control was far more efficient, even to the point that both crews and ground staff had supreme confidence in their ability to continue operations, even in poor weather.

There were more air traffic controllers, which meant less

stress and fewer mistakes. The shortage had been particularly alleviated by the arrival of eighteen experienced men from the American Civil Aeronautics Administration.

Finally came proper shifts. Pilots and their crews were now sleeping in requisitioned hotels, and for the first time they were having real rest. In October the Americans had established a training school for USAF pilots at Great Falls, Montana. It was a good beginning as it had the capacity to train up to 100 crews each month. They would arrive in Germany prepared to use instruments to fly along the corridors and needed far less time for adjustment. This would free up tired crews at the end of their tour of duty much more quickly than before.

After the potentially lethal Friday, 13 August (see Chapter 3), when aircraft were stacked up over Berlin, the drive was on to reduce accidents. General Tunner had issued a threat: 'I would reduce to co-pilot status any pilot who failed to land with ceiling and visibility greater than 400 ft and a mile. I would court-martial any pilot who did not land [if the conditions were worse].'

The practice was for pilots to be shunted to the nearest runway that had clear skies if it was impossible to attempt a touchdown in Berlin. Sometimes this meant a huge flight, adding to the strain on the already exhausted crews. On one occasion USAF pilots were directed to land at Marseilles. The RAF took a different tack – paperwork. If a pilot did not land first time, they had to fill in a form. Consequently, pilots made sure they did not have to put pen to paper.

No one ever complained about the din of aircraft landing in Berlin day and night. In fact if the inhabitants could not hear an aircraft overhead they would become anxious. The engine noise meant they had food and fuel at least for another day and that Berlin would remain free.

Up to 30,000 Berliners were directly employed by the airlift operations. Children collected aircraft numbers and made their own aircraft to land on paper runways. Many Berliners gave presents to the aircrews, such as lighters and ashtrays salvaged from scrap metal. Letters were sent to base commanders, thanking them. But for the most part none of the crews really understood what the airlift meant to the Berliners, who called it 'their' airlift and they referred to the drone above them as 'our aircraft'.

Not many of the crews had ever seen the city from the ground. At best they spent half an hour on one of the airfields before flying back to base for another sortie. Nonetheless, they were committed and absorbed in what they were doing, and were grateful that there was little time for the routines and rigours of military life, which would have been their lot on a peacetime airbase.

There was, however, one notable exception, in the shape of a quiet Mormon from Utah. Gail S. Halvorsen was a first lieutenant with the 17th Air Transport Squadron. He visited Berlin as a passenger, wanting to take moving pictures of the airlift. He arrived in Berlin on 17 July 1948. To begin with he filmed landings from a cemetery close to the end of Tempelhof runway. Standing alongside him were several children, also watching the landings.

Halvorsen was stunned that the children were not pestering him for chocolates and chewing gum. In fact they did not expect anything from him and asked nothing of him. He promised them that he would drop chewing gum and sweets from his aircraft the next time he flew into Berlin. When they asked him how they would recognize his aircraft, he said, 'Well, I'll do like I did when I was a kid over Garland, Utah. I'd fly up over a farm, wiggle the wings of the airplane at the folks, and let them know it was me.'

He came up with a simple yet ingenious delivery system. He would use handkerchiefs as parachutes and attach the sweets to them. The flare shoot became the bomb bay. As promised, he flew into Tempelhof on 18 July, saw the children, wiggled his aircraft's wings and dropped three parachutes.

This was just to be the beginning. Huge numbers of children turned up each day, hunting the skies for the wiggling aircraft. At first Halvorsen decided to ignore them, but finally gave in. He made six more drops. A few days later mail started arriving at the Base Operations Office at Tempelhof. All of the mail was addressed to either Uncle Wiggly Wings or the Chocolate Flyer.

Halvorsen was hauled in front of his squadron commander to explain. The officer said: 'Look, I'm not stupid – it's all over the front pages of the Berlin papers. You nearly hit a journalist on the head with a candy bar.' Halvorsen expected to be reprimanded. But instead he was given the official go-ahead to keep doing the drops; even Tunner approved. His drops expanded, with other pilots and crews joining in. Some units provided handkerchiefs and others gum and chocolate.

In the end Halvorsen's drops were dubbed Operation Little Vittles. Soon some 3 tons of chocolate arrived from the American Confectioners' Association, after the story had hit the headlines in the United States. Instead of handkerchief parachutes, Halvorsen began dropping boxes of chocolate through the cargo doors. By October he had six people working for him, dealing with a deluge of supplies and an equal number of letters of thanks. The German Youth Activities Group started the mass production of parachutes and at its height, Operation Little Vittles was dropping 6,000 consignments per day.

Each aircraft flown into Berlin may have had a crew of three, but at least seven other men were needed to ensure that it remained in the air. This was a huge investment in manpower. In fact in ideal circumstances each aircraft would have a maintenance crew of fifteen. The aircraft being used at the beginning of the airlift were, to all intents and purposes, obsolete. The Hastings aircraft had so many problems and requirements that these could never have been foreseen.

All of the aircraft, not to mention the crews, were not only doing a job they had never been designed to do, but they were also falling apart under the pressure. They were all flying virtually non-stop. They were all carrying maximum loads, but they were not designed for the high manifold pressure and heavy revving. The airframes were never designed to carry such huge amounts of cargo, let alone on such a repeated basis. The hydraulics, brake discs and cables were under enormous strain. Even the floors of the aircraft had been wrecked by hasty loading procedures. Consignments like coal got everywhere, clogging electrical parts and getting into control systems. Even when the aircraft landed, the pierced steel planking was no good for the tyres. Seals, gaskets and ignition wiring wore out in the engines, grit pitted the windscreens and water caused electrical faults. In fact in one case a year's supply of windscreen wiper blades were used in a fortnight.

Around 80 per cent of all aircraft came back from a sortie with a defect. The aircrews, however, kept many of these defects to themselves and just lived with them. In fact fewer than 20 per cent filled in any defect form. Some aircraft were cleared to fly with only three engines, but the aircrew relied on the ground crew to make necessary maintenance decisions and get the aircraft ready for their next block of flying.

As a result of demobilization, both the Americans and the British were suffering from a chronic lack of skilled maintenance men. The British resorted to calling up reservists and delaying demobilization. German labour could only be used in the semi-skilled areas, and in any case there were non-fraternization rules. Eventually the Americans gave in and took on eighty-five former *Luftwaffe* mechanics to be attached to each squadron. The aircraft manuals were translated into German and the men carried out vital work under German-speaking officers.

There was also a dearth of spare parts. At the beginning of the airlift the RAF was even short of screwdrivers and wrenches. Despite all of the maintenance problems, the Americans achieved a utilization rate per aircraft that was three times better than the British. This was mainly due to the fact that the C-54 was such a solidly build aircraft. It was an uneven battle: the Americans could afford to spend more money to keep them in the air, they had more spares, they had more ground staff and if there was a damaged part they used the simple expedient of ripping it out and putting in a new one. This was never the British way.

In each aircraft the RAF had a navigator, but the Americans had an engineer instead, who was responsible for monitoring the health of the aircraft and could direct the maintenance crews to deal with specific faults. From around October 1948 the Americans brought in a standardized maintenance system. Regular reports were completed on each aircraft. A colour code was used to indicate its condition. Throughout, the air and the ground crews belonged to the same squadrons so that it was easier to build up trust and have standardized procedures and understanding. The RAF used a different system, sending main-tenance crews to aircraft on an as-needed basis. In some cases the maintenance crews might never have seen that particular aircraft before and had to work from vague descriptions given to them by the crews in the case of any faults.

The RAF used a centralized system by which the officers and NCOs worked out where to deploy the teams of men. In due course they split servicing into three flights, each flight responsible for around twelve aircraft. They also brought in a card system, which described typical maintenance issues. The cards recommended the tools needed, time required and how many men would be needed to do the job. As a result, British aircraft were brought back into operation in half the time.

Comparing the aircraft in terms of maintenance, it is easy to see why the Americans had a distinct advantage. After two hours' flying the C-54 would need maintenance work taking up to an hour and a half. However an Avro York needed three hours of servicing for the same amount of flying time. It was believed that to some extent the RAF over-inspected and over-repaired their aircraft. They allowed only thirty-six minor problems in an aircraft before it was handed over to maintenance, whereas the USAF allowed 350.

The RAF initially insisted on a full service being performed for every fifty hours of flying. This was then extended to seventy-five hours and then from November 1948 to 100. Aircraft were still being flown all the way back to Britain, primarily because of the lack of hangar space and suitable accommodation for mechanics in Germany. It also cut the cost of sending equipment to Germany, and allowed the aircraft to bring in spares and additional personnel on their return.

American aircraft, on the other hand, were only given a thorough inspection after 200 flying hours. In between, spark plug and brake checks and other minor servicing procedures would be performed. To begin with all of the servicing was carried out at Oberfallenhofen. It was proposed that much of it would take place at Burtonwood in Lancashire, but it transpired that Burtonwood was hardly capable of dealing with two aircraft each day, let alone the weight of the servicing required for the airlift. It was only in March 1949 that it increased its servicing potential to six per day and it took until the middle of April for it to carry out everything required of it. In any case, American aircraft flew for 1,000 hours and then they were sent back to the United States for an overhaul.

By March 1949 it was clear from the number of aircraft accidents that the crews were exhausted. Moreover, the C-54, always thought of as being such a robust and reliable aircraft, was wearing out. The Americans figured that at least thirty-six of them would need to be totally replaced. It was out of production too and spares were short. As for the RAF, their Dakotas, which they had hoped to replace with Hastings, were still in service. It was still not easy to find enough experienced replacement crews. The Americans continued to send in new pilots via their training facility at Great Falls, but although these men arrived fresh and eager, after six months of flying they too were exhausted.

The RAF was also short of aircrew. The entire resources of Transport Command had been thrown into the operations; training and scheduled services everywhere else had been cancelled. At least the British crews were able to go home for a short period each month, but the RAF was not especially generous with their travel warrants and, in any case, there was not transport between RAF Oakington to Cambridge to enable them to catch a train.

Around this time the RAF carried out a study on 121 Dakota crews. They were asked whether tiredness and other problems affected their efficiency. The most common complaint was the irregular hours, which led to poor sleep and irregular eating habits. Only 8 per cent complained about the number of hours they were expected to fly. It was generally believed that, arising out of the study, aircrew should not be expected to fly more than eighty hours in a month.

On 27 June 1949, the first anniversary of the beginning of the airlift, General Robertson promised: 'The empty cupboard of Berlin must be filled before our pilots return to their normal tasks.' During July alone 253,090 tons of supplies were flown into the city, a record-breaking figure. It was now clear, with negotiations well underway and progress being made, that the airlift would finally be run down. It was decided to keep them going and although the flights were now reduced to a five-day week, the crews and the airmen could return to their normal duties, content in the knowledge that they had achieved their goal.

The pilots who had flown during the airlift received an enormous amount of thanks in words, but very little in deeds. Only after gentle persuasion was the USAF prepared to award their participants in the airlift a medal. The British refused to give any kind of commemoration, instead the RAF would be reviewed in front of the King at Buckingham Palace. They would then march along the Mall, into the Strand and onto Guildhall for a lunch.

Eventually the skies over Berlin were silent. The achievements of the fliers and all of the men who supported the aircraft to help them remain in the air could not be underestimated.

CHAPTER SIX

Airlift Airbases

At the peak of the airlift operations aircraft were airlifting supplies into three airfields in Berlin and using nine bases in the western zones. It was abundantly clear that the central and northern corridors into the city were the shortest routes. They were also not very far above sea level compared to the southern corridor in the US zone. As a result, by October 1948 the airlift was predominantly using airfields in the British zone, of which there were six: Bückeburg, Fassberg, Fuhlbuttel, Lübeck, Schleswigland and Wunstorf. Soon two others would be used in the British zone, including the old seaplane base at Finkenwerder and another airbase at Celle. By this stage only a pair of airfields were being used in the US zone, Rhein-Main and Wiesbaden.

The Americans had standardized their fleets to use the C-54s, each of which could carry 10 tons per sortie. In all, they were carrying 3,000 tons into Berlin each day. This compared to the mixture of military and civilian aircraft being used by the British that were lifting around 1,500 tons. It made perfect sense, therefore, to shift the main American effort from the southern bases to the shorter bases in the British zone. The first to be converted to American use was Celle. American aircraft were already operating out of Fassberg and Lübeck. Bückeburg was working as a passenger shuttle base, connecting Berlin with Great Britain.

The Combined Airlift Task Force produced a manual in

December 1948, entitled *Airlift Routes and Procedures*. This gave pilots a chart for all airlift bases, as well as approach charts for twenty-six bases around Europe.

The French had a distinct lack of transport aircraft. Most of their Douglas C-47 Transporters were being used in Indo-China. For a short period they operated three Junkers JU52s out of Wunstorf, but their contribution to the airlift ended abruptly when two of the Junkers crashed into one another. They then offered a site in the Wedding suburb, which became Tegel airfield (see below).

Tempelhof airport was a huge air terminus. It had a massive curving operations and administrative block, which had been constructed between 1934 and 1939. At the time the structure was said to be the third largest building in the world. It had served as a factory, producing Focke-Wulf Fw 190 fighter aircraft. It also had a well-equipped hospital. It was, in effect, originally designed to be the city's principal civil airport.

For a short time, it had been occupied by the Soviet 515th Fighter Air Regiment, then by the 193rd Fighter Air Division. It was the Soviets who had laid a pierced steel planking runway, extending to 4,987 ft by 120 ft.

The Americans took possession on 2 July 1945. There had been extensive damage and anything that was not concreted into the ground had been taken. The pierced steel planking had been laid on a relatively unstable foundation, making landing in poor weather hazardous.

Tempelhof was situated on a flat area in the middle of the city. The approach had to be extremely careful as the pilot had to avoid seven-storey blocks of flats on one side and a cemetery on the other. There was another hazard in the shape of a 400 ft chimney belonging to a brewery.

On 1 September 1945 C-47 Skytrain Transports, belonging to the European Air Transport Service, operated from Tempelhof. Work began in earnest to complete new runways, the first of which was completed in September 1948 and the second the following month. During the airlift the first C-47s with food from the American zone landed there.

By August 1948 the runways were beginning to crack up due to the heavy loads and the rains. Slotting in patches of work between blocks of arrivals, the repairs were carried out. The runways were strengthened and attempts were made to water-proof them by using a mixture of coarse sand, grit, tar and asphalt.

German civilians carried out the unloading at Tempelhof under American military supervision. When an aircraft radioed in its cargo the unloading teams would be forewarned what to expect. The aircraft touched down and was then given taxiing instructions by airfield control. Marshals guided it to a position on the apron. As soon as the engines were turned off a lorry backed up towards it and the chocks were jammed in under its wheels. Half a dozen labourers began manhandling the cargo or sliding it down a chute. Once the hold was clear cleaners would jump in. Coal dust was taken to a dump and flour was collected for animal feed. From here the supplies were sent by road into the centre of Berlin.

Tempelhof saw the first landing of a C-97 Stratocruiser on 4 May 1949. It was only carrying around 5 tons, but it was capable of carrying 25. This could certainly have been the shape of things to come had the blockade continued for much longer. One of its huge advantages was that the aircraft was actually in production and therefore adequate spares and replacements could always be found.

An aircraft coming into Tempelhof would call the airfield forty minutes after passing over Fulda, also known as the Kornorn Intersection. The pilot would give the airfield a position report and at the same time Tempelhof's CPS-5 radar would pick up the aircraft. The airport would instruct the pilot to turn either left or right for a minute so that the operator could be absolutely sure which blip on the radar was the aircraft in question. If at this stage the aircraft was off course it would be brought back to its correct position in the corridor. Once it reached the Tempelhof range it would pass on another position report. Depending on the weather, it would be told to contact either Tempelhof GCA or Tempelhof Tower.

If the aircraft was making a westerly landing the pilot would be told to take a heading of 360 degrees at 2,000 ft for one minute. He would then turn onto a downwind leg of 90 degrees, descending to 1,500 ft for one minute. He would then vector onto a base leg of 180 degrees and find himself at the end of the runway. He was then given final approach instructions. For an easterly landing he would follow a left-hand pattern and the downwind leg was around three minutes. This would bring the aircraft to around 6 miles to the north-west of Tempelhof, where it would then turn to its base leg heading of 180 degrees. Usually the minimum altitude at Tempelhof was 400 ft, and pilots were instructed not to go below this level.

When the aircraft landed a jeep would lead them to the space beside the loading ramp. When the aircraft left the airfield it would have to climb to between 7,500 and 8,500 ft. Aircraft would leave at three to five minute intervals. Tempelhof's two runways allowed one to be used for landing and the other for take-off. It was important that there was enough time between landings and take-offs to allow for missed approaches.

Once the aircraft had taken off it would turn at 700 ft to a heading of 255 or 260 degrees. If the take-off was westerly the aircraft would climb to 3,500 ft but if it was easterly it would remain below 1,000 ft in order to stay clear of the approach patterns of landing aircraft. By the time it got to the Wannsee Beacon it would have climbed to 3,500 ft and then would head for the Braunschweig Beacon. Here it would climb to its specified altitude and be travelling at around 180 mph. It would home in on the Fritzlar beacon, some 95 miles distant, giving a position to Fritzlar Airways. After Fritzlar they would contact Frankfurt Airways and be informed that they should either contact GCA or Rhein-Main Tower. It would continue to the Staden beacon. Air speed by now would have decreased to 140 mph and it would cross the Offenbach beacon at around 2,500 ft. It would now be vectored for its final approach. If, for example, it was landing to the east it would approach a point 7 miles to the west of the airfield and make its final approach at 2,000 ft.

A CPS-5 search radar was sited at Tempelhof in order to help avoid aircraft bunching up. It was long believed that the only factor that limited the number of aircraft that could land in Berlin was the haphazard spacing. Below the CPS-5 it was the control room, which was underneath the control tower. This consisted of half a dozen 12 inch viewing scopes. There were also large display boards that showed all inbound traffic for the three Berlin airfields. To begin with pilots operated the CPS-5 system. By March 1949, however, experienced enlisted personnel had taken over these duties.

It is testament to the usefulness of the CPS-5 system that there were no air collisions after it had been brought into use. When aircraft appeared at the 75-mile maximum range of the radar, the operators would organize them into two-minute spacing intervals before the aircraft reached Tempelhof radio range. This, in turn, allowed GCA to land them at proper intervals. Tempelhof could tell pilots the precise distance between the aircraft, which allowed them to concentrate on navigation and flying, rather than worrying whether he was going to be hit by another aircraft.

If there was a problem with the CPS-5 system or the generators powering it broke down, there would be considerable problems. The GCA radar did provide some overlap and a number of emergency landings were handled by the GCA personnel, but most of the GCA equipment was rather old; most of them were AN/MPN-1, although a CPN-4 was in use at Tempelhof.

Landings at Tempelhof were considerably more difficult than at other airfields due to the flats around the field, which meant that the GCA equipment had to be positioned at the end of the runway farthest from the approaching aircraft, so that the radar could see over the buildings. Most pilots came in high and had to be coaxed down by the GCA controllers. Because of this psychological hazard no aircraft was ever wrecked by landing too short at Tempelhof, but landing too far down the runway wrecked three.

The British airbase in Berlin was Gatow, which had been originally built as a *Luftwaffe* training base. It lacked any runways and consequently the first job was to lay a pierced steel planking runway at a length of 4,500 ft. The RAF took control of the base in 1945. It was originally designed to handle eight Tempest Mark V fighter-bombers belonging to No. 3 Squadron, and also a small number of Avro Ansons and Douglas Dakotas.

It had been a Soviet airfield for around two months, but vehicles of 2848 Squadron of the RAF Regiment claimed it on 25 June 1945. On 1 August 1945 the Royal Air Force Unit Berlin officially became RAF Gatow.

Soon after the beginning of the airlift Lieutenant-Colonel Graham, commander of the Royal Engineers in Berlin, offered his services to Group Captain Warde, the Station Commander at

RAF Gatow. It was Graham who controlled the cement in the British sector of Berlin. After consultation with the Works Services Officer, it was decided to cover the runway at Gatow with a mix of bitumen and stone. Unfortunately there was very little stone in Berlin and even less bitumen. One of Graham's officers pointed out that the Soviets had removed quite a lot of track from the railway system in the British sector, but had left the rock ballast, which had been imported from Saxony, and this could be the solution to the problem. Lorry loads were driven to Gatow, but the problem of bitumen still remained. Inside the Soviet sector, quite close to where it intersected with the British and American zones, there was a factory that produced bitumen. East Berliners did what they could to roll barrels of it through the wire into the British sector, but it was far too little for the job.

Another suggestion was to take away the road surface from bombed out areas of the city. So Graham's engineers and the men of the RAF Works Services tore off as much as they could. Over the next couple of months boilers were used to melt the bitumen and crushers to pulverise the ballast. Finally dumpers were used to cart the mixture to the runway and steamrollers to flatten it out. Graham's corner of Gatow airfield was promptly dubbed 'Dante's Inferno'.

They were desperately short of machinery, but a German driver from Leipzig drove through miles of Soviet territory to offer his services, along with his steamroller. It is still a mystery how he managed to pass dozens of checkpoints on his route.

At Gatow, as with many of the airfields, there was always the problem of theft. Heinz Michael was put in command of sixty police and 120 watch police who were responsible for guarding supplies brought in. They carried out inspections of the workers' quarters and up to 6,000 workers were searched every day when they left their shifts. In one inspection in July 1948 they found an amazing amount of sugar, tea, flour, butter, tinned meat, chocolate, cigarettes, coffee, coal, milk powder and cakes; one shift tried to steal three radio sets. It is not surprising that some of the workers did try to take things out of the airfields, undoubtedly motivated by hunger and cold. Some, however, were certainly supplying goods to the black market.

Conditions were never particularly good at Gatow and even in the winter, with mountains of coal on the airfield, Lieutenant-

Colonel Graham would sit in flying boots, a sheepskin coat, a balaclava and gloves. Eventually generators were flown in, each weighing 8,000 lb.

Throughout the airlift, Gatow provided sterling service. In March 1949 Major-General Geoffrey Bourne, the Commandant of British Troops Berlin, sent a message of congratulations to Group Captain B. C. Yard, the Station Commander. The message was dated March 12 1949:

> In addition to the sentiments expressed in my message to Air Marshal Williams I wish to add some remarks concerning RAF Station Gatow, which holds a special place for the British in Berlin.
>
> Ever since the start of the airlift, Gatow has run a 24-hour service of remarkable efficiency, accepting and despatching aircraft in all weathers. Some 582,603.1 metric tons, including vital fuels for the three western sectors, have been unloaded and delivered in Berlin; your best performance was to receive and despatch 485 aircraft in twenty-four hours using only one runway.
>
> These performances at our own British airfield in Berlin have not been achieved without great effort on the part of all who are under your command, RAF, army and German workers alike, so the British community here thank you and say, well done Gatow.

Even though by this stage the airlift was virtually over, Gatow continued to stockpile supplies for the 1949 winter. In any case, the Soviets could always repudiate the agreement that had been made.

On 15 December 1948 Berlin's third airfield, Tegel, was opened to airlift aircraft. It was situated in the French sector. There was nothing there prior to the airlift and it was built entirely to lessen the overload at Gatow and Tempelhof. Originally the area had been set aside for the delivery of supplies by parachute.

Construction began in August 1948 and after four months the airfield was ready. Around 17,000 German civilians were employed on the project, some 40 per cent of them women. They received 1.20DM per hour and received a hot meal for each shift they did. Shift patterns ensured that work continued around the clock.

A 22 in thick, tightly packed brick rubble single runway was constructed. It was 5,500 ft long and 150 ft wide. A large amount of ballast from disused railway tracks was also used on the site. In addition to the runway, aprons were also constructed, totalling 120,000 square feet. Taxiways of various widths from 50 to 120 ft were also constructed. Access roads were built, along with a link to the railway. Buildings were erected, including the control tower, operations, a warehouse, a small hangar, a transportation office, an infirmary and other sundry buildings.

The first aircraft to land at Tegel was flown by Squadron Leader A. M. Johnstone, at the request of HQ No. 46 Group, on 18 November 1948. His aircraft was a Dakota belonging to No. 30 Squadron. On board he had condensed milk, cooking oil and tractor tyres. He found that the airfield was not quite ready: most of the surface was deep in mud, although the taxiway and the runway were ideal. The airport was ideal for aircraft to land, but useless for offloading cargo and, as a result, what would have been a momentous feat in such a short time ended in frustration and Johnstone was forced to take his load back to Lübeck.

The site had indeed been a difficult one. It was an old parade ground, and four huge sand hills, each of which weighed several million tons had to be removed. Four bulldozers had to be flown in specifically for the project. Although it was in the French zone of Berlin, the French actually contributed virtually nothing to the project. The Americans paid for the bulk of the construction and eventually used this airport themselves, with the British ultimately responsible for the unloading and the emergency services.

By November 1948 the British had sent in teams to live in tents on the site. The first ceremonial flight in included Generals Cannon and Tunner, on board a C-54. A Dakota came in on the same day as Squadron Leader Johnstone, bringing in coal and taking out twenty-six undernourished children.

Two major landmarks dominated Tegel: the transmitter masts of Radio Berlin. One of them was a shade over 390 ft tall and the other 296 ft. From the outset it was obvious that they would endanger aircraft approaching the airport. General Ganeval, the

French Commandant, asked the director of the radio station and the Soviet Military Administration to remove the masts, but he was ignored. This issue reared its head again very soon.

The French finally made a symbolic contribution to the airlift at 1045 on 16 December 1948, when General Ganeval gave the order to blow up the two transmitter towers. At his wits' end with the Soviets' continued refusal even to enter into negotiations, he warned them that the towers 'would not be available after 15 December'.

He took the decision without telling either the British or the Americans about what he was about to do. He just said: 'In my opinion it is no longer possible to accept responsibility for accidents.' When the Soviet Commandant, Kotikov, said: 'How could you do such a thing?' Ganeval replied; 'With the help of dynamite and French sappers.'

An aircraft was on its way to Tegel at the time and whilst *en route* it received a message that the radio mast obstructions no longer existed.

On 14 March 1949 construction began to complete a 6,500 ft runway with an additional 1,500 ft base, so that it could be extended if necessary to take larger aircraft. Unlike the first runway, which was built primarily by hand, the airlift had allowed heavy equipment to be brought in and, as a consequence, 400 labourers and technicians completed the second. The work was completed by 4 August. The last civilian flight into Berlin landed at Tegel on 16 August 1949, an Eagle Aviation Halton.

When the airlift began the Americans already had an established airbase at Rhein-Main, close to Frankfurt. It had served as a *Luftwaffe* base, but had been pulverized by Allied bombing. By 1948 it had become the centre for the US Military Air Transport Service (MATS). Three squadrons, the 14th, 15th and 53rd, operated C-47 Transports. Collectively the units were formed under the 61st Troop Carrier Group.

Initially the airbase's 6,000 by 150 ft runway was perfectly adequate for the airlift's needs. A new one was begun that was to be some 7,000 x 200 ft, but less than a quarter of it was finished by the time the airlift ended.

Around 540 officers, 1,400 senior NCOs and 4,000 other ranks were working at Rhein-Main by August 1948. There had been considerable movements there, with new units and support services being brought in.

The Americans also used Wiesbaden. The *Luftwaffe* had also used it. By 1948 the 60th Troop Carrier Group, with its three squadrons of C-47s were based there. It was this group that provided aircraft for the mini-airlift in April 1948. It eventually became the home of General Curtis LeMay and the First Airlift Task Force.

On 15 October 1948 it became HQ Combined Airlift Task Force under General William Tunner and the 7150th Composite Wing's C-54 Skymasters arrived. In December of the same year the 317th Troop Carrier Wing moved to Celle in the British zone from Wiesbaden.

Ultimately the RAF bases at Fassberg and Celle would supersede Wiesbaden, as it took an hour and a half for a C-54 to reach Berlin from the south and only an hour from the RAF bases.

After the war, Fassberg had been used as an RAF fighter base until December 1947, when it was downgraded to a maintenance base. It had been constructed in 1936 and was originally used as a *Luftwaffe* bombing school. RAF construction teams had cleared some 5 acres of forest and laid 180 square yards of pierced steel planking, along with 5 miles of railway sidings.

It fell to Group Captain Biggar to oversee the work to convert Fassberg into an Operation Plainfare base. It was initially used by the British for their Dakotas. The huge hard standings, some 2,400 x 1,500 ft, were used by RAF Dakotas. The Dakotas remained there until 22 August 1948, when the British officially handed over the base to the Americans. Some forty, C-54 Skymasters, belonging to the 50th Troop Carrier Wing, then began to use it. A note of glamour was introduced when Colonel Jack Coulter assumed command, accompanied by his wife, the film star Constance Bennett.

Lübeck was a former *Luftwaffe* airfield that had been built in 1935. It had a railhead and after the war it became the armament practice camp for RAF fighter aircraft. It needed upgrading; including the laying a concrete road to the petrol bulk installations, amounting to some 4,000 square yards. The existing concrete runway was improved with the laying of pierced steel planking hardstands, as well as an 88,000 square yard parking apron.

Lübeck was just 2 miles from the Soviet zone and operations required particular care on the part of the pilots. It became the primary RAF Dakota base and civilian Dakotas later joined it.

In mid-September 1948 the RAF Airfield Construction Wing began converting what had been a *Luftwaffe* training centre into an airlift base at Celle. It had been built in 1935 and had later been the home of German night fighters. Initially No. 36 Wing and No. 84 Group Communications Flight had occupied it. No. 1 Barracks Equipment Disposal Unit replaced them in late 1947. The process of converting it into an Operation Plainfare airbase got underway in mid-September 1948, employing some 2,000 German workers. They constructed a runway extending to some 5,400 x 150 ft. In addition a pierced steel planking loading apron was constructed, covering 190,000 square feet. As well as the building of houses, rail facilities and fuel storage, a 9,500 x 50 ft pierced steel planking taxiway was added. It was to be handed over to the Americans in mid-December 1948, when C-54 Skymasters belonging to the 317th Troop Carrier Wing, arrived from Wiesbaden. They flew their first airlift operation on 16 December and continued all the way through to 31 July 1949, by which time the 317th had flown 288 sorties.

Wunstorf had been constructed in 1934 and although it was not a large airfield, it had been used by RAF fighter-bombers. By July 1948 there were two concrete runways, hard standings and a perimeter track. Initially, RAF Dakotas and Avro Yorks used it. There were always problems at the airfield, particularly after heavy rain, and the concrete runways were breaking up. Pierced steel planking was added and it continued to be used as a base for Avro Tudors, Lancastrians and Yorks.

Fuhlbuttel was the civil airport of Hamburg and was under the control of the Civil Aviation Commission of Germany. By 21 December 1948 it had become an airlift base, with a new 5,850 ft concrete runway running alongside an existing 4,800 ft pierced steel planking one. On 5 October 1948 some eighteen civilian Dakotas had moved out of Lübeck and had established themselves at Fuhlbuttel. One of the airfield's problems was that it did not have a GCA, although it was well illuminated.

Civilian-operated Halton Transports and RAF Hastings began using Schleswigland, close to the Baltic coast, on 25 November 1948. It had two runways, but because of its location it suffered from low temperatures, sea mist and cloud cover. It was also one of the most distant airbases from Berlin. In May 1948 No. 30 Squadron had been deployed there. It had been originally used as a civil glider airfield when it opened in 1936, but the *Luftwaffe* had taken control in 1938. Initially it was a night-fighter base, but later it was used to shuttle VIPs. In the last weeks of the war, before it was overrun, it had been used by the new German Me262 jet fighters. The Royal Air Force Regiment first occupied it in May 1945. Until the end of 1946 No. 121 Fighter Wing used it, and then it was used as an airborne forces practice camp, until June 1948.

CHAPTER SEVEN

Easter Parade

In September 1948 the combined airlift delivered some 139,622.9 tons of supplies into Berlin. This averaged out at 4,655.4 tons each day. In October they managed 147,508.8 tons, bringing the average up to 4,760.7 tons each day. By the end of October the airlift had delivered a cumulative total of 332,467 tons of cargo. This meant that the airlift was providing some 97.9 per cent of Berlin's food requirements and around 73.77 per cent of the coal requirements.

Berlin had reserve stocks of food to last them for forty-two days. Coal set aside for utilities would last fifty-three days and other coal stocks, mainly for domestic use and for industry, fifty-two days. It was possible, therefore to increase the daily food ration for Berlin inhabitants by 250 calories each day. This meant that they were no longer at starvation point and that they could begin to enjoy greater quantities of milk and sugar.

With all of these positive and upbeat results the airlift was about to face one of its greatest obstacles. This time it was not the Soviets, aircraft problems, exhausted pilots or even a dearth of supplies. Their new adversary would be General Winter. As the American Commandant in Berlin, Colonel Howley, said: 'General Winter, the unconquerable Russian general, positively frowned on us and we could almost hear the Russians guffawing through the Iron Curtain.' From now on airlift pilots would be facing thick, heavy fog and even more treacherous conditions.

It was not all gloom and doom, however, as General Clay discovered when he flew into Tempelhof in early November.

> Thanks to the effectiveness of GCA and its well-trained operators, we landed without accident but with our brakes hot. When the tower directed us to the taxiway we found the visibility so poor that we dare not move farther down the runway. We were unable to follow the jeep that was sent to guide us and we finally reached the unloading ramp guided by an airman under each wing signalling with flashlights.

Certainly the GCA systems were allowing aircraft to land in all but the very worst weather conditions. Tunner, however, was still after more aircraft. He knew that the 225 C-54s he had already at Rhein-Main, Wiesbaden and Fassberg were capable of saturating the air corridors into Berlin, but he still wanted big aircraft. He had written to Major-General Laurence Kuter, who had assumed command of Air Transport Command on 1 June 1948. Kuter replied that plans were already in place to reinforce and that he would be in a position to take action once the National Security Council had approved his plans.

By the end of September 1948 the American airlift force consisted of the 60th and 61st Troop Carrier Groups and the 1420th and 1422nd Air Transport Groups. On 30 September the 60th Troop Carrier Group's C-54s flew their last mission. The 317th Troop Carrier Group replaced them and their thirty-six, C-54s. This was not the end of the contribution from the pilots of the 60th, as many of them joined the 317th or joined other units at Fassberg, Rhein-Main or Wiesbaden.

By mid-October a dozen of the 317th's aircraft were transferred to Fassberg; a C-54 at Fassberg was worth, in tonnage terms, 1.6 at Wiesbaden, owing to the different distances to Berlin.

Clay asked for additional aircraft on two occasions during September. He wanted to be able to deliver 8,000 tons each day during good weather and 4,500 tons in poor. The navy were initially approached to provide thirty C-54s, along with sixty crews. MATS were also told to supply thirty-six C-54s as soon as crews had been trained and the USAF provided fifty aircraft during September.

Clay was still frustrated by the delays and in October he went to Washington to plead for sixty-four more C-54s. The Joint Chiefs of Staff concluded:

> With increases in personnel and funds the Berlin airlift can be continued indefinitely. Our present military power cannot effectively support the supply of Berlin by airlift on an indefinite basis, however, without such a diversion of military effort as has affected and will continue to affect the ability of the National Military Establishment to meet its primary national security responsibilities.

On 22 October President Truman gave formal authorization for the increase in airlift capability to the tune of sixty-six C-54s.

On 18 September 1948 the USAF celebrated its birthday. Tunner determined to make it a day to remember and set the wheels in motion to deliver record tonnage between noon on the 17th and noon on the 18th. During the twenty-four hours Skymasters delivered 5,000.4 tons, the C-47s 417.6 tons, the C-82s 50.3 tons and a single C-74 114.4 tons. The British added some 1,405.3 tons, making the total delivery 6,988.7 tons. On average a C-54 was being unloaded in 7.5 minutes and a C-47 in just 3.5 minutes. On one occasion German labourers unloaded 19 tons of coal in twelve minutes.

There were misgivings about whether the airlift could continue at this intensity. Some 800 aircraft could land on the three Berlin airfields per day, and in fact on one occasion, in eighteen hours 861 had landed. It was generally believed that poor weather would reduce the tonnage by around 30 per cent, but if 8,000 tons could be delivered per day then even such a 30 per cent loss would still leave the tonnage well above the 4,500 minimum.

However, this was all contingent upon these being more Skymasters. On 9 June the USAF had 258 C-54s assigned to the airlift, but only 169 were operational. Some were in the United States undergoing periodic repairs, some were with training crews in Montana, and others were scattered around Germany being overhauled. Clay was adamant that when he said he wanted 225 aircraft he actually meant 225 that were operational, not scattered around the world. He set a date of 1 January 1949 as the point at which he would absolutely need them.

By January 1949 the Americans were operating 201 air force aircraft and twenty-four navy ones in Germany. An additional sixty-seven air force and eight navy aircraft were tied up in maintenance or inspections. By the end of the month, on paper the Americans had 287 C-54s assigned to the airlift. They were fast running out of aircraft, but there was still a need for an additional twenty-five, which were not properly assigned until the April.

At its greatest strength the Americans had 312 C-54s out of the total of 441 in the USAF. At the end of January the 287 C-54s assigned to the Berlin airlift compared with 169 assigned to cover air transport routes elsewhere and forty leased by the USAF to civilian air carriers.

In November the weather closed in. Tempelhof had 5,000 cubic yards of sand on standby, which could be spread in case of ice, but there was nothing that could deal with the fog. The American Commandant, Colonel Howley said:

> The worst enemy of air operations is not cold but fog, and we had plenty of that, too – thick impenetrable fog. November and December were bad months. During November, fifteen of the thirty days were almost impossible for flying and December wasn't much better. Fog-bound November and December were the acid test of the airlift. If we could put these two normally bad flying months behind us without serious disaster to the people we were feeding, and could get well into January, we should know that we had the blockade licked.

The Combined Airlift Task Force deliveries dropped from 147,580.8 tons in October to 113,587.9 in November. This was the lowest monthly delivery total, since July. As we have seen, Berlin needed a minimum of 4,500 tons per day, but the airlift during November managed just 3,786.3.

They took advantage of good weather conditions as they appeared. On 6 November Tunner contacted his own forces and the RAF's No. 46 Group to tell them to try to make a maximum effort during the break in the weather. On 10 November some eighteen C-54s were transferred to British bases for several days.

It was also proving difficult to maintain the aircraft during the bad weather. Nothing much could be done unless the weather remained below minimum flying conditions for twenty-four hours. There was, however, an increased confidence in the airlift.

On 22 November Clay set the January daily targets at 5,620 tons. This figure included some 375 tons of American military supplies, 285 tons for the British and 113 for the French. Coal was still a considerable problem. Industry needed 2,535 tons per day and another 550 tons were needed for heating. On average, by this stage, the airlift was under delivering 1,490 tons of coal each day.

At the end of November the Americans were using several different airbases manned by different units. At Celle there was the 7480th Air Force Wing, at Rhein-Main the 61st Troop Carrier Group (Heavy) and the 513th Troop Carrier Group, at Wiesbaden 6169th Weather Reconnaissance Squadron, the 7150th Air Force Composite Wing and the 317th Troop Carrier Group, at Fassberg the 313th Troop Carrier Wing (Heavy). The 7350th Air Base Group was based at Tempelhof (with detachments at Gatow and Tegel). At Tempelhof and Frankfurt-on-Main there were air traffic control centres. Soon the 317th moved to Celle, the 513th Maintenance Supply Group and the 313th Troop Carrier Group based at Fassberg. The navy's VR-8 Transport Squadron operated as one of the 61st Troop Carrier Group squadrons, whilst the VR-6 Transport Squadron operated as a part of the 513th.

The US Chief of Staff, General Hoyt Vandenburg, visited Germany in early December. He noted that although the men were working well, they had been separated from their families for some time and at short notice. Many had been snatched from bases in Alaska, Guam and the Philippines. Vandenburg made it his duty to make sure that the men's wives and children were well looked after. He ordered overseas commanders to give special attention and also instituted Project Sleigh-bells, which was a special airlift of letters and packages between airlift personnel and their families scattered around the world.

The weather in December was not as severe as November. The airlift managed to average 4,562.5 tons each day, giving a grand total for the month of 141,438.1 tons. This was still below the total that had been achieved in October, but on the last day of 1948 alone, the Americans achieved 526 flights and delivered 5,120.4 tons into the city. At the same time the RAF delivered 1,007.4 tons, providing a total for the day of 6,127.8 tons.

The RAF's decision to convert many transporters to liquid fuel tankers had reaped dividends; they were in fact delivering far more than was actually required. There was still a major problem, however, with coal. The airlift was still not able to deliver the minimum daily requirements. Many were predicting a coal crisis in January. According to Clay's calculations, based on figures on 24 December, Berlin had nineteen days' supply of general-purpose coal and a twenty days' of home-heating coal left. New calculations set a probable requirement of 5,141 tons daily, but the airlift could only deliver an average of 3,073 tons. For the time being this would have to be enough. Most of the coal in any case was being delivered to industry and the utilities. The January allocation for households was 27,000 tons, which with a population of 2.1 million, would only give each household between 25 and 30 lb of coal.

Less problematic was the food situation. The ration calculations were based on 2,300 calories per person per day, and despite the shortage of fresh vegetables, vitamin pills and dehydrated foodstuffs were still improving nutrition.

Periodically the electricity would have to be turned off in different parts of the city. Most Berliners only had access to electricity for four hours each day, sometimes at strange hours of the day. Some meals were cooked after midnight. One particular example of ingenuity was the wife of a dentist, who pedalled a bicycle in order to provide enough electricity for her husband's drill.

The underground services were reduced by approximately 50 per cent, and trams by 40 per cent. The S-bahn was not affected because the Soviets used it themselves. The blockade had so far led to around 10 per cent unemployment in the city, but some 900,000 Berliners were still working.

US Army intelligence released a summary of the situation on 13 January 1949:

Faith in the airlift and in the willingness of the Western powers determination to remain in the city has increased since the beginning of winter. Unless the situation becomes definitely worse, the population of the west sectors of Berlin may be relied upon to support the policy of the Western powers through this winter.

January was even milder. The C-54s that had been long awaited finally arrived, maintenance was improving and there were adequate stocks of spares. January saw an average daily delivery of 5,547 tons each day. This meant a total tonnage for the month of 171,959.2 tons. Unfortunately the weather deteriorated the following month. This meant a daily average of 5,437.2 tons per day and a February total of 152,240.7 tons. By March the tonnage had dramatically improved; the Allies were delivering 6,327.8 tons each day, giving a total of 196,160.7 tons. Tonnage henceforth would continue to increase and by July, for example, the daily tonnage was 8,164.2 tons and a staggering 253,090 tons for the month.

The millionth ton of cargo was delivered to Berlin on 18 February 1949. It was now clear that the airlift was more than working. General Clay received a letter from Dean Acheson, who had replaced George C. Marshall as US Secretary of State:

The success of the airlift has enabled the Western powers to maintain their rights and discharge their obligations as prescribed by solemn international agreement and has given encouragement to the efforts of the democratic peoples of Europe to resist the use of lawless force. Our government offers its grateful commendation, in particular to the personnel of the air forces and to all units, civilian and military. We are gratified that German citizens have given their unstinted help.

The Americans lost a pair of Skymasters on 17 March. One was undergoing major repairs and another crashed. It was decided that two C-54s each month would be transferred from US Far East Air Forces from April to cover any further losses. At the same time, Far East Air Forces transferred a pair of C-54s that were undergoing repairs in the United States. It was decided that this process would continue, until a minimum number of twenty were left; this was the absolute base requirement of Far East Air Forces.

The most dramatic day of the Berlin Airlift took place on 16 April 1949. The conveyor belt system of delivering aircraft loads into the city was working to perfection. The British were operating 154 aircraft and the Americans deployed 200 Skymasters. Tunner and the planners were going for a record-breaking delivery. In Tunner's own words: 'Things were going too well. It was necessary, I thought, to do something to shake up the command.'

The event was planned in great secrecy. The weekend of 15–16April, was selected as ideal weather conditions were expected. It was decided to transport in one cargo, coal. Already 10,000 tons had been stockpiled on the airlift bases. At noon on Saturday, 15 April quotas were posted out to all commands. There were rumours that something big was happening. Everyone was determined to drive up the tonnage figures. Tunner himself flew into Tempelhof to view operations from the Berlin end, and then he flew to every base run by the British and the Americans to observe, prod and push. Seconds before the last aircraft left Rhein-Main on Sunday, 16 April, someone had totalled up the amount of coal that had been delivered into the city and painted, on a Skymaster's nose: 'Record tonnage 12941 FLTS 1383'.

For the ten days prior to the record the average airlift day had produced a delivery of 6,729 tons. After what was called the Easter Parade the average was 8,893 tons.

In the British Operation Plainfare, the civilian aircraft were being redeployed; it was not until the end of November 1948 that the manager of the civilan lift, Edwin Whitfield, was satisfied. The RAF had opened Schleswigland, which would be used by the Hastings which were just coming into service. Civilian Haltons, which had first been moved from Wunstorf to Fuhlsbuttel, were sent to join them there. In addition to this, three Skyways Avro Yorks replaced the Haltons at Wunstorf and British South American Airways were about to send Tudors there. Fuhlsbuttel was about to accept the arrival of Bond Air Services and Eagle Aviation. Henceforth Wunstorf would only have Avro aircraft.

December 1948 was a frenetic month for Gatow. Six members of parliament had arrived on the 3rd and were going to stay in Berlin to watch the elections that were due to take place there a few days later. On 9th Gatow's Forward Air Supply Organization established a new record for unloading a Sunderland flying boat. Helped by the crew, twelve men unloaded 10,020 lb of salt in just three minutes twelve seconds. On the 11th a wave of Dakota aircraft were about to arrive at Gatow when suddenly a wave of Skymasters was diverted there from Tempelhof. Between 1300 and 1400, thirty-seven aircraft landed and seventeen took off. Between 1400 and 1500, twenty-one aircraft landed and thirty-seven took off. This was a remarkable feat as there had been a runway movement nearly every minute, 112 in two hours.

On 17 December an Avro York flown by Flight Lieutenant Beeston landed the 100,000th ton of freight at Gatow. On the 20th a concert was given for the German employees at Gatow. Following this there were children's parties at which thousands were fed and huge amounts of chocolate and sweets given to them. On the 23rd the 50,000th Operation Plainfare landing was made. There had been 6,737 sorties during December, but this compared to 7,405 in November and 11,458 in October.

By the end of December, Gatow had been in operation for 187 days. Every twenty-four hours there had been an average of 278 landings. This meant that for the last six months a landing had been made, day or night, every five minutes nine and a half seconds. It had become the busiest airfield in the world, handling a ton of freight every fifty-three seconds. Moreover, only 2.6 per cent of aircraft had been forced to overshoot.

During January it was decided that Operation Plainfare should continue as a long-term commitment for at least another two years. HQ No. 46 Group was transferred to Luneburg and new flight plans were drawn up. As of 1100 on 15 January 1949, Gatow would serve Celle, Lübeck and Wunstorf, while Tegel handled aircraft from Fassberg, Fuhlesbuttel and Schleswigland. From 21 January Wunstorf was to despatch seven RAF and four civilian aircraft twelve times per day. Lübeck would provide five RAF aircraft twenty-four times a day, Schleswigland was to send two RAF and three civilian aircraft twelve times a day and

Fuhlesbuttel would send two Haltons twelve times a day, supported by any other twin-engine aircraft required.

March began badly for the British. Gatow had to be closed at 0200 on 1st due to bad weather. It was opened again at 1240, but just twenty minutes later a snowstorm hit and consequently, by 1440, just thirteen aircraft had landed and only eight had been allowed to leave. In fact all of the Western airlift bases had been closed and some aircraft were diverted as far west as Paris. Had it not been for Lieutenant-Colonel Graham, commander of the Royal Engineers in Berlin, it could have been far worse. He had been preparing for the snow and had established auto-patrols fitted with two wheels in front and an adjustable blade, which moved in staggered ranks to push the snow off the runway. He had found it difficult to get them into Berlin because they were too big to go inside an Avro York. He sent diagrams to show how they could be cut into pieces with oxyacetylene torches. Once they arrived in Gatow, his Royal Engineers then reassembled them.

Captain Bateman was on hand with his men to sand the surface when necessary. He had a simple test: he would go to the end of the runway in a jeep and then spin in a tight circle. If the jeep spun it was time to sand the runway. At a prearranged signal, flying control would start overshooting aircraft; a pair of sanding lorries would move to each end of the runway being used, and another pair would start in the middle. In this way, Bateman's men could cover 1 mile in just fifteen minutes.

On 9 March the 50,000th Berliner was airlifted out of the city. The station commander, Group Captain Yarde, formally waved her off and Group Captain Biggar led the reception committee at Lübeck.

Despite the bad weather during March, it had been possible to mount 3,795 C-54 sorties, 2,043 by RAF Avro Yorks, 1,756 by Dakotas and two by Hastings. There had been 792 flights to and from Berlin by Lancasters and Lancastrians belonging to the civilian operators, 390 Tudor sorties, 171 civilian Avro Yorks, a single Liberator and a pair of civilian Haltons. In all there had been 8,752 sorties in and out of Gatow.

It was decided that during the winter the civilian fleet would carry 550 tons of liquid fuel each day. Of this 250 tons would be kerosene, which could be used for cooking and heating. It was also planned that by 1 September the civilian fleet would be restricted to just three different types of aircraft: Tudors, Lancasters/Lancastrians and Yorks, belonging to British South American Airways, Flight Refuelling and Skyways.

By March 1949 civilian aircraft were having to fly extremely long hours in order to fill their own blocks. Despite the stresses and strains, Flight Refuelling, for example, managed to carry in 24,740 gallons of liquid fuel on 16 April alone.

It was now clear that the Berlin airlift was approaching its final stages. Up until this point, despite the awkwardness of the Soviet blockade, supplies and fuel were getting into Berlin and the most needy were being airlifted out of the beleaguered city. Sooner or later, it was figured, the Soviets would see that their strategy to try and strangle Berlin and use it as a pawn against the West was failing.

There were continual political discussions going on, despite the initial by the Soviets that they had the upper hand. Their failure to force their will on the West was beginning to be a diplomatic embarrassment and it would soon become clear they were as keen to settle the matter as the West.

CHAPTER EIGHT

End of the Airlift

E ven as late as December 1948, no one could really see any
evidence that the blockade was about to end. In fact on 7
December, Forrestal instructed the Department of the
Army to begin developing plans based on the Soviets maintaining the blockade for another three years. The Secretary of the
Army, Royall, contacted General Clay. He wanted data pro-
jections on average daily tonnage requirements. He also asked
what additional funding would be required, what ground
equipment would be needed and the number of military
personnel.

It was still clear that the tonnage still had to be increased and
it will be recalled that there were alarmist suggestions that by
the end of January 1949 Berlin's stocks would be exhausted. The
planners finally projected the city's needs between 1 April 1949
and 30 June 1950. The idea was not just to continue to deliver
Berlin's immediate needs, but to increase the standard of living
and to ensure that employment remained buoyant. It was
concluded that around 8,685 tons of cargo would be needed each
day. This would also mean that the average basic ration would
increase from 1,990 to 2,100 calories per person per day. It was
also estimated that these delivery figures would mean that food
stocks in Berlin would increase from forty-two to forty-five
days' worth.

The greater tonnage allowed certain improvements. First, at

least a third of the potato ration would be fresh potatoes during the winter months. Secondly, for morale purposes, increased coal would be set aside for domestic heating. Thirdly, domestic electricity rations would be increased from four to five hours and, hopefully to six hours each day. Fourthly, industry would be allocated more liquid fuels – diesel fuel for buses and a capacity to produce more electricity for the trams.

Raw materials would now be imported for industry and, for the first time significant amounts of consumer goods would also be flown in each day. It was, therefore, necessary to consider that the daily airlift should be 11,249 tons by July 1949.

For the Americans this would mean a considerable investment in new aircraft. In fact, in order to deliver this tonnage each day, even taking into account the British contribution, the USAF's entire C-54 fleet would have to be committed to the airlift. In actual fact only 52.77 per cent was ever in service, but the additional tonnage figures relied on 65 per cent of them being operational. This in turn would mean increases in maintenance and support facilities and a huge investment in equipment, parts and spares. It was proposed by the planners that the airlift be rationalized and that sixty aircraft should operate from each airbase. This had been shown to be the ideal number to produce maximum efficiency.

By January, of course, the airlift was using seven bases, but the planners recognized that another would have to be opened. In theory, at least, as long as the C-54s could remain operational, the airlift could continue indefinitely. But the Skymasters would not last forever. The vast majority of them would reach 14,400 flying hours by November 1952, this was considered to be second-line life for these aircraft. If the Americans wanted to fly them beyond this date they would be taking significant risks with the lives of their aircrews.

At least there was some light at the end of the tunnel. New aircraft would begin reaching Germany by 1950. There were plans afoot to deliver fifty, four-engined Boeing C-97 Stratofreighters between July 1949 and March 1950. Depending on the willingness of Congress, a further fifty-four could be added to this tally. Also authorized was the huge Douglas C-124 Globemaster II, which was a development of the C-74. It was optimistically anticipated that the first one of these would roll off the production line and be available to the USAF in May 1950. The planners had to rely on the timely delivery of these two new aircraft; there was little room for delay.

What was also necessary was a root and branch construction programme, which should begin in the summer of 1949, to improve infrastructure, runways and taxiways. Without this additional investment the airlift would be unable to continue far beyond 1952.

Consequently, on 20 December 1948, the USAF authorized an investigation into the needs for new runways, infrastructure and parking facilities to be ready in sufficient time when the C-54s were phased out and the larger aircraft came into operation, between 1950 and 1951.

At the beginning of 1949, Tunner had wanted to integrate completely all British and American operations, particularly those dealing with traffic, communications and air installation. He also wanted a single officer to be responsible for each of the three bases, as well as the control centre at Berlin, which dealt with approaching aircraft. He also proposed to move all but sixty of his existing C-54s into British bases. He, too, recognized the need to establish a new base in the British zone. He was also unhappy with Burtonwood. He believed that aircraft were there for too long and that by moving the C-54s into the British zone he could set up the 200-hour inspection system at Rhein-Main. In the end he was overruled. It was decided to keep Rhein-Main as an active operational base and to concentrate on making Burtonwood more efficient.

It seems clear that by December 1948 the Soviets had realized that their strategy in Germany had more or less failed. The Western powers, supported by German leaders, were success-fully creating a separate West Germany. There was absolutely nothing that Stalin or the Soviets could do to stop them. The key determining factor was the Berlin Airlift. Stalin could not risk brute force to further his political aims: this would inevitably lead to war. What the airlift managed to do was to allow the Western powers to negotiate with Stalin without a gun being held to their heads.

From early on the Allies had also set up a counter-blockade that had hurt Soviet Berlin and their occupation zone. The area of Germany occupied by the Soviets was deficient in coal and steel and they made no attempt to find alternative sources for these materials.

Western Germany was benefiting from the Marshall Plan, as well as the industrial muscle of the West. It was to be this factor, added to the commitment to the airlift, which was finally to break the Soviet's resolve. In December 1948 Francois Seydoux, a French political leader, made a speech in which he suggested that as far as the Soviet Union was concerned, the Berlin blockade was not just a failure, it was a positive embarrassment. This was very close to the truth.

The Soviet zone of Germany was in economic chaos due to its inability to source coal from the Ruhr. Around the same time the US Ambassador in Moscow sent a telegram to Washington: 'Berlin blockade backfired, airlift was a phenomenal practical and political success and counter-blockade pinched seriously.'

Stalin was already making moves by December 1948. He first told German Communist leaders to not be so vociferous against the West. In actual fact all they had managed to do was to alienate the non-Communists, divide Germany and Berlin and harden the West's resolve not to give in. On 30 January 1949 Stalin contacted the European Director of the American International News Service, Kingsbury Smith. He told him that he would be prepared to lift the blockade if the West did not establish a West German state and negotiations began on a Soviet/US non-aggression pact. The West did not have to jump to grab this olive branch; they had the Berlin airlift to buy them time.

In February 1949 the Soviet delegate to the United Nations, Jacob Malik, was asked by the US delegate, Philip Jessup, whether the fact that Stalin had not mentioned the currency issue to Kingsbury Smith was significant. A month went by and on 5 March Foreign Minister Molotov and the Minister of Foreign Trade, Mikoyan, were replaced with Andrey Vishinsky and Mikhail Menshikov. Could this mean that there would be a change in Soviet foreign policy?

On 15 March Jessup got his reply from Malik: it had been deliberate. Malik agreed to find out Stalin's views on lifting the blockade. He returned to Jessup on 21 March, saying an agreement might be possible. There was a meeting of the Council of Foreign Ministers, which was a condition of discussions taking place. To begin with the Soviets demanded that the West should not separate Germany until after the conference had ended, but later they abandoned this demand and an agreement was finally reached on 4 May 1949.

The Soviets lifted the Berlin blockade on 12 May 1949. The Secretary General of the United Nations announced:

> We, the representative of France, the United Kingdom and the United States of America on the Security Council, have the honor to request that you bring to the attention of the members of the Security Council the fact that our governments have concluded an agreement with the Union of Soviet Socialist Republics providing for the lifting of restrictions which have been imposed on communications, transportation and trade with Berlin.

The Soviets claimed victory. They claimed that the German people had proved to be too strong for the West, which had wanted a war. They concluded: 'War mongers had proven uncertain in the face of the growing popular peace movement.'

Despite the agreement, the Soviets still used a blockaded Berlin as a continued threat. They ensured that the Council of Foreign Ministers did not reach an agreement concerning transportation rights. Indeed interference with land transport continued for several more months. They began imposing new limitations: all rolling stock on railways passing through the Soviet zone would have to be pulled by Soviet engines, West German vehicles would not be allowed to travel on the *autobahns* and, finally, barge traffic would not be issued with permits.

Some 15,000 West German railway workers went on strike on 20 May 1949, protesting against the Soviet authorities that controlled the railways. Henceforth, they wanted to be paid in West German currency, for the Soviets to recognize their union and for fired colleagues to be reinstated. The railways were paralysed; there were bloody confrontations between Soviet-sponsored strikebreakers and the strikers themselves. Once again the airlift proved to be the only reliable means of providing supplies to Berlin.

The three military governors of Berlin, Clay, Robertson and Koenig, all determined to retain the airlift in place until huge reserves had been built up in Berlin. Together they decided that 1,100,000 tons of essential supplies would be brought into the city and that this would give the city a breathing space of four to five months. They set a target date to achieve this of August 1949.

In order to achieve this and support any future needs of the city, they recommended that two RAF heavy transport squadrons remain in Germany, as well as two USAF troop-carrier groups. They also concluded that it was essential not to mothball facilities in West Germany, but to retain them in readiness should they be required at short notice.

President Truman made the decision on 28 July 1949 that the Berlin Airlift would begin to wind down on 1 August. He had a proviso in announcing this decision, which was that provided the airlift could be re-established within ninety days, phasing out could begin. The following day both the British and the US governments announced that the airlift would begin to wind down, but that sufficient aircraft would remain in Germany and that installations would be made ready for reoccupation should the need arise.

The Americans began scaling down by transferring out of Europe all US units operating in the British zone, including the navy operation. The remaining USAF units would also be scaled down and would operate almost solely through Rhein-Main. On 1 August, as instructed, the US Navy squadrons at Rhein-Main ceased operations and began preparations to return to the United States. Mirroring their move was the USAF group at Celle.

Celle was emptied of aircraft, vehicles and supplies by 26 August and it was finally closed as an airlift base on 16 September. The closing down unit, the Erding Air Depot, then moved onto Fassberg. The airbase was closed on 26 September.

RAF airlift missions ceased on 31 August. The Combined Airlift Task Force HQ was dissolved on 1 September, leaving operational matters to the Commanding General, First Airlift Task Force, along with the Air Officer Commanding No. 46 Group.

On 30 September a C-54 lifted off from Rhein-Main, flown by Harry D. Immel, the chief pilot of the 61st Troop Carrier Group. He had been one of the first Americans to fly into Berlin fifteen months earlier. He was carrying a very common cargo, a load of coal. But this was no ordinary flight: for the Americans it was the last official flight of Operation Vittles.

During the take-off ceremony there had been a flypast by a formation of C-54 Skymasters, for the Americans the aircraft of the airlift. The epitaph of the first airlift task force read:

> At 0001, October 1, 1949, the Berlin airlift came to an end – undramatically, without fanfare. As the Command wrote 'mission accomplished', it could look back on the 15 turbulent months of operations with the satisfaction of having steered an unprecedented organization of men and aircraft through the most significant peacetime air transport operation in the history of the United States and British Air Forces.

On 23 September an RAF C-47 Dakota landed at Gatow airfield. Written on its nose were the words 'Psalm 21, verse 11'. It was a declaration of victory: 'For they intended evil against thee: they imagined a mischievous device, which they are not able to perform.'

There is some confusion in the statistics of the Berlin Airlift. The official American tallies show that 2,325,509.6 tons of cargo was flown into Berlin. This set of figures also suggests that Operation Vittles delivered 1,783,572.7 tons, whilst the British Operation Plainfare contributed 541,936.9 tons. The British, in 1956, suggested the figure was 695 tons less. Again using the US figures, they delivered 1,421,118.8 tons of coal, 296,319.3 tons of food and 66,134 tons of other miscellaneous cargo. The British delivered 164,910.5 tons of coal, 240,386 tons of food and 136,640.4 tons of other miscellaneous cargo. Included in this miscellaneous category was 92,282 tons of liquid fuels, primarily delivered by British civilian contractors.

Included in the British totals is another 146,980 tons of other cargo. In percentage terms, this suggests that the USAF brought in 76.7 per cent, the RAF 17 per cent and the British civilian operators 6.3 per cent.

Again, according to the US figures, the Combined Airlift Task Force also brought out 81,730.8 tons of cargo. The Americans flew out 45,887.7 tons of this and the British flew out the remaining 35,843.1 tons. Many of these manufactured items were stamped 'Manufactured in Blockaded Berlin'. Finally, some 227,655 military and civilian passengers were brought out of the city during the airlift.

Again the number of flights made by airlift aircraft varies. The USAF gives a total of 277,569. Of these 189,963 were flown by the USAF and 87,606 by the RAF. The GCA conducted 33,180 landings under visual flight rules and 42,205 under instrument flight rules. In addition, GCA conducted a further 3,960 landings in extremely poor conditions.

The Combined Airlift Task Force was, indeed, a truly combined force. In addition to the RAF and USAF, personnel and equipment was used belonging to the Royal Australian Air Force, the Royal New Zealand Air Force, the South African Air Force and the Royal Canadian Air Force. Two US Navy squadrons also supported the USAF.

There was enormous rivalry between squadrons, but not necessarily between services. For example, Commander James O. Vosseller's VR-8 Squadron exceeded its quota in one month by over 3,000 tons with just twelve R5Ds.

There were some seventy-nine casualties during the airlift, the majority from non-flying accidents. Thirty-one of them were Americans. In July 1948, six American C-47 Skytrains and a pair of C-54 Skymasters were involved in accidents, two occurred in flight, three on final landing approach and three on the ground. One hit a block of flats on its approach to Tempelhof on 25 July. Piloted by Charles H. King and Lieutenant Robert Stuber it crashed into the front of an apartment building in the Berlin-Friendenau district and both were killed. Another C-47 crashed into a field as it was approaching Wiesbaden.

August 1948 saw three C-47s and a pair of C-54s involved in accidents. One of the C-47s caught fire in mid-air and the two C-54s were wrecked during landing. Five C-47s and a C-54 were involved in serious accidents in September, whilst three C-47s and three C-54s were involved in minor accidents.

By the end of 1948 USAF transports had been involved in thirty-eight major and twenty-one minor accidents. On 6 December a C-54 with coal on board crashed 2 miles from Fassberg and all three of its crew members were killed.

Not all accidents led to fatalities. On 14 September 1948 a C-47 piloted by Captain Kenneth Slaker and Lieutenant Clarence Steber, was heading from Wiesbaden to Berlin. They had just entered Soviet airspace when both engines gave out. The pilots baled out and Steber was picked up the Soviet military and brought back to the US lines the next day. Slaker walked back into West Germany by himself.

On 15 November an R5D piloted by Lieutenant Commander Stephen Lucacic overran the Tempelhof runway and burst into flames. A second R5D was lost on 11 December. The aircraft was outbound from Berlin, heading for Rhein-Main when it crashed into high ground 15 miles from Rhein-Main. The skipper of the aircraft, Harry Crites was killed, but Lieutenant Joseph Norris and Ensign George Blackwood survived with serious injuries.

During the first full month of the airlift in 1948 the RAF Transport Command recorded some twenty-seven incidents. At Wunstorf a German driver hit a Dakota, an army driver backed into another, and a third was damaged whilst it was being unloaded. An unauthorized driver of a petrol bowser hit another Dakota's wing. At Bückeburg a Dakota swung off the runway as it was landing. Another flying from Wunstorf to Gatow, suffered a piston failure in the port engine. Flight Lieutenant Holmes jettisoned half his load and managed to return to Wunstorf on a single engine. Another aircraft had a fuel leak *en route* to Gatow, but it managed to return to base on a single engine. Another Dakota had to return to Wunstorf just after take-off due to carburettor problems. A Dakota flying in from Britain had even worse luck on 21 July 1948 when it was forced to make a landing at Schiphol in Amsterdam. Finally, yet another Dakota crashed near Fassberg on 24 July after a fire in mid-air.

One potentially terrifying incident took place on 7 April 1949. Flying Officer David Evans was carrying twenty-two passengers out of Gatow in his Dakota. Shortly after he had taken off from the airfield, at 200 ft, his port engine lost power. He managed to climb to 400 ft but the engine then stopped. He managed to feather the propellers and made a circuit to land, despite the strong wind. It was indeed good fortune for Evans, because later he attained the rank of Air Marshal in the Royal Australian Air Force and would clock up 764 hours of flying time, 442 by day and 322 at night, over a total of 231 sorties.

On 19 September 1948 an Avro York crashed at Wunstorf and

five of the crew were killed. On 17 November a Dakota crashed at night near Lübeck, but in the Soviet zone. Three of the crew were killed and Flight Lieutenant Wilkins, the navigator, later died of his injuries. On 24 January 1949 another Dakota crashed approaching Lübeck in bad weather, killing the signaller, Sergeant Grout and seven passengers. Two crew members and several others were injured. On 16 July a Hastings crashed on take-off early in the morning at Tegel. Sergeant Toad of the Glider Pilot Regiment, co-piloting the aircraft, was killed, as were four other crew members. Another Hastings caught fire and broke in half at dispersal in Schleswigland on 5 April. These were not the only Hastings to be involved in accidents. Others suffered accidents on 6 February, 4 April, 19 May and 18 July.

An RAF Sunderland was involved in an accident on 9 October 1948 on the River Elbe and a Lancaster was damaged on 10 March 1949 at Schleswigland. There were many accidents with the Avro York, but it is worth bearing in mind that, at one point, the aircraft was carrying 61 per cent of all supplies dealt with by the RAF. Overall it accounted for 42 per cent of all aircraft movements, so it is understandable that it had a number of accidents. The majority, however, were repaired and returned to operations. These accidents took place on 28 July 1948 at Gatow, 3 August at Wunstorf, 25 September at Wunstorf, 10 October at Gatow, 11 and 22 November at Wunstorf, 3, 14 and 15 December, at Gatow, 15 and 25 January at Gatow, 19 and 29 March at Wunstorf, 7 April at Wunstorf, 21 April at Gutersloh, 4 June at Wunstorf, 30 July at Wunstorf and 15 August, also at Wunstorf.

Nine squadrons of Dakotas, in addition to the Dakota Operational Conversion Unit, provided aircraft for the airlift, many of them made available via the lend-lease programme. Accidents involving Dakotas took place on 22 July 1948 at Gatow, 26 July at Fassberg, 3 August at both Bückeburg and Gatow, 17 and 20 September at Lübeck, 12 October at Bückeburg, 1 November at Lübeck, 6 November at Gatow, 4 January at Bückeburg and 8 May at Gatow.

The spring of 1949 saw the British deploying 150 aircraft of different types, some from the RAF and the remainder belonging to civilian operators. The USAF finally had enough aircraft to maintain the airlift for the foreseeable future, deploying 225

C-54s. For the most part around 200 of these were in daily service. There were another seventy-five being serviced or maintained and others with training crews at Great Falls in Montana.

In all, there were probably around 45,000 Germans either working as cargo loaders or carrying out other duties on the airfields. The USAF had 12,000 men and the US Navy had 800. The RAF and the British Army combined, including the Commonwealth aircrews, mustered some 8,000. In addition there were 2,000 US Army Airfield Support Command personnel, 3,000 displaced people from the Baltic states and large numbers of other civilians, including the French.

The future of the airlift for the Americans lay in the C-74. On 18 September 1948 a C-74 had carried in 150 tons of supplies, making six round trips, and being airborne for twenty hours out of twenty-four. If the Americans could muster sixty-eight C-74s, they could bring 5,400 tons into the city every day. This total compares extremely favourably with the other aircraft being used by the Americans. In order to bring in 5,400 tons each day, the Americans would have needed to have used 899 C-47s or 178 C-54s. The C-47s would need to make 39,706 trips each month, and the C-54s 13,800, whereas the C-74s would only need to make 5,400. The figures are even more striking when the number of flight hours per month are taken into account. In order to deliver the monthly tonnage C-47s would have to be aloft for 158,824 hours, C-54s for 42,888 and C-74s, for just 16,200.

The figures also compare well when taking into consideration the number of crews required. The monthly tonnage would require 1,765 C-47 crew members, 465 C-54 crew members but just 180 C-74 crew members.

The maintenance figures are also strikingly different. Just 2,700 maintenance crew members would be needed to keep the C-74s aloft, whereas 4,672 would be need to maintain a C-54 fleet and some 10,588 for the C-47s.

There was also considerable savings to be made on the amount of fuel being used by the aircraft. On a monthly basis the C-74s would need 6,804,000 gallons of fuel, the C-54s 8,577,600 and the C-47s a staggering 14,294,000.

One can only imagine the sheer logistical nightmare of keeping all of these aircraft in the skies, not to mention the paperwork involved in detailing flying logs, daily records and receipts, and checking on exactly where supplies were and where they were bound for. The crew chief on board an American aircraft would complete Air Force Form 1, which would give flight details. This was passed to Base Operations and was then sent to the Engineering Office. Together with crew flight times, this information would be entered onto Air Force Form 5, a personal record of each pilot or aircrew which showed how many hours they had flown in the day, during the night and on instruments.

The RAF used Form 700, which was normally completed by a senior technician or NCO, and would be checked by the pilot. Each aircraft crew member would use Form 414, which was the log of each flight. At the end of each month the logbooks would be handed to the squadron HQ so that the commanding officer could countersign them.

Much of the focus of the airlift operation was on what was being flown into the city. But the aircraft seldom flew back empty. Berlin was famed for many consumer and industrial products, such as cameras and loudspeakers. Even electric engines for coal mines were exported during the airlift. One of the largest items ever brought out was a grand piano; on 11 May 1949 an RAF Hastings flew a baby grand from Gatow to Schleswigland. During the airlift itself some 83,045 tons of cargo was brought out as exports from the city.

It should not be forgotten that whilst the three Berlin airports were primarily being used for the airlift operation, there were also civilian airliners flying into the city. American Overseas Airlines flew DC3s into Tempelhof, and Seaboard and Western Airlines flew DC4s into Berlin. Part of their cargo was 20,000 food parcels that arrived in the city every month.

Aviation fuel was obviously a major factor in ensuring that the airlift continued. Prior to the blockade the USAF in Europe was consuming 30,000 barrels of aviation fuel each month. This was, of course, to rise markedly once the airlift began. In July 1948, for example, the Americans alone were using 82,500 barrels each month, and in January 1949 191,000 barrels. The highest month was July 1949 when 291,000 barrels were used. It is difficult to work out the exact amount of aviation fuel used throughout the airlift, but it is probably in the region of 100,000,000 gallons.

The Americans brought their own aviation fuel over from the United States in US Navy tankers. The US Naval Transportation Service provided some twenty shiploads; 2,750,000 barrels. This whole operation needed careful planning. The aviation fuel arrived at Bremerhaven and was then conveyed by pipeline to the airfields.

Not only food and fuel was flown into the city. At the end of May 1949 a new power plant was being built in the British sector of Berlin, and huge pieces of equipment were needed to complete the project, some of which weighed 32,000 lb. C-74 Globemasters and Boeing C-97 Stratofreighters were used, as well as a C-82 Packet, to bring them in.

A short-lived experiment also involved a YC-97A Stratofreighter belonging to Strategic Air Command. In May 1949 the aircraft made twenty-seven flights into Berlin and carried more than 1,000,000 lb. Its use was cut prematurely short when it had an accident on landing at Gatow. As a result of the heavy load all of its tyres burst and the wheel hubs were ground down to the axles.

In an operation as long-lasting as this there are, of course, many staggering figures. Attempts have been made to calculate just how many miles were flown and how many sorties were achieved, but these attempts almost certainly only go as far as the official lifting of the blockade. It is probable that the Allies flew 124,420,813 miles, equal to an amazing 277,567 sorties.

Whilst much has been made of the contribution of the British civilian operators, very little has been documented about the role of American Overseas Airlines. They began flying into Berlin on 26 July 1948 and continued all the way through the airlift. In all they made 2,366 round trips between the city and Frankfurt, carrying 11,356 tons of cargo and mail, in addition to 17,242 passengers. Once the airlift was over, the airline continued to fly into Berlin twice every day, using DC3s and DC4s.

Many records, were claimed during the airlift. On 12 March 1949, for example, the weekly tonnage record of 4,644 tons was reached and between July 1948 and March 1949, the Americans made 36,797 GCA landings. At time it seemed that new records were being set and broken almost immediately. For example, on the last day of March a new monthly record was reached of 196,160.7 tons.

There were other important but less glamorous records. During March 1949, at Rhein-Main, the 61st Maintenance Squadron rebuilt a staggering 154 R-2000 Skymaster engines. This was matched by the performance of the US Naval Squadron VR-8. They spent 12.2 hours per aircraft and were operating at 155 per cent efficiency.

On 18 June 1949 the 10,000th GCA landing took place at Gatow. There was also a Skymaster operating out of Fassberg that managed to do the entire round trip to Berlin in one hour and fifty-seven minutes. It had been on the ground in Berlin for just fifteen and a half minutes. On 11 April, 922 flights were logged, having brought in 8,246.1 tons in a day.

There was also, of course, the record set by the Easter Parade on Easter Sunday, 16 April 1949, when aircraft flew more miles, made more landings and take-offs, and flew in more tons than on any other day. In the view of many people, it was the Easter Sunday exhibition that broke the back of the blockade. An incredible 13,000 tons of coal had been lifted and after that the daily tonnage totals never dropped below 9,000 tons. It was only a month later that the Soviets came to the conclusion that the blockade was not going to work for much longer.

In all, the USAF flew 189,963 sorties, and the RAF, including its civilian component, 87,606, giving a grand total of 277,569. The exact number of hours flown by the RAF is not known, but the USAF claimed 586,872 hours. There will always be dispute about some of the figures, but the Americans provide the most comprehensive range of totals and estimates. For example, they claim that between 26 June 1948 and 30 December 1949 their C-47 Skytrains flew 17,584,008 air miles. Over the same period their C-54 Skymasters flew 84,477,853 flying hours.

The British can also claim a very memorable record. On 18 February 1949 a British Avro York flew into Berlin. It was a normal cargo, potatoes, but it was the millionth ton to have landed in Berlin.

According to the Americans in their official summary of the airlift:

After the fleet had been built up to 225 aircraft, the available aircraft engaged in the mission varied between 209 and 228 until final phase out. When the phase out began on 1

August 1949 204 C-54s of the USAF and 21 US Navy R5Ds were on hand. At the beginning of the airlift, 26 June 1948, there were 102 C-47 aircraft available with a 2.5 ton capacity. The C-54s had a 10-ton capacity. From September 1948 to July 1949 5 Fairchild C82 aircraft 'flying boxcars' with a 5 ton capacity were used to airlift heavy equipment into Berlin and automobiles out of Berlin. One Boeing C97A Stratofreighter was used experimentally during May to July 1949. Also one Douglas C-74 Globemaster aircraft with a capacity of 19 tons was tested. Both the C97A and the C-74 flew approximately eighty-one flights or sorties from Rhein-Main airbase to Berlin until returned to the United States. With the arrival of sufficient C-54 aircraft the C-47 aircraft were discontinued in October 1948.

The official date of the start Berlin Airlift was always given as 26 June 1948, but in actual fact fresh milk was being flown into Berlin on both 19 and 20 June. Nearly 6 tons of supplies were flown in on 21 June and on 22 June 156.42 tons was flown in. Throughout the period 23 – 27 June on average at least 8 tons were brought into the city.

The last official USAF Operation Vittles flight took place on 30 September 1949. A C-54 lifted off from Rhein-Main airbase with a cargo of 2.5 tons of coal. Written on its side was the slogan 'Last Vittles Flight, 1,783,572.7 tons to Berlin'. However according to the Americans:

During October, 14 flights were made to Berlin with cargoes of technical and/or special supplies consigned to the airlift. The 60th Troop Carrier Group (Heavy), Rhein-Main airbase, was charged with the responsibility of transporting this cargo. On 17 October the last 'Vittles' cargo was transported to Berlin.

CHAPTER NINE

Political Settlement

The Berlin airlift had begun in order to provide enough time for the politicians to work out some sort of settlement. However, it could probably only provide a short-term solution to the dispute, and it seemed that the Soviets were in no rush to settle it.

As far as the Soviets were concerned it was the West that had broken the agreement by introducing a separate West German administration and currency. They argued that Berlin was 'the centre of the Soviet zone' and as such it was under the rule of the four powers and was 'an inseparable component part of the agreement on quadripartite administration of Germany as a whole'.

They claimed that they wanted to protect Berlin and the Soviet zone when the new currency was brought in. In effect, they rejected any kind of compromise and felt certain that they had the upper hand.

On the other hand, the Allies were determined to remain in Berlin. They also concluded that there was little point in continuing discussions until the blockade was lifted, and insisted that they would not set aside their own plans for the west of Germany in order to save Berlin.

General George C. Marshall stated publicly on July 21 1948: 'We will not be coerced or intimidated in any way under the rights and responsibilities that we have in Berlin and generally in Germany. We are not going to be coerced.'

But how could the Allies support the military garrisons and the inhabitants of Berlin? The Americans wanted to approach Stalin himself and warned that not only were the Western Allies not to be bullied, but that the Soviet action could lead to war. The British supported the idea of stationing B-29s in Britain, but this considerably increased the tension. Two squadrons arrived on 17 July 1948 and a third in August. Moreover, their deployment would solve nothing on the ground, either in Berlin or in Germany. If the Soviets decided on war Berlin would certainly fall swiftly, with some 6,500 Allies facing a Soviet force of 18,000, with another 300,000 deployed in the Soviet zone to support them.

The standing order for Allied troops in Germany was to fall back to the River Rhine and fight a defensive battle against the Soviet armies. The real question was, would the Allies drop a nuclear bomb on the Soviets? In truth it was never considered; it was certainly not a weapon that could be used to deal with the Berlin crisis. So militarily there was no solution and diplomatically there seemed no way forward.

Clay was still agitating for clearance for his armed convoy. The President, the US Joint Chiefs of Staff, the US State Department and the US Defense Department all vetoed the idea, so Clay resorted to increasing the airlift.

By 26 July it was finally agreed to make a joint Allied approach to the Kremlin. Three Western ambassadors would first approach Molotov and ask for an audience with Stalin. As it transpired Molotov was 'not at present in town', and the Foreign Ministry told the ambassadors that they would meet with a very junior and powerless Soviet Deputy Foreign Minister, Zorin. On 30 July Walter Beddell-Smith, the US ambassador, met Zorin and requested interviews with Molotov and Stalin. Yves Chataigneau, the French ambassador, met Zorin next and made the same request. Bevin's Principal Private Secretary, Frank Roberts, was standing in for the British ambassador, Sir Maurice Peterson, who had returned to London after suffering from a heart attack. Roberts summed up the interview with Zorin: 'The Russians are mainly concerned with American reactions since America alone is powerful enough to stop them.'

Bedell-Smith received a call the following day. Molotov would see him at 1900. Roberts would be granted an audience at 2000 and the French ambassador at 2200. All three men were concerned that they were about to be picked off one at a time. It was clear that this was just a rehearsal before they would be allowed to see Stalin. Indeed, after the meetings with Molotov, they were told to see Stalin at his office in the Kremlin at 2100 on 2 August. Stalin was well known for working late in the afternoon and carrying on until the early hours of the morning.

The ambassadors impressed upon Stalin that their governments had an unquestionable and absolute right to be in Berlin. There were ways of working out the problems; if the blockade was as the result of technical difficulties, these could be remedied. If it was a reaction to currency reform then some accommodation could be made about Berlin. If Stalin wanted to make the West talk to him then they would talk. But, they warned the Soviet dictator, if he intended to drive the West out of Berlin 'it could not be allowed to succeed'.

Stalin complained about the West stripping Berlin's assets, and about the technical difficulties. He pointed out that the blockade was as a direct result of the talks in London about the establishment of a West German state and currency. He was at pains to point out that he did not intend to force the West out of Berlin. His contention was that since they had set up a new German capital in Frankfurt they had forfeited their legal right to be in the city. His demands were clear: he wanted all of the London proposals to be cancelled; he wanted a four-power meeting to discuss Germany; he wanted the new German currency to be abolished; he wanted most of Germany to be demilitarized; and he wanted some control over the Ruhr.

Despite his demands Stalin had been remarkably welcoming and there did seem every chance that the blockade would be lifted. However, he laid a trap by stating that he wished the east German mark to be the only currency in Berlin. This would inevitably mean that the whole city's economy would be under the control of the Soviet zone.

Beddell-Smith wrote a cable to Washington. It read:

If one did not know the real Soviet objectives in Germany one would have been completely deceived by their attitude literally dripping with sweet reasonableness. We are in a mess over currency in Berlin and might as well be out of it on Soviet terms.

At a meeting of the Council of Ministers on Germany on 4 August Bevin was determined that Stalin would not get away with the comments he had made about the West losing their rights in Berlin, or would he accept that the reforms justified the Soviet blockade. An Allied draft announcement of the lifting of the blockade and the start of four-power talks was discussed with Molotov on 6 August, but he would not accept it: 'There is nothing here about the insistent desire of Generalissmo Stalin for the postponement of the decisions of the London Conference.'

He wanted the West to postpone the convening of the West German Assembly, which was due to take place on 1 September. He was equally tough on the currency issue: 'The three Western Allies had and could have no function whatever in connection with the control of Berlin currency once the Soviet Mark had been accepted.' He also argued that any future discussions about the city should involve one Soviet and one Western representative. Despite the fact that the Western representatives threatened that they would step up the airlift, he was immovable.

On 16 August the Western representatives had their fifth meeting with Molotov. Not much had changed. They still insisted that the restrictions imposed since 1 March be lifted, they still wanted four-power talks on Berlin and Germany; they were willing to accept the East German mark as the sole currency of the city, but under four-power supervision; and they wanted there to be no discrimination against anyone found to be in possession of Western marks.

Molotov insisted that the complete settlement should be shaped by the Soviets. He wrote a directive to be imposed by the military governors, the essentials of which were:

- Traffic restrictions that had been imposed by both sides would be lifted.
- The Western Deutchmark would be withdrawn and replaced by the Soviet currency.

It seemed clear to the West that the Soviets did not really want a settlement, and that they were happy to prolong Berlin's agony. Bevin commented: 'We cannot and will not agree to anything which will allow the Soviet government to achieve by the means of their hold over the currency of Berlin that which they have not been able to achieve by their blockade.'

The representatives met Stalin again at 0900 on 23 August. Roberts noted: 'It was clear from the start that Stalin and Molotov, who were both on their very best behaviour, were out to reach an agreement.' In fact, however, no progress was made. There still seemed to be a determination to reach some kind of agreement, but neither side was prepared to shift. There were meetings with Molotov on 27 and 30 August. At the last meeting Molotov insisted that the London proposal should be included in any communiqué. He then changed his mind and said there should be no communiqué. The argument went round and round, with no conclusion. The only decision was that all discussions concerning Berlin should be completed by 7 September.

The final directive for the talks demanded that the following steps to be taken:

- Restrictions on communications, transport and commerce between Berlin and the Western Zones and to and from the Soviet Zone of Germany, which have recently been imposed, shall all be lifted.
- The German Mark of the Soviet Zone shall be introduced, as the sole currency for Berlin and the West Mark B shall be withdrawn from circulation.

In addition to these key points, it was stated that, 'regulation of the currency circulation in Berlin is to be undertaken by the German Bank of Emission of the Soviet Zone'. Moreover, a four-power financial commission 'Shall be set up to control the practical implementation of the financial agreements indicated above'.

What concerned the Western representatives was that everything was subject to agreement by the military governors. In other words, the Soviet military government could overrule what might be agreed. When the military governors met at the Allied Control Council building on 31 August there was a strained atmosphere. The Soviet, Sokolovsky, was extremely cautious; he seemed restrained and embarrassed. Clay refused to shake hands with him and remained silent, but eventually started to contribute to the conversation, as Robertson noted: 'The fact is his forceful and efficient mind cannot bear to see things going untidily.'

It was agreed that three committees would be set up: one to look at transport, a second to consider finance and the third to deal with trade questions. Formal discussions would begin the following day. From day one Sokolovsky behaved as if there was no directive. In the end there were seven meetings, with few of them lasting more than a couple of hours. Sokolovsky's approach was to appear polite and reasonable, but not to agree to anything that he considered unacceptable.

On 4 September Sokolovsky announced that the Soviet Air Force would undertake exercises over Berlin between 6 and 15 September. It seemed clear that this was a ruse to try and threaten the corridors, but the Soviet officials did treat the manoeuvres as an exercise in co-operation, and every movement of aircraft was forwarded to their erstwhile allies.

There had been a number of demonstrations in Berlin throughout August and September, some caused by Soviet or Communist agitators. The Soviets were active in stirring up violence. The problem was that the city's government was based in the Soviet zone and as it was seen to be collaborating with the Western Allies it was a natural target for Communist agitators supported by the Soviets. The Allied military governors were adamant that Sokolovsky should uphold law and order. They saw it for what it was, an attempt to wreck negotiations.

A new round of talks began in Moscow and on 14 September Molotov told the Allied representatives that Sokolovsky had conformed strictly to the directive, although absolutely nothing had happened in the discussions on transport, finance and trade. Ultimately the talks collapsed on 18 September, on the very day that nearly 7,000 tons of supplies were flown into the city.

It did seem that the Soviet military authorities were not only trying to starve out the west Berliners, but that they were also taking steps to divide the city. Although it was occupied by four powers and it had different currency and political systems, in the early months of the blockade there was no restriction of movement. But on 18 October the Soviets curbed free movement on the pretext that it was to prevent looting and black marketeering.

There was another symbolic split – the creation of a second university in Berlin. The old Berlin University, which had opened in 1809, had been reopened by the Soviets in January 1946. But the idea for a new free university had come to the Allies in 1945. There had been significant changes in the old university: all of the Nazi Party teachers had been ousted. At the end of the war only 19 per cent of the students were from the working classes, but by 1949 this had risen to 36.2 per cent. The Soviets controlled the university with a rod of iron, making Marxism courses compulsory. Consequently, on 23 April 1948, 2,000 students flocked to a meeting in the British sector to support of the foundation of a free university in the western sectors.

On 10 May the Soviet authorities were approached to hand over Berlin University to the city's government: they refused. As a result, steps were now taken to establish a new university. In August 1948, General Clay allocated two million DM to pay the basic running costs for the first year. By September 1948 5,000 students had applied for admission, 20 per cent of them students from the old Berlin University. A further 20 per cent lived in the Soviet zone. Some 400,000 books had been collected and thirty professors and seventy junior staff filled the teaching posts. The foundation of the university was agreed on 22 September and ration books were issued to anyone who was to study or teach there. The lectures began on 15 November. It was another nail in the coffin of a united Berlin.

The unity of Berlin's administrative and political operations continued until December. The City Assembly was now meeting in the western sector, except the pro-Communist members, who still met in the East. Many of its operations had drifted over to the west. A gap was opening up between the eastern sector and the rest of the city, which was having an impact on the economic welfare of the city. By December 1948 110,000 people were either unemployed or working short hours.

Meanwhile, the British and the Americans hoped that Berlin's currency could still remain under four-power control. The East German mark was virtually worthless and the West German mark was the only currency, aside from the dollar, that had any value.

By the end of September the case of Berlin was to be discussed at the United Nations, although the British thought it would be a complete waste of time. As Sir Alexander Cadogan, who led the British delegation, said: 'If the four powers cannot agree among themselves in any conference they will not agree any more in the framework of the UN. There is no magic in the UN.'

The Americans were keener on the matter being referred to the United Nations. They wanted UN backing for any Western action, and it seemed highly unlikely that that body would come down in favour of the Soviets and suggest that the Western Allies leave the city. The British did not want any discussion about possible withdrawal, but the Americans were confident that the UN would recognize the legality of the West's cause. At the very least it gave the Allies the opportunity to discuss the situation frankly, at length and in person. The General Assembly of the United Nations met in Paris between September and November 1948, since it did not yet have a permanent home in New York.

An intensive round of private talks took place between 20 September and 5 October. The Western Allies had a new adversary in Andrei Vyshinsky, who would soon replace Molotov as Foreign Minister. Vyshinsky had a tough negotiating stance and could be abusive. In fact he even tried to undercut the Allies by suggesting that all Security Council members cut their armed forces by a third and ban the use of atomic weapons. He denied that there was any threat and made the point that the Security Council was not a competent body to deal with the crisis. On 5 October he voted with the Ukraine against even putting Berlin on the agenda. He was decisively defeated and, as a result, refused to take part in the talks.

On 22 October a neutral resolution called for the immediate end to the blockade and a meeting of the four military governors to arrange a single currency based on the eastern mark. Vyshinsky immediately rejected this proposal, stating that the East German mark's introduction and the lifting of the blockade must happen simultaneously. In the end the United Nations appointed a committee of financial experts to look at the currency problem and report back within thirty days.

The city did not wait another thirty days. The old City Assembly and the *Magistrat* ended their terms of office on 20 October, so there would have to be an election for a new City Assembly. The Western commandants only received notification on 2 October that the election would take place. They were asked to agree to polling day being 14 November. The Communists forbade their people to take part in any of the preparations and the printing works that was responsible for printing the electoral lists was sabotaged, which caused the election to be postponed to 5 December. It nevertheless happened that the 1.1m Berliners in the eastern sector were not be allowed to vote.

There was a good deal of political trickery by the Socialist Unity Party of Germany and the Soviet Military Administration itself. Posters were torn down and a poster was pasted up, depicting an air raid with the caption 'Whoever elects the warmongers votes the return of the nights of bombing'. A rally was announced for 3 December, to be addressed by the Schroeders. Around 7,000 people turned up. There were rumours everywhere: US Secretary of State Marshall was ill, the Allies would abandon the city in January, pro-Western politicians had booked seats on aircraft out of the city, Clay would be sacked and Konig was on the verge of resignation. To add a sweetener to the voters in the eastern sector, on 2 December the Soviets announced extra rations of coal and sweets for schoolchildren. 5 December, Election day, was declared a day of reconstruction by the Soviets and everyone would do an extra shift at work. Western residents that worked in the east would not be allowed to go to the polls. It was even believed that on the verge of the election the Soviets and their Socialist Unity Party of Germany allies would stage a coup in Berlin.

Some 86.2 per cent of those who were eligible to vote did so. The vote for the Social Democratic Party rose from 51.5 per cent in 1946 to 64.8 per cent in 1948, and the vote for the Christian Democratic Union fell from 24.1 per cent to 19.4 per cent, the SDP could therefore claim the majority of posts and Ernst Reuter became Mayor. However, Berlin was now a divided city.

The Socialist Unity Party held a rally between 25 and 28 January 1949, with the theme of German unity and nationalism. It seemed that the pro-Soviet party was not in a mood or a state to launch a serious threat.

The first week of January 1949 saw the eight eastern boroughs given new heads of administration. Five were Socialist Unity Party representatives and there was one each from the democratic parties. There were other changes: seven of the personnel departments were handed over to the Socialist Unity Party, whilst trade unions, education departments and other organizations became party controlled. It was decided that all city employees in the sector would have to sign a declaration of loyalty. Some 1,500 that refused were summarily sacked.

The city's finances were in shambles. An average wage-earner only received a quarter of his pay in Deutchmarks. The unemployed were paid 90 per cent of their benefits in east marks and pensioners were left destitute, with only east marks. Manufacturers were in a similarly bad state. Whilst east marks would pay their overheads, they had nothing with which to pay for their raw materials and equipment. In late December 1948, it was therefore decided that the Deutchmark would be introduced in the western zones of the city, a process that was expected would take around three weeks.

The report from the United Nations appeared in draft form on 22 December. It proposed the following:

- The Soviet Mark would be the sole currency for Berlin.
- It would be issued and controlled by the German Bank of Emission.
- Five of the eight members of the board of the bank would be nominated by the Soviets.
- Decisions would be made by majority vote.
- All existing Deutchmarks would be exchanged for east marks at a rate of one for one (about 25 per cent of their actual value).

The suggestions were roundly criticized by both the Americans and the British. Some thought it to be a poor conclusion after the results of the recent elections, and believed that it just would not work.

However, they were not prepared to reject the expert opinion of the United Nations, moreover, it would be seen as an insult to the United Nations, which could well play into Soviet hands. What they were looking for was a solution that would restore the four-power government and to have dual currency.

It was decided to go back to the Security Council with counter-proposals. The introduction of the Deutchmark to West Berlin was postponed. The technical committee of the United Nations met for the first time to discuss the currency issue on 14 January in Geneva. There were forty-two meetings in less than a month.

Bevin was still adamant that the Deutchmark should be established as a sole currency in the western sectors and believed the date of its information should be 10 March. Finally the Security Council neutrals who had proposed the introduction of the east mark gave up the attempt to enforce it on 11 February. All the postponements, disagreements and even the winter had not forced Berlin into submission. Spring was here and with it fresh hope. The prospect of sustaining the airlift had looked very bleak in October, but contrary to all expectations, it had held and despite some poor days in terms of delivery, Berlin's stockpiles were beginning to grow.

Another development of huge significance occurred on 24 December 1948, when a draft text was published to establish a North Atlantic Treaty. In addition to the proposed main members, Iceland, Norway, Denmark, Ireland and Portugal had been asked to join.

Between November 1948 and January 1949, the Ruhr Authority was established to allocate coal and steel across Germany. As part of the counter-blockade the Soviet zone received nothing. At the same time, a Parliamentary Council in Bonn began forming a constitution for West Germany, the first draft of which was ready at the beginning of January.

All the Soviet threats had been ignored and despite their demands that the West suspend unification and German self-rule, the latter had forged ahead. It was also now clear to the Soviets that Berlin could withstand the blockade; it had endured the winter. As Ernst Reuter said to the City Assembly on 1 February: 'We must not forget our obligation which we owe to the whole of Germany, which is to defend in the midst of the Soviet Zone of Occupation the high values on which our whole material and cultural existence depends.'

It was now also clear that the French were fully on board.

There had always been a suspicion that they would be the first to submit, but now they stated that they would never withdraw from the city. The counter-blockade was also biting hard and had debilitated the Soviet zone. The Soviets had forged ahead with land reform and had instituted state monopolies. Shops and storehouses were empty, and before the crops were even ready in the 1948 harvest, they had been distributed and eaten. About 65 per cent of the industrial capacity of the Soviet zone had been moved to the Soviet Union by the end of 1947. They had taken manufactured goods and raw materials and were taking up to 90 per cent of industrial output. Soviet organizations controlled around 30 per cent of the production capacity of the Soviet zone and another 40 per cent had been nationalized.

The German Economic Commission in the east projected that in 1949 production would reach 75 per cent of 1936 totals. The western zones had already exceeded that figure. By the middle of 1949 nearly 400,000 East Germans were out of work. This was in addition to at least 230,000 who were languishing in concentration camps. These figures have to be looked at in the light of the fact that there was compulsory employment in uranium mines and a requirement to work either in undesirable jobs or in the Soviet Union. The east was particularly hard hit by not being able to obtain coal or steel from the Ruhr. Brown coal was simply not a substitute for the high-quality hard coal and it affected the building of trains, electricity generation and steel production. In September 1948, the Western Allies introduced export licences for manufactured goods. The eastern zone was running out of almost all products that they could not produce themselves, from electric motors through to transmission systems and conveyor belts to lubricants. There was an A list of banned exports and a B list that required permits. Many completely innocent items found themselves on these lists purely because the West was reluctant to supply the Soviet zone with them. In October–November 1948, for example, metal deliveries to a manufacturer in Leipzig that made tanks was stopped, a whole steel rolling mill was prevented from working, and around 2 million DM of chemicals were seized.

The counter-blockade was not watertight. Illegal exporting went on and German lorry owners smuggled goods across the border, despite checks. Berlin was a centre for illegal trade. Scrap-metal merchants in the west dismantled Soviet vehicles that had been sold to them in exchange for currency or food. Some factories ran for twenty-four hours a day on electricity siphoned off from other parts of the city.

From 27 July 1948 transit rail traffic from the Soviet zone through the western zones was banned. This made it difficult for the east to trade with Holland, Belgium, Luxembourg, Scandinavia and Switzerland. Nothing, however, could stop other countries from buying products abroad and then shipping them into East Berlin or the Soviet zone. The Czechs, for example, bought 500 Ford trucks in France, which turned up in East Berlin.

With the Soviet zone almost on its knees, the Soviets could not be very confident about the effects of the blockade. Both the West Berliners and the Allies were resolved to ensure that the city was not used as a pawn. On 31 January 1949 a statement from Stalin was leaked to the press. He did not intend war and would consider gradual disarmament. He wanted to meet with President Truman. He would raise the blockade of Berlin if the Western powers postponed a meeting of the Council of Foreign Ministers and Allied transport and trade restrictions were lifted at the same time. There was no mention in his statement about the currency issue.

The new US Secretary of State was Dean Acheson. He was cautious about Stalin's offer and did not wish to look eager, but he knew he was now negotiating from a position of greater strength. He would try to find out what Stalin was ready to concede, but he was ready to turn down an offer to lift the blockade if the Soviets demanded in exchange that political and economic developments in West Germany were postponed. He wanted the Americans to remain casual with their dealings with the Soviets and therefore chose Philip Jessup, the Deputy US Representative on the UN Security Council, to have an informal conversation with his counterpart, Yakov Malik.

As we have seen, Malik claimed to know little about whether Stalin's failure to mention the currency was an accident or not, but they agreed to meet again. Jessup received a telephone call from Malik on 14 March, inviting him to the Soviet Mission offices on Park Avenue, New York. Malik read a formal statement from Moscow, which stated that Stalin had not left out the currency issue accidentally. Jessup pressed Malik about lifting the blockade: were the Soviets prepared to do this? Malik told him that he did not know and that he had only asked about the currency. He promised that there would probably be information from Moscow in a week or two.

Jessup saw him again on 21 March and was told that Vyshinsky had said that if there was an agreement to hold a Council of Foreign Ministers meeting then there could be a joint declaration on the lifting of restrictions on trade and transport. Jessup told him that he did not have the authority to agree this. Malik told him that the Soviets still believed the currency issue to be important but that this too could be discussed at the Council of Foreign Ministers.

So far information about these discussions had not been passed on to the British or to the French. The French, in particular, were not trusted; it was felt that if they were told then soon everyone would know. Just after the meeting with Malik on 21 March, however, Jessup did tell the UN representatives of the other two allies.

As we have also seen, there were moves in the Soviet Union. Molotov was about to be replaced by Vyshinsky, Sokolovsky was to be appointed First Deputy Minister for the Soviet Armed Forces and General Chuikov would take over his role as Military Governor. Meanwhile the siege continued, and it was still having an impact on Berliners' lives. Some 67,000 were unemployed and nearly 60,000 were doing a short working week.

At long last, on 20 March, the Western Allies introduced the Deutchmark. Henceforth those in the western sectors of the city would be paid in this currency. Those who lived in the western sector but worked in the eastern sector could change 30 per cent of their earnings in to Deutchmarks. Initially only 15 DM were issued to each person as it was felt that this would cover the cost of rations for the first twenty days of April. The official exchange rate was set at five to one. This meant that West Berliners could now use marketeers in the Soviet sector and buy more on the black market. Berliners who lived in the Soviet sector but worked in the west would receive 10 per cent of their wages in Deutchmarks.

Things were beginning to look up for Berlin. March had seen

a lot of snow and frost, but still the Allies had flown in 6,327.5 tons of supplies. Weather conditions were now perfect for flying and Tunner was planning an Easter present for the city. He wanted to fly in 400 tons of frozen pork, 34 kg of chocolate and 13 kg of real coffee. It was from this modest beginning that the Easter Parade airlift was born.

Other developments were going on according to plan. It will be remembered that the Parliamentary Council in Bonn was working on the West German constitution. They had a revised draft ready for 5 February 1949. There was some disagreement about how it should be framed; it was important for them to state precisely what Berlin's role would be in a new council. There was still no agreement by mid-March, but matters were brought to a head on 20 March, when the People's Council in the east, after 'consulting the broad masses,' unanimously opposed a united democratic German republic. This put the matter firmly back in the West's court. An immediate constitutional settlement was required.

Elsewhere, the final draft for the North Atlantic Treaty was ready and representatives of the twelve proposed member states met in Washington. The treaty was signed on 4 April 1949. Things were now beginning to fall into place: there was a solid Western alliance and the beginnings of a West German state, and the Soviets now appeared to want to talk. There was, however, still a need for caution. There was still the distinct possibility of shutters being pulled down, and dangerous confrontation could occur.

The next round of the talks between Jessup and Malik were now due. A statement was read to Malik; it was tough, and required the Soviets to move on the matter of Berlin and the blockade. They agreed to meet once again on 11 April. The conversation kept coming back to the problem that the Soviets believed that the West German government should not be established until the Council of Foreign Ministers' meeting had taken place. Jessup continued to say that if the Council of Foreign Ministers' meeting took place during the next six weeks there would not yet be a West German government.

There was also an important omission in the Soviet stance. Vyshinsky had suggested a reciprocal lifting of trade and transport restrictions between the eastern and western zones, but at no point was Berlin actually mentioned. Whether this was deliberate is not clear; perhaps Vyshinsky thought he was dealing with fools.

There was still political wrangling over the German constitution. The parties were under pressure from Washington and London to come to a conclusion. Finally General Clay put his foot down. He believed he knew what was best for Germany and was determined to hold out until he got what he wanted. The main thrust was the establishment of German Basic Law (which was brought in, in May 1949 and lasted until December 1993). On 20 April 1949 he said: 'I am not trying to run this show. If you want to judge the German political situation here, please simply give me instructions and take away my discretionary power. My real suggestion is that you let me come home tomorrow.'

He was bitter that four year's work was being destroyed. But on 21 April, a large majority in Bonn finally approved the draft and it seemed that the German constitution could finally be framed. Clay still did not agree as it did not quite conform with what he had in mind. General Bradley, the US Chief of Staff, contacted him on 22 May: 'We as soldiers in our long careers have often had to carry out orders with which we did not entirely agree.'

Clay already knew about the Council of Foreign Ministers meeting and refused to allow the prospect of it to derail his efforts. On 24 April the German parties were in full discussion and redrafting, and a new basic law was brought before the military governors for approval on 25 April. This took just an hour and a half.

Clay refused to comment on whether or not the blockade was about to be lifted. On 17 April he had even denied stories that it was: 'There have been no signs of any Russian approach here and if it had happened at government level I am absolutely sure I should have heard about it.'

He was speaking in all honesty. The US State Department had not told him about the Jessup/Malik talks and he was rather put out when he found out about them. Washington was keen for there to be some agreement, but the British were still not eager. Bevin in particular thought that the Soviets would try their best to postpone the ratification of the North Atlantic Treaty and the creation of the West German Republic.

On 26 April, Tass, the Soviet news agency, gave a brief account of the conversations between Jessup and Malik. It suggested that once a date for the Council of Foreign Ministers' meeting had been set the blockade would be lifted.

By the time Jessup and Malik met on 29 April nearly everyone had been brought up to date with the discussions. Malik had a full communiqué ready and he proposed that the Council of Foreign Ministers should meet between 10 and 14 June in Paris. He also said that the blockade would be lifted a week before this. Jessup was suspicious as to why the Soviets wanted to wait until June for the meetings. Malik replied that they wanted to make sure that the UN General Assembly had finished and that Andrei Gromyko, the Soviet representative at the UN, was in Moscow so that he could run the Foreign Ministry in Vyshinsky's absence. Jessup was not keen to continue conversations without the presence of the British and French. Malik, on the other hand, was firmly of the opinion that it would be better for just the two of them to talk, as they could sort out the matter much quicker. The West German elections were due on 15 July, barely a month after the lifting of the blockade.

There was still considerable disagreement about when the blockade had begun. The Soviets considered 30 March 1948 to be the date, although in actual fact problems had arisen far earlier than this. On 2 May 1949 Jessup sent Malik a note, which stated that in the opinion of the United States, 1 March was the starting date for the blockade. It also stated that as far as the Allies were concerned, the blockade should be lifted on 12 May and the Council of Foreign Ministers' meeting should begin on 23 May.

Amazingly Malik replied the next day, agreeing each of the three points. It was also agreed that on 4 May all three Western diplomats would meet Malik at the UN delegation offices on Park Avenue in New York. It seemed success was just around the corner.

Bevin told a jubilant House of Commons about the deal on 5 May. He particularly praised everyone involved in the airlift and also commented on the courage and restraint of the Berliners. Similar thanks came from Robertson and Clay. What was notable in the text of the agreement that was issued on 5 May was the fact that there was no mention of the two currencies.

On 9 May the West German Parliamentary Council approved

the Basic Law. This meant that a federal republic could now be established in the west of Germany. Significantly, the new constitution was passed on the fourth anniversary of Germany's surrender in 1945. Once it came into force civilian high commissioners replaced the military government. It was also decided that since the question of Berlin had not been fully established, the new German government would be based in Bonn. It had been suggested that Frankfurt should be the new capital, but this had been rejected. Others looked for a site in the British zone, but there was not a single city that could accommodate a government because there was still damage from the pulverizing air raids during the war. It was always the intention that Berlin would become the capital of a united Germany once again, but for the time being it would have to be Bonn.

On 10 May 1949 the Soviets finally published orders regarding the lifting of restrictions, which would take place on 12 May. There were some petty restrictions, such as the fact that goods trains would be restricted to sixteen a day and passenger trains to six, and that they must be drawn by Soviet zone engines.

On the evening of 11 May Berlin was bathed in light for the first time in years; the current had been turned on from the Soviet zone. The military had spent the last twenty-four hours tidying up the city: trimming verges, and painting fences and buildings. A few seconds after midnight a corporal of the Royal Corps of Military Police opened an iron gate at Helmstedt. Within seconds cars and lorries were moving through. An American car from Berlin crossed in the other direction two hours later. A British military train set off from Helmstedt station at 0123: it was pulled by a West German train, driven by West German drivers. The train was full of officials, journalists and soldiers. In the darkness of the night, the song 'It's a Long Way to Tipperary' could be heard. The blockade was over.

CHAPTER TEN

Legacy of the Airlift

W as the Berlin blockade really over? It seemed so when the first trucks arrived in the city. But the aircrews would continue to fly in food and fuel to build up stockpiles. There were, however, luxuries by Berliners' standards too: real coffee and tea arrived, ingredients for baking, fresh fish, oranges and other fruits. Farmers from the east were selling their wares in Berlin's markets, but there was still suspicion. If it was this easy for the Soviets to lift the blockade, how easy would it be for them to reimpose it?

Western intelligence heard that on 6 May the Soviet zone had been told to begin stocking up now the counter-blockade was lifted. There was suspicion that once the East German economy had re-established itself, the blockade would be reimposed. It was the Allies' intention to continue to supply Berlin until the situation returned to normal; for now things were not normal – only sixteen freight trains were allowed into Berlin each day, there were roadblocks everywhere, there were two rival city administrations and, of course, two competing currencies.

The Berliners wanted a united city, and they wanted strong ties with the rest of West Germany. The blockade may have been lifted, but the political situation had not been solved. What the Berliners feared most of all was that what the Soviet's could not achieve through the blockade they would get in Paris from the Council of Foreign Ministers. If there was a centralized

163

government and the Western occupation troops were withdrawn, the Communists would take over, and reparation payments would be extorted beyond reasonable limits. For now, although they were an island in the sea of the Soviet zone, they would have to make do with what they had.

Celebrations to mark the end of the Berlin blockade on 12 May went well. The Western military governors met twelve of the Parliamentary Council at a meeting of the City Assembly. Clay was warmly welcomed. The City Assembly heard that West Germany would strive to maintain ties with Berlin. The Allied pilots were thanked and the names of those who had died during the airlift were read out. It was also decided that the square in front of Tempelhof would be renamed Airbridge Square.

Nearly 200,000 Berliners had gathered outside the City Hall. The Mayor told them: 'We have not finally succeeded. We want self-government. We want to rebuild our city. Our trains must run again to Stettin and Breslau and we shall live again unfettered by inter-zonal passes.'

The Soviets were still being very awkward. All trains running into Berlin had to use Soviet-supplied engines and crews. Timetables were changed without consultation, military trains were held up and some 90 per cent of all goods manufactured in the city were forbidden to be exported. Of the sixteen freight trains travelling to Berlin each day, only about five were allowed to return. Since June 1948 the Soviets had appropriated some 5,000 wagons and this ploy added to that number.

On 16 May the Soviets promised eighteen trains per day, but this was not fulfilled. Germans had to carry letters of recommendation or permits. Barge traffic could move but was interrupted by the introduction of transit permits and the requirement to provide crew lists. Trucks could not travel on the *autobahn* at night. By 18 May there were no fewer than 400 food trucks waiting at Helmestedt because the Soviets were now demanding an Economic Commission stamp on contracts. The Department of Interzonal Trade of the Economic Commission decided on 18 May that only trucks supplying the Allied garrisons could use the *autobahn* from Helmestedt. Special permission was required for all other traffic.

There was therefore in effect a semi-blockade still in

operation. So the airlift continued, bringing in 250,834.5 tons. By the end of the month Soviet restrictions were getting even tighter and over the last ten days of May, only 39,831 tons were brought in by road, 12,484 by barge and 70,915 by rail. The Soviets had already begun diverting mail trains, which would not be released, so mail had to come in by aircraft. Worryingly there was also significant Soviet fighter activity over Berlin and along the air corridors. On 27 May the Soviet Air Safety Centre announced that there would be ground-to-air firing along the Bückeburg corridor, supposedly in connection with Red Army manoeuvres.

The Council of Foreign Ministers began their talks in Paris on 23 May. By then the city's railway workers were on strike about the currency in which they were paid. Some 15,000 railway workers who lived in the western sectors, were receiving their wages in east marks. The immediate solution seemed to be to exchange them for Deutchmarks. It was even suggested that extra rations would be given to these workers and shops set up in which they could buy food in east marks, but in early May, unconvinced, they voted for a strike. At midnight on 20 May, 16,000 workers refused to operate the railway network. The following day Soviet and East German police took over Berlin's stations. They fought with strikers, and the police opened fire. The British sent in military police and took control of Charlottenburg. The next day they captured Zoo Station. Elsewhere there was more fighting.

The workers were offered 100 DM if they would return to work on 26 May. The following day their spokesman agreed to the suggestion that all rail tickets would have to be paid for in Deutchmarks and that this would provide the necessary currency to pay 60 per cent of their wages in that currency. But the strikers wanted to be paid only in Deutchmarks, and in the end turned down the offer. In actual fact they were better off as they were, receiving both union strike pay and unemployment relief in Deutchmarks. In a ballot on 2 June the men voted overwhelmingly to continue the strike.

Another offer was made, which was also turned down on 14 June. On 26 June came the final offer. The Western military commandants would provide enough funds for the railway workers to be paid in Deutchmarks for three months. Relief payments would also now stop. The strikers now had no real option, and the strike came to an end. It had meant, however, that the 240,325 tons of supplies that had been flown into Berlin during June had actually been consumed rather than stockpiled.

Meanwhile, in Paris, it was clear that some agreement would have to be reached as the Soviets were continuing to prevent free traffic in and out of Berlin. However, there seemed to be little way forward. The West would not accept a unified Germany on Soviet terms. It was felt that a centralized government sponsored by the Soviets would not guarantee even basic civil liberties. The Western powers were prepared to reintroduce four-power control, but they would not allow a return to the veto, which could block any further way forward.

The US State Department had presented what they called Plan A, on 15 November 1948. This had called for a civilian four-power body to frame policy, free German elections under supervision and a provisional government to draw up a constitution. It had also suggested that the American forces would withdraw to Bremen, the British to Hamburg, the French to their own border and the Russians to Stettin. It seemed as if the dust was going to be brushed off this idea. Many believed, however, that withdrawal would be foolish and would only result in an easy occupation of more of Germany by the Soviets. The American military was not happy to withdraw and the British Chiefs of Staff pointed out that they would lose vital airfields and would be 300 miles from Berlin.

The Soviet suggestions were clear enough. They wanted to restore the Allied Control Council and have an individual veto. They wanted to establish a German State Council, under the control of the military governors. The Western powers put forward their ideas on 28 May. They wanted a unified country, subject only to civilian high commission guidance.

Berlin came onto the agenda on 2 June. The West suggested city-wide elections and full powers to the city's own government. The military governors would no longer have veto power. The Soviets' counter-proposal included the military governors having control of trade, fuel, power, finances, transport, communications, police, appointments and dismissals, as well as an individual veto. The meetings were really getting nowhere and things became worse when the Soviets demanded the withdrawal of the Deutshmark from Berlin. The question of traffic into and out of Berlin came up on the agenda on 12 June. All that could be agreed was that traffic would be normalized as far as possible. This left enormous room for manoeuvre.

Some things were improving in Berlin: the *S-bahn* reopened on 1 July and the majority of the trains were running by the following day. One of them brought back 100 children that had been evacuated during the blockade. Letters were beginning to arrive in the Western sector.

Road traffic, however, was taking a long time to return to normal. Initially the Soviet authorities insisted on signatures for food permits. On 13 July, for example, there was a 12-mile queue of lorries waiting to get into Berlin, so slow was the checking of documents. The Americans declared their intention of sending a weekly convoy of sixty trucks under the protection of military police bringing supplies for their garrison.

As the autumn arrived the Soviets were still squeezing Berlin. People were beginning to stand up to their intimidation, however, and the West had proven that enough food and supplies could be flown into the city. In fact it was now believed that the city's food supplies would last for around seventy days. The decision had been taken in June to close Rhein-Main's warehouses and henceforth fly in supplies only from Wunstorf or Fuhlsbuttel. July saw 253,090 tons of supplies flown into the city. A pair of troop carrier groups belonging to the USAF and two heavy transport squadrons of the RAF would remain in Germany for the foreseeable future.

On 12 August the airlift switched to a five-day week. The final civilian operator's flight touched down at Tegel on 16 August. The RAF's Yorks stopped flying on 26 August, the Hastings on 6 September, the Dakotas on 23 September and finally the C-54s on 30 September.

September had seen 14,898.6 tons delivered to Berlin, even though the airlift was being run down. The aircrews could go home happy, knowing that the job had been done well. Air power which had originally been created for destructive purposes in the war had actually maintained the peace.

Berlin still found it difficult to pay for itself: the city had received some 500 million DM from the military governors in interest-free advances against exports for the period June 1948 to

June 1949 alone. An additional 275 million DM had been borrowed from the American and British zones of occupation. The French had loaned them 2 million DM and a further 20, million DM had been raised in special taxes. The majority of the loans terminated when the blockade ended, but the city was still overspending by some 2 million DM each month. In June 1949 it had been unable to pay its employees and by September it had a budget deficit of 800 million DM. One of the major contributions to this overspending was the influx of refugees from East Berlin and the Soviet zone. On average at least 1,300 were still arriving each week. By August there were also 200,000 unemployed. The airlift workers and staff that had worked for the military government had now swelled the ranks of the wageless. Money was beginning to run out and industrial production was still only 20 per cent of the figure it had achieved in 1936.

There were some high points, however. Daimler Benz decided to start up the manufacturing of diesel engines again in the city, Siemens started to rebuild some of its plants and Telefunken decided to set up valve manufacturing in Berlin. Marshall aid was beginning to arrive: the first instalment would be 95 million DM, followed by a second payment of 60 million DM.

The city still remained vulnerable, however. In May 1952 the East German government cut off telephone links and early the following year bus traffic and trams were suspended. The security of Berlin required the Allies and the Germans to be in it for the long haul.

Marshall Plan aid propelled the new West German Federal Republic into massive growth. Exports were boosted; there were cheaper imports, fewer labour disputes, reductions in tariffs and fairly liberal trade laws. Between 1950 and 1955 the average West German's income rose by 12 per cent, unemployment was met head-on and was plummeting. The West Germans were keen to enjoy the fruits of their labour and desperate to purchase consumer goods. They had suffered six pre-war years of austerity under the Nazi government, followed by a war, which had led in turn to utter destruction. They had then faced near starvation in the first four years after 1945. By the time the occupation of Germany formally ended in 1955, West Germany had become one of the most prosperous states in Europe.

However, this success barely touched West Berlin. The

Berliners could only dream of economic miracles, high standard of living, productivity and a full wage packet. The population, despite the influx of East German refugees, was still only a third of what it had been in 1936. The city, of course, had borne the brunt of Allied bombing, particularly after the Normandy landings in June 1944. The city had been pulverized, and once the Soviets had stormed Hitler's capital, they had systematically looted and removed over 500 factories, shipping them east.

As Berlin was now no longer a capital, public-sector jobs were no longer needed; it has been estimated that around 175,000 of these jobs were lost. The import/export business had suffered too, and banking, finance, insurance, hotels, catering, the stock market and a host of other trades and professions had moved west into the new Federal Republic. Around half a million jobs had been lost. The blockade simply compounded Berlin's agony.

In 1950 the unemployment rate in West Berlin was 300,000; even two years later it was hovering at around 270,000. On 4 January 1952 the Third Transference Law was passed by the federal parliament in Bonn. Henceforth West Berlin would become part of the legal and financial system of West Germany. It could now enjoy subsidies, and treaties and laws passed by or entered into by the West German government were applicable to West Berlin.

The US State Department despatched Eleanor Lansing Dulles, the sister of Allen W. Dulles and John Foster Dulles to discover what could be done about Berlin. By 1953 Allen would be the head of the Central Intelligence Agency and John the Secretary of State. Eleanor made dozens of trips to Berlin and to the Federal Republic, trying to sort out programmes of construction and support. She said of Berlin:

> In 1953 the economy of the city was faltering, and production was at a low level. Some thought there could be only a small amount of improvement. Using a more optimistic approach, a many-sided program was initiated. This included continuing aid to industry, building up the stockpile, subsidizing housing for refugees in Berlin and in the Federal Republic, improving public relations, and varied measures not developed under other aid programs. The

new attention to the city of Berlin was to be so comprehensive as to give a clear impression of the usefulness of an
imaginative American and German approach to the needs
and support which could be given. Some of the impact
projects met with initial resistance from Berlin and from
some financial officers in Bonn. They were obliged to ration
sparingly the supporting German budget funds. We
Americans, on our part, had to stress the overall needs of
the economy and the long-run interests of the city as well as
propaganda and political issues. Without impairing these
various considerations, consulting together, we developed
a balanced and dependable program.

By 1957 unemployment in West Berlin had dropped below
100,000 and by 1960 it was only 10,000. Enormous strides were
being made in West Germany and even more East Germans
wanted a part of it. This was no great surprise, as they had had
their human rights violated on so many occasions. There was at
least one defining anti-human rights moment in virtually every
year from 1950 to 1959.

In 1950 the Soviets created a Ministry of State Security. Also in
1950 a single-list election took place, with a supposed 99.7 per
cent vote for the candidates, who had already been selected by
the Soviets. In 1950 alone, 197,788 East Germans fled to the west.

In 1951, nineteen young people were sentenced to a total of
130 years imprisonment after being denounced by the Ministry
of State Security. Workers could no longer negotiate about wage
agreements. The outflow of East Germans to the west that year
amounted to 165,648.

In 1952 a new law was introduced which allowed the confis-
cation of all property that belonged to people that had left East
Germany or East Berlin. A security zone was established, which
was often referred to as the 'death strip'. Despite this, 182,393
East Germans risked death to escape to the west.

In 1953 the East German government increased working
hours by 10 per cent with no increase in pay. There was a strike
by building workers and an uprising on 17 June. In the aftermath eighteen people were sentenced to death and 1,200 people
were sentenced to a total of 4,000 years imprisonment. That year
East Germany haemorrhaged 331,390 people.

In 1954 there was another election using the single-list system, again with a supposedly high turnout. The Communists campaigned against religious teaching in schools and in that year 184,198 East Germans left the country.

In 1955 there were strong moves against private industry and state co-operatives were created in the countryside. Some 252,870 East Germans were unconvinced by the changes and fled to the west.

In 1956, in a test trial, two men and a woman were tried because they had 'encouraged flight from the republic'. All three of them were sentenced to life imprisonment. Private industry was forced to allow state participation in management and funding. In that year 279,189 East Germans fled west.

In 1957 new passport laws were introduced. Henceforth anyone making an unauthorized journey outside of East Germany would be sentenced to a mandatory three years imprisonment. A massive 261,622 East Germans chose to ignore this new law to escape East Germany.

In 1958, nineteen students from Tena University were sent to prison under the terms of a new law that outlawed 'slandering the state'. Compulsory polytechnical education was introduced, which meant that for a stated period of time schoolchildren had to work either in agriculture or industry. East Germany lost 204,092 people to the west.

In 1959 the universities and technical colleges were purged. In Dresden five students received prison terms amounting to thirty-seven and half years.

The US State Department and the Central Intelligence Agency also tried to provoke the Soviets and undermine the stability of East Germany. In the 1950s they launched the highly controversial food project programme, of which Eleanor Dulles said:

> The thought was, somehow, to make a gesture to demonstrate our concern for those whose homes and jobs were in the Soviet zone. Fifteen million dollars were allocated for this general purpose in July [1953]. The method adopted was to give our food packages to all who came to get them. To permit immediate action the supplies were borrowed from the stockpile already in Berlin, later replaced by shipments from America. The people who

streamed into the city during the next weeks were making a gesture of solidarity with the West. They came in many cases from afar. Their expenses often exceeded the value of the gift. The Communists, faced with this act of defiance, hesitated to impose obstacles for those seeking food, but they finally decided to harass, and even arrest, many of those travelling to Berlin. It was decided to halt the program to lessen the danger to the residents of the Zone. The funds remaining were spent in other ways for their benefit. Some of the subsequent programs were classified [secret or covert operations].

There were indeed covert operations underway, as there had been since victory in 1945. Western intelligence used Berlin as a listening post. It could gather information there about what was going on in Eastern Europe. It was also an ideal place to recruit agents, who would be offered financial assistance, or perhaps help in getting their families to the West. Refugees would often provide information on a free basis. One major intelligence-gathering effort was the Berlin Tunnel Operation. A tunnel was constructed by the Central Intelligence Agency, snaking out into the eastern sector of the city, allowing them to monitor telephone calls. In their own assessment; it produced literally tons of trivia and gossip, but provided little in the way of high-grade secret information that could be used by the agency's intelligence analysts. Whatever the shortcomings of the operation, however, it caused immense embarrassment to the KGB.

Spying was a two-way pastime. Amongst the refugees were trained Communist agents; hundreds of low-grade agents tied up Western counter-intelligence, whilst high-grade agents slipped in. Moles were established by the Soviets, many of which were not discovered for twenty or thirty years. A prime example was the case of Gunther Guillaume, who became the personal advisor to Chancellor Willy Brandt, and was only unmasked as an East German spy in 1979.

The airlift had proved beyond doubt that a whole city, could be supplied by air. During the war British and American aircraft had ranged far and wide, delivering supplies to conventional ground troops or paratroopers or, in many cases, to isolated agents co-operating with guerrilla fighters and partisans. The

Air Transport Command had provided sterling service during the war. It had even operated, as some described it, as an airline in olive drab. The American Troop Carrier Command had brought cargo and aircraft over from the United States, and both had contributed to the airlifts into China.

But how had the concept of airlift operations evolved? Back in the 1930s the Germans had developed Junkers JU52s as eighteen-seat airliners that could also be used as either bombers or troop transports in time of war. Twenty JU52s had been sent to Spanish Morocco when the Spanish Civil War broke out in 1936. Franco and the bulk of the Nationalist army were trapped there and unable to cross the Strait of Gibraltar. Between August and September 1936 the German aircraft transported 20,000 troops in 677 flights and dropped them into Seville in Spain. Without this airlift assistance it is highly unlikely that Franco would have ever won control of Spain.

Other nations were desperate to have their own transport aircraft. The United States used modified airliners, converting the Douglas DC-3 to the C-47 Skytrain. The British opted for transport bombers, including the Vickers Victoria. The American system would prove to be one of the most effective. By simply replacing the large cargo door with a smaller one, the C-47 could be converted into a paratroop carrier, the C-53 Skytrooper.

The Germans had shown that airlift troops were capable of taking and holding ground. They had done this in 1940 against Belgium and Holland. Thousands also dropped and died on Crete in 1941. In terms of sheer numbers, it was, however, three Allied operations that saw airlift capacity extended to its ultimate. Thousands were dropped during D-Day, thousands more in Operation Market Garden and even more when Allied paratroopers dropped beyond the Rhine in the latter stages of the war.

The Berlin Airlift, however, was not an offensive operation. The aircraft were not armed and they did not drop bombs or paratroopers. This was the way operations had been run in China, Burma and India. The C-4s flown into China during the five-hour, 700-mile route, faced almost as many hazards those following the narrow corridors towards Berlin. Even then it was recognized that flying C-47s was no easy task. One veteran of the Flying Tigers said: 'Flying a P-47 in combat was not as dangerous as flying a C-47 across the hump.'

The most significant aspect of this operation, however was the individual who took command of it in September 1944. What he learned then about tonnage requirements, planning and reduction of accidents, would stand the Berlin airlift in good stead. His name was William Tunner, and at that time he was a brigadier-general.

Tunner's contribution to the Berlin Airlift has already been noted. After Berlin he was again involved in airlift operations, during the Korean War, when for the first time transport helicopters reinforced aircraft, providing an additional facet to airlift deliveries. No longer would there be a need for a permanent airfield – cargo could be dropped to troops who had been cut off, reinforcements could be brought in and the wounded taken out. Conventional transport aircraft, however, were still used to bring in vehicles, medical supplies, food, fuel and ammunitions.

The biggest challenge for airlift operations during the Korean War occurred in the winter of 1950. United Nations troops were in the process of withdrawing from the Chosin Reservoir. The Chinese had destroyed a 20 ft bridge. Tunner, who was confident that he could bring out the 12,500 men, proposed an air evacuation. The marine Major-General Smith refused the offer and said, 'We walked in here and we're going to walk out.' Incredibly, American transporters, aided by a Greek unit, dropped a steel bridge in eight sections, twice the amount needed, and within a day the UN troops had constructed the bridge and could continue their retreat.

The capability of airlift operations had increased by the 1990s to the extent that during the Gulf War of 1991 the US had brought in a third of their personnel by air. They also airlifted in 75 per cent of all of their supplies. By this stage they were using C-5s and C-141s. It is testament to the development of transport aircraft that the C-5s, in just twenty-one days, brought in the tonnage equivalent to what had been achieved during the whole Berlin Airlift. As one pilot said: 'You could have walked across the Mediterranean on the wings of C5s, C-141s and the commercial aircraft moving across the region.'

After the first Gulf War the Americans developed the Air Mobility Command, which was used in Bosnia and allowed

American troops to be airlifted to anywhere in the world. During Operation Enduring Freedom in Afghanistan C-17 Globemasters transported the first US marines into action. In the words of the late British Prime Minister, Winston Churchill: 'Transport is the stem of the rose.' He knew that without air support land operations would be almost impossible.

Berlin's geographical location made it the pivotal point in post-war world politics. Eisenhower's administration saw West Germany as the means by which the United States could contain the Soviets in Europe, which had been US policy since the end of the war. The Americans believed it was imperative that West Germany become part of a political, economic and military alliance. Once this had been achieved, then it would stand as the first line of defence against the Soviets and their satellites in Europe.

Over the course of just a decade, Germany had shifted from being an implacable enemy to a partner and an ally. By 1954 West Germany had been granted its sovereignty, which was followed by the Soviets granting sovereignty to their zone, East Germany. The key date was 23 October 1954, when the Paris Protocols were signed ending the military occupation of West Germany as from 5 May 1955. At the same time West Germany was formally admitted into the North Atlantic Treaty Organization (NATO). The Western European Union also accepted West Germany as a full member.

The Soviets were keen to follow suit. The Warsaw Pact was signed on 14 May. This was a military alliance designed to act as a counterbalance to NATO. So two military alliances opposed one another across a line drawn through Germany.

NATO was a hierarchical organization under the leadership of the United States. In assuming leadership responsibilities, the United States undertook to station considerable numbers of troops, supported by a potent air force, in Europe for the foreseeable future. It was also necessary to begin to frame an overall defence strategy for the Western countries of Europe. By admitting West Germany into NATO, rather than allowing the Europeans to create their own set of military alliances,the risk of a potentially strong third bloc was averted.

Lord Ismay was the first Secretary General of NATO, holding the position from 1952 until 1957. His view of its role was: 'To keep the Americans in, to keep the Russians out, and to keep the Germans down.'

US policy was primarily to contain the Soviets and their allies, a major element of which was to integrate West Germany into a defensive alliance. This could best be achieved, in their eyes at least, by placing the defence of West Germany directly under US military command and control.

West Berlin was crucial to the containment and defence policy. It was, in effect, a tripwire. Any aggressive action under-taken, by the Soviets directly or by their East German vassals, would entail the destruction of the Allied garrisons in the city. This would have to be achieved either before or simultaneously with a major offensive in the west. To have ignored Berlin, there-fore would have risked massive reinforcement and disruption of lines of communication and supply. The city was surrounded by Soviet and East German troops. For the Soviets it was still a huge irritation – a bright and beckoning place in a sea of East German grey.

Western Europe could not just rely on the ability of NATO forces to resist a Warsaw Pact offensive in a ground and air war. The United States was not willing or able to deploy hundreds of thousands of men and billions of dollars worth of equipment in Europe, so they would never be able to match the Warsaw Pact man for man, machine against machine, which would have been the traditional approach. Instead Eisenhower developed a policy dubbed 'new look', which called for a nuclear deterrent. He would use nuclear weapons, as a 'massive retaliation' should the Warsaw Pact tanks roll across the West German border or seek to seize West Berlin.

This retaliation did not consist of strategic nuclear weapons, which would almost certainly have to be fired from US soil. That was asking for the Soviets to strike back directly at the United States. Worse still was the fear that the Soviets would fire their missiles first, leaving the United States impotent under a blanket of destruction and radiation. In order to avoid this unacceptable risk and to keep the defence of Europe as cost-effective as possible, the American armed forces were supplied with tactical nuclear weapons. In Eisenhower's words: 'In the event of hostilities, the United States will consider nuclear weapons to be as available for use as other munitions.'

In 1954 General Alfred Gruenther, the NATO Supreme Commander, warned that a future war in Europe would involve nuclear weapons, and NATO approved the deployment of tactical nuclear weapons in December 1957.

As part of the overall integration and defence plan, West Germany would have to muster some 500,000 troops for their new army, the *Bundeswehr*, supposedly, a condition for being admitted into NATO. In fact by the close of 1956 they had only recruited 67,000. The figure had increased significantly by 1959, when it stood at 230,000 men, but the shortfall meant that tactical nuclear weapons would be all the more needed.

Nikita Khruschev, the Soviet Premier from 1958 to 1963, tried to resolve the pressing issue of Berlin. The continued division of the city had not worked to the advantage of the Soviets or their creation, East Germany. An incredible two million East Germans had crossed the border and entered either West Berlin or West Germany. It was a crippling number of people and it had already brought East Germany to its knees.

Once again Berlin provided the backdrop for another major confrontation between the Western Allies, led by the United States, and the Warsaw Pact, backed by the Soviets. In 1958, Khruschev, suggested a redefinition of the status of Berlin. He wanted a new treaty between the four Allied powers that won the war against Germany. He proposed that Berlin should become a free city as a solution to their growing emigration problem. He issued an ultimatum to deal with what the Soviets considered to be an anachronism. He called on the West to withdraw their troops from the city. This ultimatum was rejected in no uncertain terms.

In 1957 the Soviets had successfully launched their Sputnik, illustrating that they were capable of launching projectiles into space. Khruschev was using the very real threat of nuclear weapons as a means of permanently changing the status of Berlin. Eisenhower considered the idea of transforming Berlin into a free city to be a reasonable one, with one proviso: that the free city status should incorporate the whole of Berlin, including the Soviet sector and not just the western sectors.

A Paris summit between Eisenhower and Khruschev in 1960 floundered as a result of the crisis that had been caused when the Soviets had shot down a U-2 spy plane over their territory, capturing the pilot, Gary Powers.

John F. Kennedy became US President in 1960. It seems that he viewed the Berlin situation in a very similar way to Eisenhower. He simply would not bow to the Soviets. His main policy shift with regard to Europe was an increasing commitment to conventional forces rather than a nuclear deterrent. Dean Acheson led a senior advisory group to look at the Berlin crisis. They were charged with coming up with new policy recommendations that would work. Acheson's group recommended that two or three additional US divisions be deployed in Europe and that the ready reserve of US troops be increased.

By 1961 the continuing drain on the population of East Germany had reached epidemic proportions: around 30,000 refugees were leaving each month and on one day alone, 12 August 1961, 4,000 fled. Huge numbers were still using East Berlin as their entry point into the west. The Soviets and the East Germans knew that they had to do something.

On 13 August 1961 the East Germans began to construct a wire fence around West Berlin, which would ultimately be transformed into the Berlin Wall. It was to be a potent symbol of the physical division of the city, not only representing the division between West and East Berlin, but symbolising the partitioning of West and East Germany and the drawing of the lines between the United States and its allies and the Soviet Union and the Warsaw Pact.

When the Soviet Union collapsed in 1991 the wall had already been torn down and the city of Berlin reunited. The new goal of NATO was the containment of the Russian Federation. Gradually it has come to encompass some of the former Warsaw Pact countries, including Poland, Hungary, the Czech Republic, Slovakia and Bulgaria.

The Berlin Airlift was the first Cold War victory. The excitement and relief that had accompanied victory over Germany in 1945 quickly evaporated as former allies stood against one another for control of Europe. In hindsight we can see that the Berlin blockade had its seeds as far back as the Yalta Conference in 1944. It was here that the fateful decision had been made to divide Germany into occupation zones and, more importantly, to divide Berlin itself into four sectors and create an island in the middle of the Soviet zone. Again in hindsight it was probably inevitable that it would cause major problems.

Too many assumptions were made, too little was written down, agreed and signed. There was too much reliance on inference and on the false assumption that allies battling against the Germans in 1944 would be similarly allied to one another once Germany had been defeated. Even the Potsdam Conference in 1945 had not seen any real progress in sorting out what the problems would be in occupied Germany. It had already become clear that the Soviets had very different views of Germany and the future of post-war Europe from the Western allies. The two blocs opposing one another sprang up very quickly. General Clay said during the Berlin airlift itself: 'When Berlin falls, Western Germany will be next. If we withdraw, our position in Europe is threatened and Communism will run rampant.'

From haphazard beginnings, the Allies, principally the British and the Americans, conducted an operation of hitherto unknown scale to support the city. In the end very few individuals lost their lives during the Berlin airlift, it was not a shooting operation, but it was nevertheless very much a military campaign. But it cost Great Britain £17 million to support Berlin during the blockade, the West Germans contributed 150 million DM, and the United States, in addition to the vast commitment of men and equipment, had put in $350 million. These were vast sums of money for the 1940s.

Little is said of the contribution of some of the less well-known operations of the airlift. Aircraft of Coastal Command, in the shape of Sunderlands, flew supplies into the lakes in West Berlin. These supplies had been brought to the port of Hamburg by vessels such as HMAFV *Bridport*, an RAF vessel originally assigned to the Air Sea Rescue and Marine Craft Section.

I am proud that on board the ship was John Francis Sutherland, my late father. 'Johnnie' remembered well the fevered activities and the ferrying of supplies using vessels that had previously been used to pick up downed airmen during the war. The men of the Air Sea Rescue and Marine Craft Section were there because Calshot, the former training base of the section, was home to 201 and 230 Flying Boat Squadrons. They had travelled to Hamburg in early July 1948 and were operating on the River Elbe. There were also detachments from Coastal Command. Amongst the mass of supplies flown into the city after unloading from HMAFV *Bridport* and other vessels were sacks of salt, millions of cigarettes and German mark notes. The Air Sea Rescue and Marine Craft Section was there to support the flying boat squadrons and generally to respond to aircraft emergencies in the area, as well as providing necessary muscle.

The success of the Berlin Airlift, and indeed the shape of Cold War Europe, owed much to the political will of the West, but more to the resilience of the countless aircrews and others working during the operation. The Berliners were determined to live through any privations and deny the Soviets their prize of a Communist-dominated Europe. Berlin did not fall and nor did the morale of the Berliners.

To live in a united Berlin, the capital of a united Germany once more, would have to wait another forty years. But wait the Berliners did.

Appendix I

RAF Units used During Operation Plainfare, June 1948 – September 1949

Unit	Aircraft
No. 10 Squadron	Douglas Dakota CIV*
No. 18 Squadron	Douglas Dakota CIV
No. 24 Squadron	Douglas Dakota CIV, Avro York C1, Avro Lancastrian II
No. 27 Squadron	Douglas Dakota CIV
No. 30 Squadron	Douglas Dakota CIV
No. 40 Squadron	Avro York C1
No. 46 Squadron	Douglas Dakota CIV
No. 47 Squadron	Handley Page Hastings C1
No. 51 Squadron	Avro York C1
No. 53 Squadron	Douglas Dakota CIV, Handley Page Hastings C1**
No. 59 Squadron	Avro York C1
No. 62 Squadron	Douglas Dakota CIV
No. 77 Squadron	Douglas Dakota CIV
No. 99 Squadron	Avro York C1

No. 201 Squadron	Short Sunderland GRV
No. 206 Squadron	Avro York C1
No. 230 Squadron	Short Sunderland GRV
No. 238 Squadron	Douglas Dakota CIV***
No. 242 Squadron	Avro York C1
No. 297 Squadron	Handley Page Hastings C1
No. 511 Squadron	Avro York C1
No. 235 Operational Conversion Unit	Short Sunderland GRV
No. 240 Operational Conversion Unit	Douglas Dakota CIV
No. 241 Operational Conversion Unit	Avro York C1
No. 114 (MEDME) Detachment	Douglas Dakota CIV

* No. 10 Squadron – effective from October 1948 – absorbed No. 238 Squadron.
** No. 53 Squadron – re-formed as a Hastings Squadron on 1 August 1949.
*** No. 238 Squadron – renumbered No. 10 Squadron in October 1948.

The Airlift in Figures (Figures from British Sources)

MONTHLY TONNAGES

Month	US Flights	US Tonnage	British Flights	British Tonnage	Total Flights	Total Tonnage
June/July 1948	8117	41188	5919	29053	14036	70241
August	9796	73632	8252	45002	18048	118634
September	12905	101871	6682	36556	19587	138427
October	12139	115793	5943	31245	18082	147038
November	9046	87963	4305	24629	13351	112592
December	11655	114572	4834	26884	16489	141456
January 1949	14089	139223	5396	32739	19485	171962
February	12051	120404	5043	31846	17094	152250
March	15530	154480	6627	41686	22157	196166
April	19129	189972	6896	45405	26025	235377
May	19365	192247	8352	58547	27717	250794
June	18451	182722	8049	57602	26500	240324

TOTAL MILEAGE

British	32,358,951 (including civilian operations)
RAF only	24,692,603
British direct flights only	30,858,951
American	92,061,862
Total mileage	124,420,813

TOTAL SORTIES

RAF	65,857
British civilian	21,984
American	189,963

Total tonnage (short tons)

RAF	394,509
British civilian	147,727
American	1,783,573
Total tonnage	2,325,809

Highest daily tonnage achieved

05/07/49	British – 2,314.5 (RAF 1,755)
16/04/49	American – 10, 905

Total deaths

18 RAF
10 British civilians
31 Americans
9 Germans

APPENDIX III

Chronology

Date	Event
1948	
11 June	All Allied and German railway freight traffic between the western zones and Berlin suspended by the Soviets for two days.
16 June	Soviets walk out of the Allied *Kommandatura* meeting in Berlin.
17June	Operation Knicker plan prepared by HQ BAFO.
18 June	Western powers announce a currency reform, with effect from 20 June.
21 June	Last food train enters Berlin.
22 June	EUCOM directs USAFE to airlift supplies to Berlin garrisons; 156 tons delivered in sixty-four sorties.
24 June	Soviets suspend all surface communications with Berlin.
25 June	First eight RAF Dakotas arrive at Wunstorf.
26 June	Airlift (Operation Vittles) begins with thirty-two flights by USAFE Douglas C-47 Skytrains from Wiesbaden to Tempelhof.
28 June	USAFE orders C-54s to be transferred from Alaska, the Caribbean and Tactical Air Command units. LeMay forms airlift Task Force, commanded by Brigadier-General Joseph Smith.

30 June	RAF operation renamed Carter Patterson.
1 July	Avro Yorks flown to Wunstorf from RAF Transport Command. Soviets withdraw completely from the *Kommandatura*.
3 July	Avro Yorks commence airlifting dehydrated potatoes into Gatow.
5 July	RAF Sunderland flying boats join the airlift, flying from Finkenwerder to Havel Lake.
7 July	First coal shipments arrive at Gatow on C-54s.
8 July	First fatal US crash of a C-47, near Wiesbaden.
10 July	HQ British Army Air Transport Organization moves to the Schloss, Bückeburg.
12 July	Construction work began at Tempelhof.
16 July	Gatow's new concrete runway completed.
19 July	British airlift operation renamed Operation Plainfare.
20 July	Clay flies to Washington for meeting with President Truman. Fifty-four C-54s, 105 C-47s, forty Avro Yorks and 50 Dakotas now involved in the airlift.
23 July	Major-General William H. Tunner to command provisional Task Force HQ. Eight additional squadrons of nine C-54 Skymasters each provided by USAF.
25 July	Second fatal crash of C-47 in Berlin centre. Two crew members killed.
27 July	Tunner and advance party of Task Force Headquarters travel to Wiesbaden with the first two squadrons. Flight Refuelling begin operations at Buckeburg with three Avro Lancastrian Tankers.
29 July	RAF Dakotas transferred from Wunstorf to Fassberg.
30 July	Two new squadrons of C-54 Skymasters arrive. 1,918 tons airlifted by the USAF.
31 July	New daily record for airlift of 2,027 tons in 339 sorties.
3 August	Two new squadrons of Military Air Transport Service C-54s leave United States for Germany.

4 August	First day of the civilian volunteer lift: one Halton and one Liberator from Scottish Airlines out of Wunstorf. Nine Dakotas out of Fassberg and two Hythe flying boats out of Finkenwerder. USAF has a new record of 2,104 tons.
5 August	USAF airbase at Oberpfaffenhofen designated as maintenance depot. New airfield begun at Tegel. First Berlin-manufactured goods flown out to the western zones.
6 August	Ciros Aviation sends one Dakota to Fassberg.
7 August	Combined airlift sets a new record – 666 sorties and 3,800 tons.
8 August	Flight Refuelling moves to Wunstorf. More Ministry Air Transport Services C-54s leave the USA.
10 August	C-54s leave Japan and Hawaii for Berlin. New record lift – 2,437 tons in 346 sorties.
12 August	Combined airlift delivers 4,742 tons in 707 flights. Estimate of daily average requirements is 4,500 tons.
13 August	Black Friday. Tunner demands revised flight pattern and experienced air traffic controllers.
14 August	Scottish Airlines Liberator withdrawn from the airlift. First Douglas C-74 Globemaster arrives in Berlin.
17 August	Douglas C-74 makes first airlift – 22 tons of flour into Gatow.
20 August	RAF Dakota squadrons move from Fassberg to Lübeck.
21 August	C-54 Skymasters begin operations from Fassberg. Little Vittles drops sweets to Berlin children.
24 August	Two C-47s crash in thick fog; four aircrew killed. New USAF record – 3,030 tons in 395 sorties.
26 August	Eagle Aviation join the airlift with their Halton at Wunstorf. USAF deliveries pass the 100,000-ton mark.
27 August	Scottish Airlines Dakota withdrawn.
28 August	All civilian aircraft based at Fassberg move to Lübeck.
31 August	USAF new daily record – 3,124 tons.

1 September	Burtonwood replaces Oberpfaffenhofen as maintenance depot for C-54s. 19,000 German civilians employed at Tegel.
2 September	Tunner's request for air traffic controllers sees twenty join airlift.
3 September	Airflight arrive at Wunstorf with their Tudor Freighter.
8 September	Record tonnage now 3,320 tons for USAF.
9 September	Record tonnage now 3,329 tons for USAF.
10 September	Record tonnage now 3,527 tons for USAF.
13 September	Record tonnage now 3,610 tons for USAF. First three Fairchild C-82 Packets arrive at Wiesbaden.
14 September	Record tonnage now 3,936 tons for USAF. Scottish Aviation's Liberator withdrawn from airlift.
15 September	RAAF Dakota aircrews arrive in Lübeck.
17 September	Skyflight's Halton Freighters start flying from Wunstorf.
18 September	US Air Force Day – 6,987.7 tons delivered, including 5,583 tons of coal. German guests visit USAF bases at Wiesbaden and Rhein-Main. Silver City's two Bristol Wayfarers join airlift out of Wiesbaden.
19 September	First fatal RAF crash; five aircrew of an Avro York die when their plane crashes on take-off at Wunstorf.
21 September	British Nederland Air Service joins airlift at Lübeck with their one Dakota. First SAAF Dakota aircrew leave South Africa bound for the UK. Thirty-six more C-54s leave Tokyo bound for the airlift.
23 September	British South American Airlines commences operations from Wunstorf with two Tudor Is, as does a Viking of Transworld Charter.
24 September	Hornton Airways Dakota arrives at Lübeck. The Douglas C-74 Globemaster I makes its last flight to Berlin.
25 September	Replacement Training Unit at Great Falls established to train C-54 crews.

26 September	Test flights to Berlin by Tudor Tanker aircraft begin with diesel oil.
30 September	USAFE withdraw their Douglas C-47 Skytrains from the airlift.
1 October	C-47s taken off the lift, leaving only C-54s and C-82 Fairchild Packets.
2 October	One crewman killed at Rhein-Main when a fire truck collides with a C-54 Skymaster.
4 October	Discussions begin between the Soviets and the United Nations Security Council in New York. C-74s begin transatlantic support flights.
5 October	All British civilian aircraft based at Lübeck are moved to Fuhlsbuttel, near Hamburg.
6 October	World Air Freight's Halton begins flying from Wunstorf. Skyflight withdraw from the airlift.
7 October	RAF Transport Command decide to operate Handley Page Hastings aircraft on the airlift.
8 October	World Air Freight's Halton crashes at Gatow, with no casualties.
14 October	Tunner appointed Commanding General of Combined Airlift Task Force, incorporating USAF and British operations. The 1,000th C-54 Skymaster flight leaves Wiesbaden.
15 October	Lieutenant-General John K. Cannon takes over as Commanding General of the USAFE.
16 October	Lancashire Aircraft Corporation's three Halton Freighters begin flying out of Wunstorf.
17 October	British aircraft fly 454 tons into Gatow in twenty-four hours.
18 October	Three USAF aircrew die in C-54 Skymaster crash 4 miles from Gatow. Some 10,000 ex-pilots, radio operators and flight engineers recalled for duties in Europe by the USAF.
19 October	Sivewright Airways' one Dakota joins the airlift at Hamburg. RAF Dakotas begin moving German civilians from Gatow to Lübeck.
20 October	BOAC's three Dakotas arrive in Hamburg.

21 October	President Truman directs USAF to place sixty-six more C-54 Skymasters on the airlift.
26 October	Soviets reject the UN Security Council bid to terminate the blockade. RNZAF aircrews arrive in Lübeck.
27 October	US Navy squadrons VR-6 and VR-8 begin moving from the Pacific to Germany to join the airlift.
28 October	Airflight Tudor Freighters converted into tankers.
29 October	Tegel opened as Berlin's third airlift terminal.
30 October	Lancashire Aircraft Corporation's Halton Tankers begin operations out of Wunstorf.
1 November	No. 47 Squadron's Hastings arrive at Schleswigland.
3 November	CALTF aircraft fly the 300,000th ton into Berlin.
5 November	Operations commence at Tegel.
8 November	The US Navy's first three Douglas R5D Skymaster transports arrive at the airlift.
9 November	The US Navy planes start carrying cargo into Berlin.
10 November	Trent Valley Aviation, Ciros Airways, Air Contractors and Kearsley Airways withdrawn from the airlift. Airwork's Bristol Freighter arrives in Hamburg.
11 November	The first Hastings transport is operated on the airlift.
14 November	British Nederland's Dakota and two Vikings withdrawn from the airlift. Bond Air Services move their Haltons from Wunstorf to Hamburg.
15 November	Sivewright and Air Transport withdrawn from the airlift. Completion of transfer of maintenance crews from Oberpfaffenhofen to Burtonwood.
16 November	Skyways joins the airlift at Wunstorf with their three Yorks.
17 November	RAF Dakota crashes in Soviet zone, near Lübeck and three aircrew instantly killed, with the fourth dying later in hospital.
18 November	Hornton Airways withdrawn from the airlift. The first RAF Dakota flew into the new airfield at Tegel.

20 November	Eagle Aviation moved from Wunstorf to Hamburg.
21 November	British South American Airways commences operation with their Tudor Tankers out of Wunstorf.
22 November	The 500,000th ton flown into Berlin by CALTF [Combined Air Lift Task Force] aircraft.
23 November	Westminster Airways withdraw their Dakotas from the airlift. Seven killed when Flight Refuelling's Lancaster crashes in England.
24 November	Silver City Wayfarers return to UK. Lancashire Air Corporation's Haltons moved to Schleswigland.
25 November	BOAC withdraw from the airlift. Schleswigland opened for operations.
26 November	All civilian Dakotas withdrawn from the airlift.
29 November	British South American Airways withdraw one Tudor Freighter.
5 December	Second runway at Tegel begun.
6 December	USAF C-54 Skymaster crashes on take-off at Fassberg, killing three of the crew-members.
7 December	Tegel airfield officially opened.
8 December	Captain Utting, the Chief Pilot of Airflight, knocked down and killed by a truck on the tarmac at Gatow.
9 December	Silver City's two Bristol Freighters arrive in Hamburg. The Combined Allied airlift delivers 6,133 tons.
11 December	British American Air Services' Haltons begin flying out of Hamburg. US Navy's R5D-Skymaster crashes in the Taunus Mountains.
15 December	Aquila Airways withdrawn from the airlift. Finkenwerder closed. All RAF Sunderlands and civilian Hythe flying boats withdrawn from the airlift because of ice on Havel Lake. 317th Troop Carrier Group's C-54 Skymasters move to Celle in the British zone from Wiesbaden.

16 December	Lancashire Aircraft Corporation ceases to operate their freighters – now converted to tankers.
	5,000th landing by a civil aircraft made by Skyways' York.
	USAF announce that C-54 Skymasters to be increased to 225 by the end of the month.
	Total load carried to date by civilian aircraft now 26,170 tons.
20 December	Operation Santa Claus gets underway with presents for 10,000 Berlin children.
24 December	World Air Freight's one Halton Freighter arrives in Hamburg.
25 December	RAF Dakota out of Lübeck flies into Gatow on the 50,000th landing by an airlift aircraft.
26 December	Over the last six months, 700,172.7 tons have been airlifted in 96,640 sorties.
31 December	100,000 flights by the Allies completed.

1949

2 January	Skyways' first Lancastrian tanker arrives at Wunstorf.
7 January	USAF C-54 Skymaster crashes at Burtonwood, killing six crew-members.
8 January	British South American Airways withdraw their second Tudor I from the airlift.
14 January	A USAF C-54 Skymaster crashes near Rhein-Main, killing three crew-members.
15 January	Tegel airport opened to civilian aircraft.
	Three civilian aircraft ground personnel killed at Schleswigland in an accident involving an RAF Hastings.
18 January	USAF C-54 Skymaster crashes near Fassberg, killing the pilot.
24 January	RAF Dakota crashes at night in the Soviet zone. Wireless operator and seven German passengers killed.
	250,000th ton of coal flown from Fassberg to Tegel.
25 January	British American Air Services converted Halton Freighter begins tanker operations from Schleswigland.

29 January	Westminster Airways begin flying their Halton Tanker from Schleswigland.
31 January	CALTF achieve highest monthly total to date – 171,960 tons.
3 February	British aircraft achieve highest tonnage to date in 24 hours and 293 sorties – 1,736 tons.
5 February	Silver City withdraws from airlift.
12 February	Airwork withdraws from airlift.
15 February	Air Ministry decides not to deploy flying boat on the airlift in the future.
18 February	RAF York flies in the 1,000,000th ton of supplies.
19 February	Scottish Airlines rejoin airlift with two Liberator tankers out of Schleswigland.
26 February	New tonnage record – 8,025 tons in 902 sorties.
4 March	Clement Attlee visits airlift base and facilities at Bückeburg.
11 March	50,000th German civilian flown from Lübeck to Gatow by the RAF.
15 March	No. 46 Group RAF Transport Command moved to Lüneberg from Bückeburg. Skyways York crashed near Gatow, killing three crew-members.
21 March	Lancashire Aircraft Corporation's Halton crashed near Schleswigland, killing three crew-members.
22 March	RAF Dakota crashes inside the Soviet zone, near Lübeck, three die.
31 March	Highest monthly tonnage to date – 196,160.7 tons. The 61st Maintenance Squadron at Rhein-Main claims new USAF record – 154 engines rebuilt during the month. US Navy Squadron VR-8 sets record of 155 per cent efficiency.
1 April	Civil Airlift Division formed. HQ No. 46 Group from RAF Transport Command transferred to BAFO.

7 April	Tempelhof GCA radar crews set new high by handling 102 aircraft over a six-and-a-half-hour period. C-54 Skymaster out of Fassberg completes round trip in one hour fifty-seven minutes, with a turnaround time of fifteen minutes thirty seconds.
11 April	Highest tonnage to date in twenty-four hours – 8,246 tons in 922 sorties. RAF and British civilian aircraft out of Wunstorf achieved 1,135 tons – highest total to date from that base.
16 April	Flight Refuelling moved from Fuhlsbuttel to Wunstorf. Tunner's Easter Parade flies 12,940 tons of coal, food and other supplies in 1,398 sorties, British contribution is 2,035 tons.
21 April	Work commenced on third runway at Gatow.
25 April	Rumours begin of the Soviets' desire to lift the blockade.
30 April	World Air Freight's Halton crashed near Tegel in the Soviet zone. Four crew-members killed.
1 May	Civil Airlift Division joins HQ No. 46 Group at Lüneberg.
2 May	Rhein-Main sees the arrival of a Boeing YC-97A Stratofreighter to join the airlift.
4 May	The Stratofreighter lifts its first 10-ton load to Tempelhof. Big Four delegates announce the lifting of the blockade on 12 May.
7 May	Ernest Bevin visits Berlin.
9 May	Highest British tonnage in twenty-four hours – 2,617 tons.
10 May	Flight Refuelling's Lancastrian force-lands in the Soviet zone – no casualties.
12 May	The blockade is lifted at 0000. Rail lines and highways to be reopened.
22 May	British civilian aircraft achieve a record – 1,009 tons in 132 sorties.
31 May	Airflight Tudors withdrawn from the airlift. 100,000th ton delivered by civilian aircraft.

1 June	100,000th ton of liquid fuel flown in by a British civilian Lancastrian from Fuhlsbuttel.
	Rotation scheme for RAF squadrons started.
8 June	Airlift includes 8 tons of mail.
19 June	Skyways York crashes near Wunstorf; no casualties.
24 June	Airflight's Avro Lincoln tanker arrives at Wunstorf.
26 June	Skyways Lancastrian burned out near Gatow; no casualties.
	British record again passed – 2,244 tons in twenty-four hours.
30 June	Highest daily total achieved by RAF and civilian aircraft – 2,263 tons in twenty-four hours.
2 July	USAF C-54 Skymaster flies in the 2 millionth ton.
12 July	British civilian airlift running down.
	Airflight's Lincoln withdrawn.
	British American Air Services, Lancashire, Scottish and Westminster ceased to operate.
	Schleswigland closed to civilian operations.
13 July	Liquid fuel target reduced to 14 tons daily.
17 July	Skyways' Lancastrian Tankers withdrawn.
21 July	British deliver their 500,000th ton.
24 July	Berlin's Military Government announces a stockpile of food to last eighty-eight days.
29 July	Fassberg holds a parade to commemorate lives lost during the airlift.
1 August	US airlift operation termined.
	Rundown of RAF operation.
	USAF cease their operations at Celle.
10 August	Flight Refuelling and British South American Airways withdraw from airlift.
12 August	British civilian aircraft withdraw from Fuhlsbuttel
15 August	Bond Air Services, Eagle Aviation and World Air Freight withdraw and Skyways cease operations from Wunstorf.
16 August	End of British civilian airlift, with all charter aircraft withdrawn.
22 August	Night flying on the airlift ceases.
29 August	RAF York squadrons cease operations.

1 September	HQ CALTF disbanded. USAF operations from Fassberg ceases. Tegel closed.
23 September	RAF Dakota aircraft cease operations.
30 September	Last flight of a USAF C-54 Skymaster.
6 October	RAF Hastings cease operations.
15 October	No. 46 Group closed at Lüneberg.

Statistics for the First Year of the Airlift

(26 June 1948 – 26 June 1949)

TONNAGE AND PLANES

	Planes	Tons	% Contribution to US Total	% Contribution to Combined Total
US Tempelhof Airbase	115,103	829,500.7	56.2	42.2
US Gatow Airbase	59,861	383,894.6	25.9	19.5
US Tegel Airbase	36,457	261,517.8	17.9	13.3
Total US Figures for 3 Airbases	211,421	1,474.913.1		75
Total Brit. Tonnage for 2 Airbases		486,708.5		25
Combined Figures for 5 Airbases		1,961,621.6		

Operation Vittles

July – December 1948 Compared with January – June 1949

1948

Months	Incoming Cargo Tempelhof	Outgoing Cargo Tempelhof	Trucks Utilized	Total Personnel per Shift
July	38713	1311	108	344
August	63515	1754	108	537
September	61688	2090	106	593
October	61158	2552	104	641
November	48521	1924	101	679
December	66744	4050	79	608
Total	340339	13681	606	

1949

Months	Incoming Cargo Tempelhof	Outgoing Cargo Tempelhof	Trucks Utilized	Total Personnel per Shift
January	68282	3383	74	548
February	59395	2352	66	545
March	76347	3251	61	516
April	95066	4193	61	516
May	88432	3536	59	512
June	82339	2564	59	464
Total	469861	19309	380	

It will be noted that the average decrease in personnel covering the six month period is 17 per cent; that is, the last six months of 1948 contrasted to the first six months of 1949.

Percentage of Cargo Handled by Three Fields

1948

Months	Total Berlin	Percent Tempelhof	Percent Gatow	Percent Tegel
July	67297	58	42	–
August	114357	56	44	–
September	136386	45	55	–
October	146267	42	58	–
November	111559	43.9	56	0.06
December	138224	47	37	16
Total	714090			

1949

Months	Total Berlin	Percent Tempelhof	Percent Gatow	Percent Tegel
January	166099	41	38	21
February	145894	41	42	17
March	191313	40	36	24
April	226598	41	34	25
May	238474	38	32	30
June	229931	36	33	31
	1198309			

It will be noted despite an average 17 per cent personnel reduction, that the total tonnage for the first 6-months of 1949 was 50 per cent greater than the total during the last 6-month period of 1948 for all airfields.

Soviet Harassment Incidents during the Airlift Operations

Buzzing	77
Close Flying	96
Flak	54
Air to Air Fire	14
Flares	59
Radio Interference	82
Searchlights	103
Air-Ground Fire	42
Ground Fire	55
Ground Explosions	39
Rockets	4
Balloons	11
Chemical Laying	54
Bombing	36
Unidentified Objects	7
Total	**733**

Documents Regarding the Partitioning of Germany and Berlin

Memorandum to the President

I enclose herewith a copy of a telegram from Ambassador Winant, outlining the present status of the work of the European Advisory Commission. There is likewise enclosed a copy of the draft protocol regarding the zones of occupation in Germany and the administration of 'Greater Berlin' which is referred to in Ambassador Winant's telegram.

Cordell Hull
Department of State
Bureau Division—CE
ENCLOSURE
TO
Letter drafted 9/11

Memo to the President
London
Dated September 9, 1944
Rec'd 7:22 p.m.

Secretary of State,
Washington.
US Urgent

NIACT 7430, September 9, Midnight
PERSONAL AND SECRET TO THE SECRETARY AND
UNDER SECRETARY

This morning Ambassador Gousev told me that as chairman of
the European Advisory Commission he was calling a meeting
for Monday afternoon. We have already forwarded the draft
surrender terms, which have been accepted without conditions
by the US and USSR Governments and by the British subject to
conditions which, I have been informed by Mr Eden, will be
cleared. Gousev told me that he is now in a position to agree to
recommend acceptance by the EAC of the German protocol
covering zones, leaving in blank the designation of the US and
UK zones with the understanding that the US Government
and the UK Government will decide on their respective
zones and areas of occupation in Germany and Berlin. That
means that this document will have received informal clearance
in all other respects from the three governments and is recommended by the commission.

We will have before us this week officially the question of
control machinery, basic proclamations and orders, as well as
the protocol on Austria in which I have already gotten agreement for tripartite control with US participation limited to a
small contingent force. We are now analyzing the recommendations of the other Allied Governments with respect to the
treatment of Germany. You are also aware of our work
on the Bulgarian armistice terms; we are proceeding to formu-
late the terms for Hungary.

I would greatly appreciate your getting this message to the
President together with a copy of the German protocol.

WINANT

3rd August, 1944

EUROPEAN ADVISORY COMMISSION
DRAFT PROTOCOL

Between the governments of the Union of Soviet Socialist Republics, the United Kingdom and the United States of America, on the zones of occupation in Germany and the administration of Greater Berlin. (as amended at the meeting held on 2nd August, 1944)

The Governments of the Union of Soviet Socialist Republics, the United Kingdom of Great Britain and Northern Ireland, and the United States of America have reached the following agreement with regard to the execution of Article 11 of the instrument of surrender of Germany:

1. Germany, within her frontiers as they were on the 31st December, 1937, will, for the purposes of occupation, be divided into three zones, one of which will be allotted to each of the three Powers, and a special Berlin area, which will be under joint occupation by the three Powers.

2. The boundaries of the three zones and of the Berlin area, and the allocation of the three zones as between the USSR, the UK and the USA will be as follows:

Eastern Zone
The territory of Germany (including the province of East Prussia) situated to the East of a line drawn from the point on Lübeck Bay where the frontiers of Schleswig-Holstein and Mecklenberg meet, along the western frontier of Mecklenberg to the frontier of the province of Hanover, thence, along the eastern frontier of Brunswick; thence along the western frontier of Anhalt; thence along the western frontier of the Prussian province of Saxony and the western frontier of Thuringia to where the latter meets the Bavarian frontier; thence eastwards along the northern frontier of Bavaria to the 1937 Czechoslovakian frontier, will be occupied by the armed forces of the USSR, with the exception of the Berlin area, for which a special system of occupation is provided below.

Northwestern Zone
The territory of Germany situated to the west of that defined above, and bounded on the south by a line drawn from the point where the western frontier of Thuringia meets the frontier of Bavaria; thence westwards along the southern frontiers of the Prussian provinces of Hessen-Nassau and Rheinprovinz to where the latter meets the frontier of France will be occupied by the armed forces of the UK.

Southwestern Zone
All the remaining territory of Western Germany situated to the south of the line defined in the description of the North-western zone will be occupied by the armed forces of United States.

The frontiers of States (Lander) and provinces within Germany, referred to in the foregoing descriptions of the zones, are those which existed after the coming into effect of the decree of the 25th June, 1941 (published in the Reichsgesetzblatt, Part I, No. 72, 3rd July, 1941).

Berlin Area
The Berlin area (by which expression is understood the territory of 'Greater Berlin' as defined by the law of the 27th April 1920) will be jointly occupied by the armed forces of the USSR, UK and USA assigned by the respective Commanders-in-Chief. For this purpose the territory of 'Greater Berlin' will be divided into the following three parts:

Northeastern part of 'Greater Berlin'
Districts of Pankow, Prenzlauerberg, Mitte, Weissensee, Friedrichshain, Lichtenberg, Treptow, Kopenick will be occupied by the forces of the USSR.

Northwestern part of 'Greater Berlin'
Districts of Reinickendorf, Wedding, Tiergarten, Charlottenberg, Spandau, Wilmersdorf will be occupied by the forces of the UK.

Southern part of 'Greater Berlin'
Districts of Zehlendorf, Steglitz, Schoneberg, Kreuzberg,

Tempelhof, Neukolln will be occupied by the forces of US.

The boundaries of districts within 'Greater Berlin' referred to in the foregoing descriptions, are those which existed after the coming into effect of the decree published on 27th March, 1938 (Amtsblatt der Reichshauptstadt Berlin No. 13 of 27th March, 1938, page 215).

3. The occupying forces in each of the three zones into which Germany is divided will be under a Commander-in-Chief designated by the Government of the country occupying that zone.

4. Each of the three Powers may, at its discretion, include among the forces assigned to occupation duties under the command of its Commander-in-Chief, auxilary contingents from the forces of any other Allied Power which has participated in military operations against Germany.

5. An Inter-Allied Governing Authority (*Komendatura*) consisting of three Commandants, appointed by their respective Commanders-in-Chief, will be established to direct jointly the administration of the 'Greater Berlin' area.

6. This protocol has been drawn up in triplicate in the Russian and English languages. Both texts are authentic. The protocol will come into force on the signature by Germany of the Instrument of Unconditional Surrender.

Lancaster House
London, S.W.1.
3rd August, 1944

Bibliography

'Airlift Gets Navy Lift', *All Hands* no. 384 (February 1949): 11.

'Airlift Over, MATS Resumes World-Wide Schedules', *All Hands* no. 394 (Dec. 1949): 50.

'Airlift Workers Get Award', *Naval Aviation News* no. 293 (May 1949): 11.

Anderhub, Andreas. *Blockade, Luftbrucke und Luftbruckendank*. Berlin: Presse und Informationsamt des Landes Berlin, 1984.

Arnold-Forster, Mark. *The Siege of Berlin*. London: Collins, 1979.

Baldwin, William C. 'Eers and the Berlin Airlift, 1948–1949'. Engineer. April 1998: 35–7.

Barker, Dudley. *Berlin Airlift : An Account of the British Contribution*. London: HMSO, 1949.

The Berlin Airlift: A Brief Chronology. Scott Air Force Base IL: Military Airlift Command, 1988.

'Berlin Airlift, a brief chronology, part 2', *Mobility Forum* Vol. 7, No. 4 (July–August 1998): 26.

'Berlin Airlift, the first use of airlift as an instrument of national policy', *Mobility Forum* Vol. 7, No. 3 (May–June 1998): 14–15.

'Berlin Airlift Rugged', *Naval Aviation News* No. 294 (June 1949): 11.

Bible, Dale F. *Genesis of Air Mobility: The 'Hump' and the Berlin Airlift*, Maxwell AFB: Air War College, Air University, 1995.

British Army. *Notes on the Blockade of Berlin: From a British viewpoint in Berlin*. Berlin: Headquarters, British Troops, 1949.

Buffet, Cyril. *Mourir pour Berlin: la France et l'Allemagne, 1945–1949*. Paris: Armand Colin, 1991.

Bunker, William B. 'TC in the Vittles operation', *Defense Transportation Journal*, Vol. 54, No. 3 (June 1998): 22–23.

Castellon, David. 'Operation Vittles: the Berlin Airlift, 1948–1949', *Air Force Times*, Vol. 58, No. 47 (29 June 1998): 12–16.

Charles, Max. *Berlin Blockade*. London: Wingate, 1959.

Christensen, Daniel W. 'Navy Air in the Berlin Airlift', *Naval Aviation News*, Vol. 78, No. 2 (January–February 1996): 34–37.

Clay, Lucius D. *Decision in Germany*. Garden City, NY: Doubleday, 1950.

Collier, Richard. *Bridge Across the Sky*. New York: McGraw-Hill, 1978.

Curtiss, John. 'Insecure peace, 1947–1949', *Royal Air Force Air Power Review*, Vol. 1, No.1 (1998): 102–8.

Davison, Walter Phillips. *The Berlin Blockade*. New York: Arno Press, 1980.

Donovan, Frank Robert. *Bridge in the Sky*. London: Hale, 1970.

Flintham, Victor. 'Berlin aircraft, 1948–1949', in *Air Wars and Aircraft: A Detailed Record of Air Combat, 1945 to Present*. New York: Facts on File, 1990.

Gann, Timothy D. *Decision from the Sky: Airpower as a Decisive Instrument of National Power*. Carlisle Barracks, PA: Army War College, 1997.

Gerhardt, Gunther. *Das Krisenmanagement der Vereinigten Staaten Wahrend*. Berlin: Duncker & Humblot, 1984.

Giangreco, D.M. and Robert E. Griffin. *Airbridge to Berlin – the Berlin Crisis of 1948, Its Origin and Aftermath*. Novato, CA: Presidio, 1988.

Gimbel, John. *The American Occupation of Germany: Politics and the Military, 1945–1949*. Stanford CA: Stanford University Press, 1968.

'Global supply and maintenance for the Berlin Airlift, 1948–1949', in *Logistics Dimensions: Selected Readings*. Gunter Annex, AL: Air Force Logistics Management Agency, 1998.

Grathwol, Robert P. and Donita M. Moorhus. *American Forces in Berlin: Cold War Outpost, 1945–1994*. Washington: Dept. of Defense, Legacy Resource Management Program, Cold War Project, 1994.

Grose, Peter. 'Boss of occupied Germany: General Lucius D. Clay', Foreign Affairs, Vol. 77, No. 4 (July–August 1998): 179–85.

Halverson, Gail. 'Operation Little Vittles', *Mobility Forum*, Vol. 8, No. 2 (March–April 1999): 26–30.

Halverson, Gail. 'Uncle Wiggly Wings: An interview', *Air Power History*, Vol. 36, No. 1 (Fall 1989): 26–9.

Harrington, Daniel F. *Air Force Can Deliver Anything: A History of the Berlin Airlift*. Ramstein, GE: USAFE Office of History, 1998.

Haydock, Michael D. *City Under Siege: the Berlin Blockade and Airlift, 1948–1949*. Washington: Brassey's, 1998.

Hindrichs, Guenter and Wolfgang Heidelmyer. *Documents sur Berlin, 1943–1963*. Munich: R. Oldenbourg Verlag, 1964.

Hoppe, Billy J. *Lieutenant General William H. Tunner in the China-Burma-India 'Hump' and Berlin Airlifts: A Study in Leadership in Development of Airlift Doctrine*. Maxwell AFB: Air War College, Air University, 1995

Interview with Colonel Gail S. Halvorsen, USAF-Ret, 13 May 1988. (Military Airlift Command Oral History Program Interview No.1). Scott Air Force Base IL: Office of History, Military Airlift Command, 1988.

Jackson, Robert. *Berlin Airlift*. Wellingborough: Patrick Stephens, 1988.

Kaufer, Mary Anne. *A Register of the Berlin Airlift Documents*. Scott Air Force Base IL: Office of History, Military Airlift Command, 1989.

Keiderling, Gerhard. *Die Berliner Krise 1948/49*. Berlin: Akademie-Verlag, 1982.

Launius, Roger D. 'Berlin Airlift: Constructive Air Power', *Air Power History*, Vol. 36, No. 1 (Spring 1989): 8–22.

—— 'Berlin Airlift: refining the air transport function, 1948–1949'. Airlift. 10, no.2 (Summer 1988): 10–17.

—— 'Lessons learned: The Berlin Airlift', *Air Power History*, Vol. 36, No. 1 (Spring 1989): 23.

Launius, Roger D. and Coy F. Cross II. *MAC and the Legacy of the Berlin Airlift*. Scott Air Force Base IL: Office of History, Military Airlift Command, 1989.

—— 'Tunner Airlift Philosophy', *Mobility Forum*, Vol. 7, No. 3: 16–17.

Man, John. *Berlin Blockade*. New York: Ballantine Books, 1973.

Miller, Charles E. *Airlift Doctrine*. Maxwell AFB: Air University Press, 1988.

Miller, Roger G. *To Save a City: The Berlin Airlift, 1948–1949*. Washington: Air Force History and Museums Program, 1998.

—— 'Global Supply and Maintenance for the Berlin Airlift, 1948–1949', *Air Force Journal of Logistics*, Vol. 22, No. 2 (Summer 1998): 33–40.

—— 'Anchors aweigh: the U.S. Navy', *Air Power History*, Vol. 45, No. 3 (Fall 1998): 48–51.

—— 'Eagles Victorious, a Summary and Accounting', *Air Power History*, Vol. 45, No. 3 (Fall 1998): 66–71.

—— 'Freedom's Eagles: The Berlin Airlfit, 1948–1949', *Air Power History*, Vol. 45, No. 3 (Fall 1998): 4–39.

—— 'French Eagles, Too', *Air Power History*, Vol. 45, No. 3 (Fall 1998): 59.

—— 'Hauling the Freight: the U.S. Army', *Air Power History*, Vol. 45, No. 3 (Fall 1998): 52–58.

—— 'Lion's Eagles : The Royal Air Force', *Air Power History*, Vol. 45, No. 3 (Fall 1998): 40–47.

Milton, T. Ross. 'Berlin Airlift', *Air Force Magazine*, Vol. 61, No. 6 (June 1978): 57–68.

—— 'Inside the Berlin Airlift: Fifty Years Later, the Task Force Chief of Staff Reflects on Operation Vittles', *Air Force Magazine*, Vol. 81, No. 10 (October 1998): 48–51.

—— 'Why the Airlift Succeeded', *Air Force Magazine*, Vol. 71, No. 5 (May 1988): 210.

Morris, Eric. *Blockade: Berlin and the Cold War*. London: Hamilton, 1973.

Murphy, David E., Sergei A. Kondrashev and George Bailey. *Battleground Berlin: CIA vs KGB in the Cold War*. New Haven CT: Yale University Press, 1997.

'Naval Personnel Praised For Berlin Airlift Work', *All Hands*, No. 394 (December 1949): 48.

'Navy Refits Vittles Planes', *Naval Aviation News*, No. 299 (November 1949): 14.

'Navy Squadrons Lead Pack', *Naval Aviation News*, No. 293 (May 1949): 11.

'Navy Wins Airlift Honors', *Naval Aviation News*, No. 299 (November 1949): 15.

'Navy Wings Over Berlin', *Naval Aviation News*, No. 291 (March 1949): 1–5.

Parrish, Thomas D. *Berlin in the Balance, 1945–1949*. Reading MA: Addison-Wesley, 1998.

Pearcy, Arthur. 'Berlin Airlift', *AAHS Journal*, Vol. 34, No. 3 (Fall 1989): 196–212.

—— *Berlin Airlift*. Shrewsbury: Airlife, 1997.

Pernot, Francois. 'Point aérien de Berlin et l'armée de l'Air'. *Revue historique des armées*, Vol. 215 (June 1999): 51–62.

Pirus, Douglas L. 'Berlin Airlift: A Pictorial', *AAHS Journal*, Vol. 23 (Fall 1978): 230–233.

Powell, Stewart M. 'Berlin Airlift', *Air Force Magazine*, Vol. 81, No. 6 (June 1998): 50–63.

Rodrigo, Robert. *Berlin Airlift*. London: Cassel, 1960.

Scherff, Klaus. *Luftbrucke Berlin*. Stuttgart: Motorbuch-Verlag, 1976.

Schuffert, Jake. 'Cartoons of Jake Schuffert', *Air Power History*, Vol. 45, No. 3 (Fall 1998): 60–5.

Shlaim, Avi. *The United States and the Berlin Blockade, 1948–1949*. Berkeley CA: University of California Press, 1983.

Shokair, Abdul A. *Berlin Airlift*. Maxwell AFB: Air War College, Air University, 1990.

Sherman, Jason. 'Golden Vittles: The Golden Anniversary of the Berlin Airlift, Operation Vittles, Harkens Back to Hard Times and Unsinkable Spirits', *Armed Forces Journal International*, Vol. 135, No. 10 (May 1998): 20.

Smith, Jean Edward. *Lucius D. Clay: An American Life*. New York: Henry Holt, 1990.

Smith, Jean Edward, ed. *Papers of General Lucius D. Clay: Germany 1945–1949*. Bloomington, IL: Indiana University Press, 1974.

Smyser, W. R. *From Yalta to Berlin: The Cold War Struggle over Germany.* New York: St. Martin's Press, 1999.

'Soviet View of Berlin Airlift', *Air Power History*, Spring 1989: 24–5.

Special Study of Operation Vittles: The Story of the Berlin Airlift, an Enormous Technical Achievement That Has Revolutionized the Role of Aviation in Transportation and Logistics. New York: Conover-Mast, 1949.

Steury, Donald P., ed. *On the Front Lines of the Cold War: Documents on the Intelligence War in Berlin, 1946 to 1961.* Washington, DC: CIA Staff History, Center for Military Intelligence, 1999.

Stivers, William. 'Incomplete Blockade: Soviet Zone Supply of West Berlin, 1948–1949', *Diplomatic History*, Fall 1997: 569–602.

Surba, C.F. 'Berlin Airlift: Lessons Learned Still Apply', *National Defense*, Vol. 69 (September 1984): 50–6.

Tunner, William H. *Over the Hump.* New York: Duell Sloan and Pearce, 1964.

Tunner, William H. 'Over the Hump: the Berlin Airlift'. *Mobility Forum*, Vol. 8, No. 4 (July–August 1999): 20–5.

Tusa, Ann and John. *The Berlin Airlift.* New York: Atheneum, 1988.

'Two Navy Air Transport Squadrons Fly Record Loads into Berlin Via Airlift', *All Hands* No. 390 (August 1949): 33.

United States. Air Force. *Berlin Airlift: The USAFE Summary.* Berlin: USAFE, 1949.

Westerfeld, Scott. *Berlin Airlift.* Englewood Cliffs, NJ: Silver Burdett Press, 1989.

Wilhem, Karen S. 'Berlin Airlift: Foreign Policy Through Logistics'. *Air Force Journal of Logistics*, Vol. 11 (Winter 1987): 6–8.

Woods, P.R. 'Thirty Years On: The Berlin Airlift: A Reassessment'. *Royal Air Forces Quarterly*, Vol. 18, No. 3 (Autumn 1978): 226–238.

Wragg, David. *Airlift: A History of Military Air Transport.* Novato, CA: Presidio Press, 1986.

Westerfeld, Scott. *The Berlin Airlift.* Englewood Cliffs NJ: Silver Burdett Press, 1989.

Index